ISSUES BEFORE THE 41ST GENERAL ASSEMBLY OF THE UNITED NATIONS

An annual publication of the United Nations Association of the United States of America

John Tessitore and Susan Woolfson, Editors

Lexington Books
D.C. Heath and Company/Lexington, Massachusetts/Toronto

Published simultaneously in Canada
Printed in the United States of America
Casebound International Standard Book Number: 0–669–14013–9
Paperbound International Standard Book Number: 0–669–14012–0

The paper used in this publication meets the minimum requirements of American National Standard for Information Sciences—Permanence of Paper for Printed Library Materials, ANSI Z39.48-1984. ∞™

86 87 88 89 90 8 7 6 5 4 3

Contents

I. **Dispute Settlement and Decolonization 1**

  1. Making and Keeping the Peace 1
      The U.N. Role in Conflict Resolution 1
      The United Nations and Peacekeeping 3
  2. The Middle East and the Persian Gulf 4
      The Iran-Iraq War 4
      The Arab-Israeli Conflict and the Occupied Territories 8
      International Terrorism and U.S.-Libyan Hostilities 12
      Lebanon 16
      UNRWA 19
  3. Africa 20
      The African Development Crisis 22
      Southern Africa 26
          South Africa 26
          Namibia 30
          South Africa and the Region 32
  4. Central America 33
  5. Afghanistan 36
  6. Indochina 39
  7. Cyprus 41
  8. Other Colonial and Sovereignty Issues 44

II. **Arms Control and Disarmament 47**

  1. Weapons in Outer Space 49
  2. Nuclear Weapons and the Superpowers 51
  3. The Spread of Nuclear Weapons 55
  4. Chemical, Conventional, and Other Weapons 58
  5. Comprehensive Disarmament 60

III. **Economics and Development   63**

    1. The World Economy in 1986   63
    2. Money and Finance   67
       The Debt Crisis   68
       The Role of International Institutions and Cooperation   71
    3. Trade   74
       Oil, Commodities, and Agricultural Products   74
       Trade in Manufactures and Services   76
    4. Transnational Corporations, Science, and Technology   79
       Code of Conduct for Transnational Corporations   80
       Transnational Corporations and Apartheid   81
       United Nations Conference on Science and Technology for
         Development   82
       The International Transfer of Technology   83

IV. **Global Resource Management   85**

    1. Food and Agriculture   85
    2. Population   91
    3. Energy   98
    4. Environment   100
    5. Law of the Sea   104
    6. Antarctica   107

V. **Human Rights and Social Issues   111**

    1. Human Rights   111
       Standard Setting   113
       Country-Specific Issues   117
    2. Refugees   120
    3. The Status of Women   124
    4. The Information Issue   128
    5. Other Social Issues   131

VI. **Legal Issues   137**

    1. The International Court of Justice   137
    2. The Effectiveness of the Organization   139
    3. Peace and Security   140
    4. Economic Relations   142
    5. International Organizations and Host Country Relations   144
    6. Violence by Individuals and Groups   145
    7. Outer Space   147

8. The International Law Commission   148
9. Other Legal Issues   149

VII.   Administration and Budget   151

1. U.N. Budget and Finance   151
2. Personnel and Administration   154

Appendix   159
Principal Organs of the United Nations

Index   173

Contributors

Don Babai (The World Economy in 1986, Money and Finance, and Trade sections, with Stephan Haggard) is an Assistant Professor of Government and an Associate of the Center for International Affairs at Harvard University.

Libby Bassett (Environment section) is a writer and editor and a consultant on international environment and development issues.

Michael J. Berlin (Making and Keeping the Peace, Central America, Afghanistan, Indochina, Cyprus, and Other Colonial and Sovereignty Issues sections) writes on the United Nations for *The Washington Post* and *The Inter Dependent* and is the diplomatic correspondent of *The New York Post*.

Sandra Bieniek (Transnational Corporations, Science, and Technology section, with Debra L. Miller), a recent graduate of Barnard College, will be continuing her studies in international political economy in the Ph.D. program at Columbia University.

Linda Griffin (Human Rights section), Director of Publications at the Carnegie Council on Ethics and International Affairs, assisted in a three-year research project that examined the role of religiously based relief and development agencies in overseas refugee relief work.

Stephan Haggard (The World Economy in 1986, Money and Finance, and Trade sections, with Don Babai) is an Assistant Professor of Government and an Associate of the Center for International Affairs at Harvard University.

John W. Harbeson (Africa section), Director of International Studies and Professor of Political Science at City College, City University of New York, is the author of *Nation-Building in Kenya: The Role of Land Reform,* among many books and articles on Africa.

Aaron Karp (Arms Control and Disarmament Chapter), who has taught at Columbia and Rutgers universities and has worked at the U.S. Department of State and the Arms Control and Disarmament Agency, is a Ph.D. candidate in political science at Columbia.

Lee Kimball (Law of the Sea and Antarctica sections) is the Executive Director of the Council on Ocean Law and serves as a consultant on Antarctic issues to the International Institute for Environment and Development.

Fred Lister (U.N. Budget and Finance section), a consultant to UNA-USA's U.N. Management and Decision-Making Project and the author of *Decision-Making Strategies for International Organizations,* served the United Nations in a variety of capacities during a career as an international civil servant that spanned 34 years.

Debra L. Miller (Transnational Corporations, Science, and Technology section, with Sandra Bieniek) is Assistant Professor of Political Science at Barnard College. She has written extensively on the political economy of direct foreign investment and technology transfer and has recently completed a study of the Mexican informatics sector for the National Science Foundation.

Larry Minear (Food and Agriculture section) works in Washington as Representative for Development Policy of two U.S. nongovernmental organizations, Church World Service and Lutheran World Relief.

Bruce Nichols (Refugees section), Director of Ethics and Foreign Policy Programs at the Carnegie Council on Ethics and International Affairs, is author of *At Home in No Man's Land,* a study of U.S. church and state involvement in international refugee programs.

Sterett Pope (The Middle East and the Persian Gulf section) writes a monthly column on the Middle East for *World Press Review.*

Ruth Raymond (Personnel and Administration section) is Research Associate for UNA's U.N. Management and Decision-Making Project.

David J. Scheffer (Legal Issues Chapter), formerly an attorney with Coudert Brothers, is an International Affairs Fellow of the Council on Foreign Relations.

Neal Spivack (Population, Information, and Other Social Issues sections) is a Contributing Editor of *The InterDependent.*

John Tessitore (Co-Editor) is Director of Publications at UNA-USA.

Janet Torsney (The Status of Women section) writes about women, energy, population, and other development issues for a variety of publications.

S. Dana Wolfe (Energy section) is a graduate student of United Nations and International Studies at New York University.

Susan Woolfson (Co-Editor) is Managing Editor of Publications at UNA-USA.

Preface

The United Nations Association of the United States of America (UNA-USA) is a national organization dedicated to strengthening the U.N. system—and the role of the United States within that system—so that the world body can better meet its many critical challenges. It is toward this end that UNA compiles its annual volume, *Issues Before the General Assembly*. Here, under a single cover, the reader may find the latest developments affecting the many issues of concern and debate that come before the U.N. General Assembly. The list—reflected in the table of contents of this volume—is a long and varied one; but many will note that it changes little from year to year. Indeed, we have all come to realize that such problems as conflict resolution, arms control, and third world development are not to be "solved" in the conventional sense of the word. Rather, these issues are the object of ongoing efforts and, at best, incremental improvements; and it is precisely for this reason that *Issues,* by identifying and articulating such efforts from one General Assembly to the next, has proven so useful to scholars, government officials, and students of international affairs.

Among those working toward the success of the United Nations must be counted the men and women who have contributed to this volume. Each has generously taken up the task in addition to an already full workload, and each has done so with the dedication that can only come from a deep personal commitment to the subject matter. To these scholars, journalists, professionals, and foreign affairs students we express our gratitude and admiration.

Of our editorial interns special mention must be made. Mr. Brian Gerber, Ms. Ellen Ribner, Mr. Alex Robarts, and Ms. Toni Wein spent several months under the direction of the authors locating, assembling, and sorting through great masses of background and support data. It is no exaggeration to say that without their tireless, voluntary efforts the timely production of this volume would have been impossible. For their hard work and good spirits we are very much in their debt.

Finally, our thanks go to the many men and women of the United Nations who gave so generously of their time and attention to our project, providing documents, assisting authors and interns, and making invaluable comments and suggestions on the early drafts of each chapter.

John Tessitore
Susan Woolfson

I
Dispute Settlement and Decolonization

1. Making and Keeping the Peace

The U.N. Role in Conflict Resolution

Despite hopes that peacemaking—the U.N.'s primary function—would be reinvigorated in the wake of the 1985 U.S.-Soviet Geneva summit meeting and the critical self-examination that surrounded the United Nations' 40th anniversary celebrations, the United Nations produced no tangible progress in the months preceding the 41st General Assembly. The agenda before the United Nations had been set by Secretary-General Javier Pérez de Cuéllar in his first annual report in 1982. At that time he outlined ways in which his own office, the Security Council, and (to a lesser extent) the General Assembly could serve as more effective forums for the settlement of disputes between nations. These issues were addressed in general terms by all of the heads of state who attended the General Assembly in October 1985, and by a ministerial meeting of the Security Council held on September 26.

In practice, each of these organs tried to apply the theory in limited areas. The General Assembly adopted a resolution in December [A/Res/40/50; vote: 97–7, with 39 abstentions] asking the chairman of the Organization of African Unity (OAU) and the Secretary-General to work toward direct negotiations between Morocco and the Popular Front for the Liberation of Saguia el Hamra and Río de Oro (Polisario) on a cease-fire and referendum in Western Sahara, which Morocco has annexed. Indirect negotiations on the basis of this resolution began in April 1986 at U.N. Headquarters, and a second round was held in May.

In February, the Security Council sought to create a basis for negotiations between Iran and Iraq by unanimously adopting a resolution [S/Res/582/1985] that deplored the "initial acts" that launched the Persian Gulf war (an oblique reference to the Iraqi invasion), and called for an immediate cease-fire, the withdrawal of all forces to the frontiers, the return of prisoners of war, and the start of a dispute-settlement process. A month later, in a statement by the

President of the Security Council [S/17932], the Council members tried further to satisfy Iran's demand for condemnation of the Iraqi aggression by condemning the Baghdad regime by name for frequent use of chemical weapons, in violation of the 1925 Geneva Protocol. However, these measures did not satisfy the Iranians, who continued to boycott the Council meetings. As a result, the Secretary-General's efforts to mediate the dispute remained dormant.

Regional organizations were similarly frustrated in their efforts to create mechanisms to deal with ongoing local problems. The OAU made no significant progress in Chad or the Western Sahara, nor did the Contadora Group advance in its attempt to negotiate conflict in Central America.

Both the Council and the Assembly took strong stands against terrorism in 1985. The Council issued a statement in October, following the hijacking of the Italian cruise liner *Achille Lauro* and the killing of an American passenger, condemning terrorism "in all its forms, wherever and by whomsoever committed" [S/17554]. On December 18, it unanimously condemned all acts of hostage-taking [S/Res/579(1985)]. Nine days earlier, the Assembly had adopted by consensus a resolution condemning all acts of terrorism but upholding the legitimacy of struggles for liberation [A/Res/40/61]. Diplomats saw these actions, with their show of unanimity, as a significant base upon which future agreements could be negotiated.

The Secretary-General or his representatives continued to maintain a watchdog role on the Persian Gulf war, the Middle East, Central America, Democratic Kampuchea (Cambodia), the Falklands/Malvinas, East Timor, and Korea, but they detected no openings for U.N. actions to move these disputes toward settlement. U.N. mediation was more active on Cyprus and Afghanistan, but success still proved elusive.

In March, Angola called upon Pérez de Cuéllar to take the lead in negotiations on the independence of Namibia. These talks had been pursued by U.S. Assistant Secretary of State Chester Crocker, in conjunction with the South African demand that Namibian independence be linked to the withdrawal of Cuban troops from Angola. But after Jonas Savimbi, leader of the Angolan rebel group UNITA, was received by President Reagan at the White House, Angola broke off the dialogue with the United States. Pérez de Cuéllar dispatched his Special Representative for Namibia, Martti Ahtisaari, to Angola in March and again in May to determine what role the United Nations could play in the matter; but his prospects were limited by U.N. resolutions obliging him to reject any link between Namibian independence and the Cuban withdrawal.

In July, Pérez de Cuéllar, acting in his personal capacity, issued an arbitration ruling that resolved the dispute between France and New Zealand over the bombing by French agents of the Greenpeace ship *Rainbow Warrior,* which resulted in one death. Both governments accepted the Secretary-General's verdict, involving a formal apology and monetary compensation by France and the transfer of two French agents from a New Zealand jail to a French overseas territory for a period of three years.

The United Nations and Peacekeeping

U.N. peacekeeping operations historically have arisen from the institution's peacekeeping efforts, and have served as the most visible mechanism by which dispute-settlement agreements arranged under U.N. auspices can be instituted or preserved. The prospects for future U.N. peacekeeping operations, therefore, depend on the fruition of peacemaking in Namibia, Western Sahara, Cambodia, the Persian Gulf, and Afghanistan (the most likely future arenas for the presence of blue-helmeted U.N. observers or peace forces). The United Nations currently maintains three peacekeeping forces: in Cyprus, on the Golan Heights between Israel and Syria, and in southern Lebanon.

The **United Nations Interim Force in Lebanon (UNIFIL)**, established in March 1978, was bypassed by Israeli troops during the 1982 invasion. Since then the Israelis have withdrawn to a security zone on the Lebanese side of the frontier, leaving the 5,825-member force unable to fulfill its mandate of patrolling the border. In April 1986 the mandate of UNIFIL was renewed for just three months, instead of the usual six, at the insistence of France, which sought to increase pressures to resolve the financial and military problems plaguing the operation.

The financing of peacekeeping operations has always been a sensitive political issue—and a strain on the overall U.N. budget. Over the years, states which object to the peacekeeping operations for various reasons have adopted the practice of withholding operating funds. Such actions have resulted in a deficit of well over $200 million in the peacekeeping accounts. Through March the UNIFIL deficit stood at $237.7 million—more than its annual budget of about $144 million [S/17965]. In April the United States began withholding $21 million a year, half its annual share of the UNIFIL budget and 15 percent of the operation's yearly cost. But the Soviet Union, which had withheld $152 million, its share of UNIFIL payments since 1978, announced that it would start paying its $18 million annual portion of the costs. Several of the troop-contributing nations, Norway in particular, warned that they might pull out of the force because of the military vulnerability of their contingents, and the cuts in reimbursements caused by the financial strains. But all nine troop-contributors finally agreed to stay. The mandate of the force was routinely renewed for six more months in July 1986.

The two other peace forces continued to operate effectively. The 1,331-member **United Nations Disengagement Observer Force (UNDOF)** has patrolled the Golan buffer zone with no major incidents since June 1974. With the cooperation of the Syrian and Israeli authorities, UNDOF has continued to perform its operations effectively, and in June 1984 it facilitated an exchange of Israeli and Syrian prisoners of war. Its term was renewed by the Security Council through November 1986, at a cost of about $36 million a year. The 2,328 member **United Nations Peace-keeping Force in Cyprus (UNFICYP)**, established in 1964, patrols the "green line" between the Greek-Cypriot and Turkish-Cypriot communities, and its mandate runs through December 1986. UNFICYP is financed solely by voluntary contributions, at a cost of about $28 million a year, and had a deficit of $134 million through December 15, 1985.

A second type of U.N. peacekeeping operation involves unarmed observers, of officer rank, who patrol, monitor, and report, rather than interposing themselves physically between combatants. The **United Nations Military Observer Group in India and Pakistan (UNMOGIP)**, a small team of observers, has patrolled the line of control in Kashmir agreed between the two countries in 1972. The **United Nations Truce Supervision Organization in Palestine (UNTSO)**, originally established in 1948 to supervise the truce declared by the Security Council after the first Arab-Israeli war, still functions in various capacities in the region. It includes both American and Soviet officers, and some 50 of its members are stationed in Beirut. A small number have been stationed in Baghdad and Teheran since June 1984 to verify complaints by Iran and Iraq about attacks on civilian population centers.

Brian Urquhart, the man who helped to devise the concept of peacekeeping under Ralph Bunche and succeeded him as head of U.N. peacekeeping operations, retired in February 1986 after more than 40 years as an international civil servant. He was replaced by Marrack Goulding, a former British foreign service officer.

The 33-member **Special Committee on Peacekeeping Operations** was established in 1965 to help solve the crisis over peacekeeping finances that threatened to tear the United Nations apart at that time, and to draw up guidelines to govern the conduct of all such U.N. operations. U.N. peacekeeping operations are not equipped to achieve resolutions of the conflicts that sparked the outbreak of fighting in each situation. Rather, they are charged with ending hostilities and separating the parties involved. Such stabilization of a conflict is often the most that can be achieved. The 41st General Assembly is to consider the committee's reports of peacekeeping finances and guidelines, but no progress toward consensus is expected [A/41/50, item 75].

2. The Middle East and the Persian Gulf

The Iran-Iraq War

After nearly six years of fighting, the Iran-Iraq war continues with little hope of resolution. Iraq, which invaded its neighbor in September 1980, has sought to end the conflict since 1982, when its armies were driven back to the Iraqi border; but Iran has repeatedly refused to negotiate pending the overthrow of Iraq's government and the payment of war reparations by a successor regime in Baghdad. Meanwhile, the protracted fighting has inflicted **heavy casualties** on both sides, resulting in hundreds of thousands of dead, and over a million wounded and dislocated.

The United Nations has played a mediatory role in the conflict through a number of channels. Iraq has regularly solicited U.N. mediation on the basis of Security Council resolutions. Iran has preferred to communicate directly with Secretary-General Javier Pérez de Cuéllar while ignoring the good offices of the Council, arguing that the Council has shown a pro-Iraq bias in its resolutions. Recurrent charges on both sides of chemical warfare, bombardment of civilian populations, and mistreatment of prisoners of war have prompted visits to the front by various U.N. commissions and a **tour of the Gulf by the Secretary-General** during the spring of 1985. None of these efforts has produced more than temporary results, much less momentum toward an eventual settlement of the war, though the United Nations has succeeded in stationing observers in the two capitals.

As hostilities have dragged on, both countries have raised massive armies: Iran currently maintains an estimated 1,200,000 men under arms, many of whom are irregular volunteers; while Iraq has put more than half a million troops into the field [*Middle East*, 4/86]. Since 1982, when Iraq assumed a defensive posture, neither side has gained a strategic advantage over the other. Baghdad has fortified its positions with earthworks and artificial lakes, and has accumulated a formidable arsenal of state-of-the-art weapons systems. Against this technical advantage, Teheran has pressed its indisputable edge in morale and manpower. For the past four years Iranian armies have mounted punishing spring offensives, while staging desultory feints and probes all year round. These maneuvers have brought only minor territorial gains at the cost of tens of thousands of lives each year; but Iran's leadership seems determined to pursue an open-ended war of psychological and economic exhaustion.

Both countries have continued to attack oil facilities and tanker traffic on the Persian Gulf. In 1982, Iraq declared an "exclusionary zone" in the Gulf and announced its intention to stop all "enemy vessels" carrying Iranian oil. In February 1984, Iraq began in earnest to interdict tanker traffic carrying Iranian oil, causing consternation among other Arab governments on the Gulf, and leading to Iranian threats to arrest Gulf shipping entirely by closing the Straits of Hormuz. Unchastened by a June 1984 Security Council resolution condemning attacks on tankers in international waters, Iraq (and to a lesser extent Iran) has continued such attacks intermittently in an effort to cripple Iran's capacity to export petroleum, a commodity upon which the economies and state revenues of both countries dearly depend.

In August, Iraq scored a major aerial victory when at last it succeeded in crippling Iran's vital oil terminal at Kharg Island. Iraqi claims to have leveled Kharg proved premature; tankers continued to take delivery at the huge oil complex. But Iranian petroleum exports fell dramatically during the next six months, from 1.5 million barrels a day (mbd) in July 1985 to a reported 0.7 mbd in March 1986 [*Middle East,* 4/86]. Taken together with plummeting oil prices on world energy markets, Iran's setback at Kharg has resulted in a severe reduction of Iranian oil revenues—from $1.3 billion a month in late 1985 to $420 million in March 1986 [*The Christian Science Monitor,* 3/7/86].

Iraq, on the other hand, has increased its oil exports substantially over the last year. In the early phases of the conflict, Iran shut down 80 percent of Iraq's peacetime production capacity by razing Iraqi port facilities on the Gulf in 1980 and then persuading its ally Syria to close the Iraqi-Syrian pipeline in 1982. But the widening of the Iraqi-Turkish pipeline and the construction of a second pipeline through Saudi Arabia to the Red Sea, which began operation in late 1985, have boosted Iraq's oil exports considerably from a wartime low of 0.65 mbd three years ago to 1.7 mbd in March 1986 [*Middle East,* 4/86]. Reversing Iran's longstanding edge in export capacity and revenue base, these developments pose new fiscal problems for Teheran. Nevertheless, Iran's leaders regularly announce new measures designed to put their country on a war footing for the next generation.

In late February 1986, Iran launched its fifth spring offensive in as many years. With the assistance of Kurdish rebels, Iran seized the small Iraqi border town of Suleimaniyya in the mountainous northern sector of the front. But this northern thrust proved a diversionary tactic to prepare a massive **siege of Fao,** Iraq's southern-most port on the Gulf. In a week of fighting, Iran ferried 30,000 troops across the Shatt al-Arab waterway and pushed Iraqi forces from the Fao peninsula. Iraqi attempts to recapture Fao failed, even after a massive counterattack in which Iraq's elite Presidential Guard was badly mauled. By the end of March, Iran had secured its beachhead at Fao and established firm supply lines across the Shatt. Casualties were heavy: at Fao, Iraq reportedly lost 10,000 men, as many as had died during the whole of 1985, with Iranian losses presumably running much higher [*Middle East,* 4/86].

On February 18, Iraq obtained a four-day debate at the Security Council. Six days later, the Council unanimously passed a resolution calling, as usual, for an immediate cease-fire. The February 24 resolution also deplored "the initial acts which gave rise to the conflict," referring for the first time to Iraq's invasion of Iran in 1980 [S/Res/582]. Despite this concession to Iran, which has consistently demanded that the United Nations condemn Iraq as the aggressor, the resolution produced no tangible results at the front.

Iran's capture of Fao marked more of a psychological than a strategic victory. Fao itself has little military importance, since the city is separated from the rest of Iraq by virtually impassable marshes. But Iran's demonstration of tactical ingenuity and unshakable political will has undermined Iraq's morale. In the face of Iraq's six-to-one superiority in the air, Iran was able to transport and supply tens of thousands of troops over the Shatt al-Arab, a waterway several miles wide and thought invulnerable to attack. Iraq's reluctance to commit infantry to the battle, and the huge losses and poor performance of the best Iraqi troops, further discouraged Baghdad.

Responding to Iranian allegations of renewed Iraqi use of **chemical weapons**, Secretary-General Pérez de Cuéllar sent a special U.N. commission of inquiry to the Gulf in March 1986 to investigate the charges. The commission's report cited clear evidence that Iraq had used mustard gas bombs in February 1986 to a far greater extent than it had in 1984. A statement issued by the President of the Security Council in March condemned Iraq's use of chemical weapons, which, it noted, was "in clear violation of the Geneva Protocol of 1925" [S/17191].

The battle for Fao, which lies less than ten miles from Kuwait, renewed concern among Arab states in the region that the Iran-Iraq war might spread to other parts of the Gulf. At the end of February 1986, the Gulf Cooperation Council (GCC)—a regional organ formed by Bahrein, Kuwait, Oman, Qatar, Saudi Arabia, and the United Arab Emirates in November 1984—convened an emergency session, strongly condemning the latest Iranian offensive. The GCC also approved the lifting of 0.35 mbd of Saudi and Kuwaiti oil on behalf of Iraq. The GCC's press releases, which spoke of "coordinating defense strategies against a possible spread of the war," differed sharply in tone from the proceedings of the GCC summit of November 1985, which had adopted a more conciliatory posture toward Iran and prompted some talk of a GCC "peace initiative."

The renewal of battle on the ground in 1986 has been accompanied by an **escalation of hostilities in the air**. Iraq has stepped up its attacks on tankers calling on Iranian ports, prompting Iran to raid ships loading at Saudi Arabia, Kuwait, and the United Arab Emirates in retaliation. In the first four months of the year, Iraq and Iran together attacked more than 40 tankers in the Gulf, six less than the figure recorded for all of 1985 [*The New York Times*, 5/18/86]. Following the GCC's emergency meeting in February, and its announcement of renewed financial and diplomatic support for Iraq, Iran has again begun to attack tankers calling on GCC countries. In April and May, Iranian helicopters launched a series of raids on Saudi tankers, the first time Iran systematically threatened Saudi shipping since June 1984, when Saudi warplanes downed an Iranian fighter over the Gulf [*The New York Times*, 5/13/86].

A **superpower confrontation** in the Gulf appears unlikely. Although both the United States and the Soviet Union claim neutrality in the conflict, both in fact favor Iraq. Relations between Washington and Teheran remain acrimonious; and the United States has recently restored diplomatic ties with Baghdad, severed in 1967 during the Six-Day War. Removing itself from the radical Arab Rejection Front, Iraq has softened its position on the Palestine question considerably; and significantly, Washington has recently removed Baghdad from its list of sponsors of state terrorism, where Iran still occupies a prominent place. The Soviet Union signed a 20-year Treaty of Friendship and Cooperation with Iraq in the seventies, and while deeply critical of Iraq's initial invasion of Iran, the Soviet Union renewed shipments to Iraq of new model weapons, accompanied by Soviet military advisors, in 1982. Relations between Moscow and Teheran have been strained, although the Soviet Union permits its allies to supply Iran with missiles.

The conflict between Iraq and Iran is likely to continue as a war of attrition. Observers generally agree that both sides lack the logistical and military capacity to score a decisive victory. Iraq has a distinct advantage in matériel; but Baghdad, whose initial invasion of Iran was both costly and unsuccessful, shows no inclination to renew an offensive strategy. Iran, which has proven itself willing to sustain casualty rates far higher than those suffered by Iraq, lacks the technical and economic resources to defeat its adversary in battle. Over the past four years, Iranian leaders at times expressed their frustration over the tragic waste and futility of the war, only to be overruled by the tenacious Ayatollah Khomeini.

The General Assembly has not passed a resolution on the Iran-Iraq war since the 37th Session of 1982–83. At the request of Iraq and the GCC, the Security Council has held several debates on the war over the last year; and it passed its most recent resolution calling for an immediate cease-fire in February 1986. Although Iraq has often stated its desire to abide by Security Council resolutions, Iran has refused to honor the decisions of the Council, charging that they consistently favor Iraq. Iran was especially critical of a resolution the Council passed soon after Iraq's invasion in September 1980, because it called for an immediate cease-fire while Iraqi troops were still on Iranian soil [S/17084]. The Security Council's February 1986 resolution, which, without naming Iraq specifically, condemned the original invasion of Iran, has not changed Teheran's hostile attitude. Iran's relations with Secretary-General Pérez de Cuéllar, cordial from the start of the conflict and strengthened by the Secretary-General's visit to the Gulf in the spring of 1985, are far more promising. Should Teheran tire of the war and its tremendous costs, it may turn to the Secretary-General for help in ending it.

The Arab-Israeli Conflict and the Occupied Territories

Nearly forty years after the formation of the state of Israel, the Arab-Israeli conflict continues. Hopes for reviving the moribund Middle East "peace process" were raised in early 1985 when Palestine Liberation Organization (PLO) Chairman Yasir Arafat and Jordan's King Hussein signed the **February 11 Agreement**, which opened the possibility of direct negotiations between Israel and a joint Jordanian-Palestinian delegation. Both Jerusalem and

Washington responded with encouraging démarches during the spring and summer of 1985; but hopes for peace talks were dashed by the inability or unwillingness of the PLO leadership to commit itself to a negotiating course. In February 1986, King Hussein publicly abandoned the effort, and the "peace process" ground to a halt.

The United Nations remains on the margins of the peace process in the Middle East. The General Assembly has condemned Israel relentlessly for its occupation of the West Bank and the Gaza Strip, but Israel has rejected these U.N. actions, decrying the pro-Palestinian sympathies of the world body. In the Security Council, the United States continues to veto many of the resolutions that are critical of Israel.

A central issue of the Arab-Israeli conflict remains the **Palestine question.** Israel has never conceded Palestinian rights to self-determination, and considers the PLO as an outlaw "terrorist" organization. The Palestinians, for their part, have refused to recognize the state of Israel without a reciprocal concession from the Israelis, and the PLO continues to proclaim its right to "armed resistance" within Israel and the occupied territories. Israel is willing to negotiate on the basis of U.N. Security Council resolutions 242 and 338, the former guaranteeing legitimacy and "the right to live within secure and recognized borders" to "every state in the area" (though its interpretation of 242 differs from that of other parties). The PLO will not accept resolution 242 as the basis of a settlement since it makes no mention of Palestinian self-determination and addresses Palestinians only as a refugee problem. The United States, which has brokered several bilateral agreements between Israel and Arab states since the Yom Kippur War of 1973, will not negotiate with or recognize the PLO until the organization accepts without reservation Israel's right to exist by accepting resolution 242. The Arab countries, while loudly championing the Palestinian cause, have generally pursued their own state interests, when necessary at the expense of the Palestinian people.

The February 11 Agreement of 1985 between Jordan and the PLO appeared to offer a way out of this impasse. The accord called for negotiations between Israel and a joint Jordanian-Palestinian delegation in the context of a broad international conference. It envisioned an eventual **confederal linkage** of Jordan and a Palestinian entity consisting of the West Bank and the Gaza strip. The new formula suggested a PLO retreat from its long-held goal of an independent Palestinian state; and Jordanian officials interpreted the accord as an implicit acceptance by the PLO of Security Council resolution 242, which PLO leaders denied.

Spurred by the support of Egyptian President Hosni Mubarak, the United States announced in May that it would meet with a joint Jordanian-Palestinian delegation, provided that no members of the PLO were included. Washington was initially critical of an international conference that it believed might enhance Soviet influence in the Middle East and complicate the negotiations, but eventually accepted the idea of an international forum that would lead to more limited talks.

In June 1985, Israel announced its own peace plan calling for direct and unconditional negotiations between "parties interested in peace." The plan did not include the PLO, but "Palestinians who are not PLO" were welcome [*The New York Times*, 6/11/85]. Israel pushed momentum for a breakthrough a step further in September when Israeli Prime Minister Shimon Peres addressed the U.N. General Assembly and stated his willingness to negotiate with a joint Jordanian-Palestinian delegation. Mr. Peres said he was prepared to travel to Amman to start direct peace talks which might "be initiated with the support of an international forum, as agreed upon by the negotiating states" [A/40/PV.42 p.59]. In a separate statement, the Prime Minister indicated he might welcome an international peace conference of the kind advocated by King Hussein if the Soviet Union were willing to restore diplomatic ties with Israel, severed 18 years before during the Six-Day War [*Newsweek*, 11/4/85].

These calls for negotiations for peace were soon followed, however, by a new round of international terror and reprisal. In late September two Israeli sailors were found dead in Barcelona and days later four Israeli tourists were killed in Cyprus. Holding Arafat responsible for these crimes, Israel responded by sending Israeli warplanes over 1,500 miles of water to bomb the PLO headquarters in Tunis, killing 73, including 12 Tunisian civilians [*Newsweek*, 10/14/85]. Chairman Arafat survived unscathed to announce that Israel had "bombed the peace process." Charging that Israel had intended to kill him and derail direct negotiations, Arafat now demanded fresh assurances from the United States and Israel to bring the Palestinians to the peace table [*Newsweek*, 10/14/85].

Such assurances were not forthcoming, especially after Palestinian gunmen hijacked the Italian cruise liner *Achille Lauro* in early October, taking the passengers hostage and killing an American tourist. Although Arafat condemned the action, the *Achille Lauro* affair badly damaged his credibility, as strong circumstantial evidence indicated that Abu Abbas, a colleague of Arafat's and the head of a tiny PLO faction, had sent the highjackers on their mission. Cresting a wave of increasing terrorism in Europe and Palestinian violence in the occupied territories, the *Achille Lauro* affair incited Western opinion against Arafat and his long-standing policy of "gun and olive branch," a two-track approach combining "armed struggle" in Israel and the occupied territories with a willingness to pursue peace negotiations.

European impatience and growing tensions between Jordan and the PLO surfaced in mid-October, when planned talks between the British Foreign Secretary and two members of the PLO's Executive Council had to be cancelled. The Palestinians refused to affirm their acceptance of resolution 242 [*The Economist*, 10/19/85] and Jordanian officials, who had brokered the talks, withdrew. The failed London meeting reportedly resulted in a rift within Fatah, the mainstream and largest PLO faction headed by Arafat, over whether the PLO should accept Security Council resolutions 242 and 338 without further assurances from Washington concerning Palestinian rights [*The New York Times, 12/15/85*].

PLO hesitation over resolutions 242 and 338 finally prompted King Hussein to abandon the February 11 Agreement. In a long and bitter speech broadcast over Jordanian television in February 1986, the King announced his decision "to close another chapter in the search for peace." Hussein said he could not cooperate with the PLO leadership "until such time as their word becomes their bond, characterized by commitment, credibility and constancy"[*The Christian Science Monitor, 2/20/86*].

Hussein's withdrawal from the peace process was preceded by the beginning of a Jordanian-Syrian reconciliation, marked by a visit by the King to Damascus in November 1985. Many saw this as an effort by Hussein to cover his flank with Syria. Syrian President Hafez al-Assad had been strongly opposed to the February 11 Agreement, which he saw as ignoring Syrian interests, in particular Syrian concern over Israel's formal annexation of the Golan Heights in 1981.

Since King Hussein's break with the PLO, **prospects for a negotiated solution to the Arab-Israeli conflict** appear darker than ever. Many Palestinian moderates feel that peace must be made now before Israel's annexation of the occupied territories becomes irreversible, if it is not already so. Israel now controls, directly or indirectly, over 50 percent of the West Bank, where more than 140,000 Israelis live in some 110 settlements and East Jerusalem [*The New York Times, 1/26/86*]. But mutual hostility and intolerance are growing in Israel and the occupied territories, especially among a new generation of Jews and Arabs who have grown up since the Six-Day War.

In the **occupied territories**, sporadic bombings and attacks have increased sharply over the last year, according to Israeli police minister Haim Bar-Lev [*Middle East, 11/85*], as have the inevitable Israeli reprisals and preemptive police measures. With the aborting of the February 11 Agreement, Israelis placed new hope in their policy of appointing independent non-PLO mayors in the West Bank. The assassination of Zafer al-Masri, the mayor of Nablus appointed last year by Israel with the approval of King Hussein, dealt a blow to this policy, however.

The 40th Session of the General Assembly passed a number of resolutions denouncing Israel's occupation of the West Bank and the Gaza strip. The resolution on **"The situation in the Middle East"** [A/40/168] repeated the General Assembly's conviction that the Palestine question is the core of the Arab-Israeli conflict. It also reiterated the Assembly's support of the PLO as the just representative of the Palestinians and its condemnation of Israel's "aggression, policies and practices against the Palestinian people." The resolution further deplored Israel's occupation of the Golan Heights, and called for a U.N.-sponsored international peace conference to negotiate a comprehensive regional settlement.

The 41st Session of the General Assembly will debate these issues once again, and there seems little reason to suppose they will be treated much differently from the past.

International Terrorism and U.S.-Libyan Hostilities

In 1985 and early 1986, a number of bombings, hijackings, and assassinations again brought the problem of terrorism to the attention of the international community, and led to a series of Israeli and American reprisals and "preemptive" measures, culminating in a U.S. raid on the Libyan cities of Tripoli and Benghazi in April 1986. All these actions spurred a number of debates and resolutions at the United Nations, where terrorism has long been a scabrous subject. Delegates have been unable to agree on an acceptable definition of the word. A special U.N. committee convened in 1972 to discuss the topic, for example, quickly bogged down in semantic squabbles.

Nevertheless, the 40th Session of the United Nations broke new ground in the debate surrounding terrorism by adopting a number of Security Council and General Assembly resolutions in December 1985 and January 1986 (see below). American and Israeli reprisals and actions to combat terrorism also prompted debates in the Security Council, where the United States vetoed various resolutions condemning the actions.

Never far from the headlines, terrorism returned to the international agenda with a vengeance in June 1985 when **Lebanese Shiite gunmen hijacked a TWA airliner** and held its passengers hostage in Beirut, killing an American citizen and demanding the release of 750 Shiites detained by Israel in southern Lebanon and later transferred to Israel. The hostages were released in late June; and the next day Israel freed some 300 Shiites from its prisoner-of-war camps. This exchange was the fulfillment of an informal "linkage" Syrian President Hafez al-Assad had negotiated with the Lebanese hijackers, persuading them to release their hostages [*The Washington Post*, 7/3/85]. Throughout the crisis, both the United States and Israel had refused to make formal concessions to the air pirates; and Israel later insisted that its release of Shiite detainees had nothing to do with the TWA hostage crisis.

In the United States, the crisis aroused public pressure to retaliate, and President Reagan stated that American restraint and patience had limits, and that America might well strike back at terrorists in the future. Citing a number of attacks against Americans in June, including the assassination of four U.S. marines in El Salvador, the President called terrorism "a criminal threat to civilization" that was "no mere domestic problem" [*The New York Times*, 6/22/85].

In delimiting this growing problem, the U.S. administration did, however, make some allowances for political expediency, as when in a July speech President Reagan seemed to strike Syria from a U.S. list of "states sponsoring terrorism" in apparent gratitude for President Assad's good offices during the TWA hostage crisis. The omission was particularly glaring in light of reports Arab sources had published in June, which alleged that an "anti-American strategy" involving the systematic use of terror had been formulated jointly by the foreign ministers of Iran, Syria, and Libya during a summit held in Teheran in January 1985 [*The Wall Street Journal,* 6/19/85]. Iraq was also formally deleted from the list in 1985, following a U.S.-Iraq rapprochement.

A new cycle of terror and reprisal began in September 1985 with an upsurge of **Palestinian attacks against Israelis in Europe and the occupied territories.** Following the Israeli bombing of the PLO headquarters in Tunis, Tunisia protested to the U.N. Security Council, which in early October adopted a resolution condemning the raid as an "act of armed aggression . . . in flagrant violation of the Charter of the United Nations." The resolution also requested that U.N. member nations "take measures to dissuade Israel" from further such actions, and allowed that "Tunisia has the right to appropriate reparations as a result of the loss of life and material damage" it had suffered [S/Res/573 (1985)]. The U.S. vote for the resolution, one of the Council's sharpest criticism of Israel, reflected a shift in White House reaction from the initial approval of the raid as a "legitimate . . . expression of self-defense" [*Newsweek,* 10/14/85].

Three days later, **Palestinian gunmen seized the Italian cruise liner *Achille Lauro*** on its way to the Israeli port of Ashdod via Alexandria, Egypt. The seajacking prompted a statement by U.S. Ambassador Vernon Walters, President of the Security Council, that members of the Council condemned "terrorism in all its forms, whenever and by whomsoever committed" [S/PV.2618]. Secretary-General Javier Pérez de Cuéllar also deplored the seizure as "criminal and unjustifiable" and further condemned "all acts of terrorism" without qualification [PR SG/SM/3763].

The dénouement of the *Achille Lauro* affair provided another landmark in the history of international terror and reprisal. After PLO cadres arrived to assist Egypt in negotiating with the hijackers, the ship was soon released, but not before the gunmen had killed an American tourist. Egypt, which later claimed it had no knowledge of the death, then pledged free passage for the hijackers and the PLO negotiators to Tunis. But the EgyptAir liner carrying the Palestinians was diverted by American jets to Sicily; and U.S. officials announced their intention to try the terrorists and Abu Abbas, the head of a tiny PLO faction who U.S. authorities contended had both sent the terrorists on their mission aboard the *Achille Lauro* and negotiated the ship's release. A confrontation between Italian and American security units on a Sicilian airbase left the Palestinians in the custody of Italy, which released Abu Abbas, citing lack of proof for the American charges. Egypt protested vigorously the action of the United States, but did not seek recourse at the United Nations.

In December 1985, the General Assembly adopted a draft resolution of the General Assembly Legal Committee condemning "as criminal all acts, methods and practices of terrorism, whenever and by whomever committed" [A/C.6/L.31]. The resolution was passed by a vote of 113 to 1 (Cuba voted against) with 2 abstentions (Burkina Faso and Israel). Its passage marked the first time Warsaw Pact nations had ever supported as a bloc a measure against terrorism at the United Nations, a breakthrough perhaps explained by the kidnapping of four Soviet diplomats, one of whom was killed, in Beirut two months before, as well as by the slight thaw in U.S.-Soviet relations that followed the Reagan-Gorbachev summit in Geneva in November [*The Economist*, 12/6/85]. A Security Council resolution adopted later in December also condemned "unequivocally all acts of hostage-taking and abduction" without reference to their cause or context [S/Res/579 (1985)]. A resolution adopted without a vote on the basis of the report of the Legal Committee struck a different tone, citing "causes underlying international terrorism ... *inter alia* colonialism, racism and flagrant and mass violations of human rights and fundamental freedoms and those involving alien occupation" [A/40/1003].

In late December, the double **bombing of the Rome and Vienna airports** altered the terms of the ongoing debate on terrorism by sparking a new U.S. campaign against terrorism directed specifically at Libya. In early January 1986, the U.S. State Department issued a White Paper which accused the state of Libya, and its leader Colonel Muammar el-Qaddafi in particular, of planning and sponsoring numerous acts of international terrorism, which, the paper charged, "Qaddafi has used as one of the primary instruments of his foreign policy" [*The New York Times* 1/9/86]. Declaring the need for punitive action, the U.S. Government ordered all Libyan assets in the United States frozen, and asked its North Atlantic Treaty Organization (NATO) allies to consider similar measures. The NATO allies demurred, demanding proof of Libyan involvement in the Rome/Vienna attacks, especially in light of an Italian intelligence report which indicated that the airport bombers had come to Europe via Damascus.

Instead, it was **Israel** that made the next move against Libya, when, in early February, it **intercepted a Libyan airliner** bound for Damascus. Israeli officials explained that they had good reason to believe that PLO terrorist leaders were on the plane; but finding only a group of indignant Syrian officials on board, they quickly released the airliner. Libya protested the Israeli "hijacking," accused the United States of assisting "the Zionist air pirates," and brought a complaint to the Security Council [*The New York Times*, 2/5/86]. The United States vetoed the resulting Council resolution.

The U.S. representative at the Council, Vernon Walters, issued a separate statement saying that the diversion of civilian aircraft "may be justified" as a legitimate act of self-defense "if the responsible terrorists are clearly on board and every precaution is taken to assure the safety of the plane." Walters's statement marked the first time the United States had challenged a long-standing rule of international law condemning such airplane diversions. Walters did, however, deplore the recent Israeli action, opining that Israel had failed to meet "the rigorous and necessary standard" the United States had observed when it diverted an EgyptAir plane over the Mediterranean in October 1985 [InterDependent 3-4/86].

In March and April, the United States escalated its campaign against Libya with a series of armed reprisals against Libyan warships, bases, and cities. In late March, elements of the U.S. Sixth Fleet staged naval maneuvers off the Libyan coast, crossing the 30°30′ parallel into the Gulf of Sidra, which Libya claims as its territorial waters. Earlier in the month, Colonel Qaddafi had dubbed this parallel "the line of death," and warned that Libya would defend itself if U.S. forces crossed the line. Six hours after the Sixth Fleet took up Qaddafi's challenge, Libya launched four SAM-5 missiles, drawing American attacks on Libyan gunboats, coastal missile installations, and radars [The Economist, 3/9/86]. Although the original U.S. rationale for the maneuvers in the Gulf of Sidra concerned the need to demonstrate "the freedom of navigation in international waters" on behalf of all nations, U.S. officials later admitted that the naval action had been primarily intended as a punishment for Colonel Qaddafi's crimes.

A further escalation of U.S.-Libyan hostilities occurred in mid-April when F-111 and naval bombers dispatched from Great Britain and the decks of the Sixth Fleet **attacked the Libyan cities of Tripoli and Benghazi**, bombing alleged terrorist camps, communications centers, military bases, and Qaddafi's headquarters and sometime residence outside Tripoli. The Colonel survived, but later announced that the raid had caused 37 casualties, wounded two of his sons, and killed his adopted daughter.

In a speech broadcast hours after the raid, President Reagan said he had acted in response to the bombing of a discothèque in West Berlin, which had killed an American serviceman and a Turkish woman the previous week. Reagan announced he had "clear" and "precise" proof of Libyan responsibility, and insisted that his response would "diminish Col. Qaddafi's capacity to export terror," and "provide him with reasons to alter his criminal behavior." Finally, the President stated that the United States would act again against terrorism "if necessary." Once again, U.S. officials provided a provocative post mortem, denying any American intention to kill Qaddafi, but admitting that a coup d'état by the Libyan military against Qaddafi would be "a good idea" [Time, 4/28/86].

In the two days that followed the attack, Lebanese kidnappers dumped the bodies of three Western hostages in the mountains outside Beirut, and an

American diplomat was shot in Khartoum, the victim of an allegedly Libyan-inspired assassination attempt.

Libya appealed to the Security Council, this time prompting a U.S. veto of a draft resolution condemning "armed attacks by the United States" as well as "all terrorist activities, whether perpetrated by individuals, groups or states." Australia, Denmark, France, and the United Kingdom also opposed the draft. Following the vote, the Council heard statements by India, Cuba, and Ghana deploring the American raid and "demanding peace and de-escalation" [S/4831].

Actions of the General Assembly and the Security Council during 1985, together with measures by the United States and its allies during the same period and the first half of 1986, marked a major escalation of efforts by the international community to deal with terrorism. Some antiterrorist actions by the United States in particular will doubtless continue to be politically unpopular in the United Nations, but at the same time the attitude toward terrorism itself within the international community has become considerably less equivocal.

Lebanon

The situation in Lebanon continues to deteriorate amid sectarian strife and public disorder. Israel's withdrawal from southern Lebanon to a six-mile-wide "security zone" north of the Israeli border prompted new hopes for the peaceful resolution of Lebanese internal disputes; but in the absence of a functioning central government, or a national consensus on how to restore one, Lebanon's many private armies continue their sectarian disputes. Syria, which still maintains some 25,000 troops in the country, has not been able to impose peace in Lebanon. In December 1985, Syria brokered the Damascus Accord between leaders of the Christian, Shiite, and Druze militias in Lebanon; but weeks later the agreement collapsed following a revolt by the Lebanese Forces, the Maronite Christian militia.

The United Nations, like most external actors, has been frustrated in its efforts to move war-torn Lebanon toward peace. The United Nations Interim Force in Lebanon (UNIFIL), which was sent to southern Lebanon in 1978 to help restore Lebanese authority in the area after an Israeli incursion, has been hampered in its mission by Israel's refusal to withdraw entirely from Lebanon and also by the harassment of local militias, especially the Israel-backed South Lebanon Army (SLA). The unilateral withdrawal of Israeli troops from most of southern Lebanon, which was accomplished in three phases between January and June 1985, has not quelled Shiite violence directed against Israel's presence in the country. U.N. attempts to mediate an agreement between Israel and Lebanon in 1985 broke down owing to differences between the parties involved. The U.N. Security Council has been unable to act in southern Lebanon because of disagreements within the Council.

Violence has persisted between the militias of Lebanon's many religious and ethnic communities. In May 1985, the Shiite Amal militia, assisted by the Christian-dominated Sixth Brigade of the Lebanese Army, stormed three Palestinian camps in Beirut in an effort to establish Shiite control over the camps and forestall a return of Palestinian guerrillas. "The war of the camps," which cost over a thousand lives during May and June, did not succeed in driving Palestinian defenders from their homes, and it was revived briefly in March 1986. Another turf war broke out between Shiite and Druze militias in November 1985. Five days and some 70 deaths later, a new "green line" was drawn through West Beirut demarcating Shiite and Druze enclaves in the city [*The Economist*, 1/4/86].

The anarchy of Lebanon has been aggravated by tensions and battles not only between, but also within, the country's fractious religious sects. The Lebanese Forces (L.F.), the Maronite militia which achieved dominion over Lebanon's Christian community during the early eighties by crushing rival Maronite militias, remains particularly prone to internecine strife. In March 1985, the Lebanese Forces revolted against President Amin Gemayel, charging he had become too subservient to Syria. In May, an L.F. countercoup was staged by Elie Hobeika, the Maronite commander who had led the Christian massacres of Palestinians at Sabra and Shatila in 1982.

Hobeika was willing to come to terms with Syria, and his rise to power gave momentum to a new Syrian campaign to mediate an interconfessional agreement to bring peace to Lebanon. Syria decided to present a new plan to the leaders of Lebanon's three most powerful militias—Hobeika's L.F., Walid Jumblatt's Druze militia, and Nabih Berri's Shiite Amal—rather than work through the country's political institutions and the civilian leaders of Lebanon's numerous religious sects, as previous Syrian plans had tried to do.

After much backing and filling, Syria persuaded Hobeika, Berri, and Jumblatt to sign the **Damascus Accord** in December 1985. The new agreement, intended as a first step toward the reconstruction of a peaceful Lebanon, mandated a cease-fire to be enforced by Syrian troops with the full support of the three signatories, who pledged to promote the "strategic integration" of their militias and sectarian fiefs into a revitalized Lebanese government. Constitutional reform would involve greater power-sharing for underrepresented Lebanese minorities, especially the Shiite Moslems, while maintaining the Maronite presidency and reducing Christian representation in parliament from a bare majority to a strong plurality [*Middle East*, 2/86].

But in January 1986, another coup shook the L.F., bringing to power Samir Geagea, who denounced the Damascus Accord as a total surrender of Christian power in Lebanon. Battles between Hobeika and Geagea LF factions left 300 dead, bringing Hobeika's defeat and sealing the collapse of the

Damascus agreement. Skirmishes between the L.F. and smaller Christian militias followed, and a new Shiite Amal attack on Palestinian camps broke out in March. Violence as usual had returned to Lebanon [*The Economist*, 1/25/86].

Meanwhile, **fighting along Israel's security zone** in the south continued. Guerrillas of the Shiite fundamentalist organization Hizbollah conducted raids against Israeli and SLA positions; and in February a platoon of Israeli soldiers was kidnapped, prompting an Israeli raid on Shiite villages in a futile effort to retrieve them. In March, the Hizbollah launched Katyusha rockets on settlements in northern Israel. Since the Israeli invasion of Lebanon in 1982, an estimated 2,000 Palestinian guerrillas, many of them followers of Yasir Arafat's moderate wing of the PLO, have returned to Lebanon. Most are busy defending Palestinian camps in Beirut, but some have found their way into southern Lebanon. Wishing to prevent further Israeli incursions into Lebanon, the moderate Shiite Amal movement is hostile to any Palestinian armed presence in the country, and Amal militiamen arrested a group of Palestinian guerrillas near Tyre in March 1986. The radical Shiite Hizbollah, however, opposes all collaboration with the state of Israel, and is reportedly assisting Palestinian infiltration into southern Lebanon [*The Economist*, 4/5/86].

Another war between Syria and Israel in Lebanon remains unlikely, despite rising tensions between the two countries in the spring of 1986. In 1985, Israel's withdrawal from most of southern Lebanon relaxed Syrian-Israeli tensions, restoring Lebanon to the status of a buffer zone separating the armies of Israel and Syria. Following the withdrawal, Israel announced that it would not tolerate Syrian occupation of any Lebanese territory it had evacuated; and in May 1986 it expressed concern about Syrian preparation of more forward military positions in Lebanon, closer to Israel. Syria posted Soviet SAM missiles just over the Syrian-Lebanese border, effectively denying Israeli reconnaissance planes access to eastern Lebanon. In April and May of 1986, Syria began digging a series of tank and artillery trenches 15 miles north of Israel's security zone [*The New York Times*, 5/19/86]. A further irritant has been Israel's concern over Palestinian penetration of southern Lebanon. Israel continues to raid Palestinian and Shiite positions in southern Lebanon; and in December 1985 it launched an air and ground attack against Palestinian positions in the Syrian-controlled Bekaa Valley.

UNIFIL, which now has almost 6,000 troops in southern Lebanon, continues to pursue its peacekeeping role, although its mandate prevents it from using force to stop guerrilla attacks and Israeli countermeasures. Israel's refusal to evacuate its security zone has prevented the peacekeeping force from deploying to the international border; and UNIFIL's mission has been further frustrated by the harassment of the Israeli-backed SLA, which held 21 UNIFIL soldiers hostage for a week in June 1985 [*The Washington Post*, 6/17/85]. UNIFIL casualties during the first three months of 1986—3 dead and 13 wounded—were up dramatically from the previous three-month period. In

April, the Security Council met and extended UNIFIL's mandate until July 1986. Secretary-General Pérez de Cuéllar expressed concern over the many obstacles to UNIFIL's mission and noted that UNIFIL was facing a financial crisis, prompted in part by the United States Congress's decision to withhold roughly 50 percent of the assessed U.S. contribution to the force in 1986 [*Press release, S/4830*].

The 40th Session of the General Assembly took no action on the situation in Lebanon, although the 39th Session had adopted a resolution urging "international action" to promote the reconstruction and development of Lebanon. The Lebanese Government has sought not to involve the General Assembly in order to avoid linking Lebanon's internal situation with the Arab-Israeli conflict in the eyes of the international community.

A larger role for the United Nations seems unlikely unless the various factions decide to settle their differences through negotiations rather than force. Even then, external actors in the conflict could likely block any U.N. efforts that they saw as compromising their political interests.

UNRWA

The United Nations Relief and Works Agency for Palestine Refugees in the Near East (UNRWA) was established in 1949 to provide humanitarian supports to Palestinian refugees pending a political settlement of the Arab-Israeli conflict. Today, the agency provides education, health, and welfare services to over 2.1 million eligible refugees, 100,000 of whom UNRWA considers special hardship cases to be provided with emergency food rations and shelter materials.

UNRWA's operations have cost in excess of $200 million a year over the last several years and were budgeted this year at $194 million. Last year, however, the agency weathered a severe financial crisis when an initial budget in excess of $250 million faced a sudden and serious shortfall, forcing UNRWA to make "major cuts in services to Palestinian refugees." These cuts were greatest in education but also involved reductions in staff and expenditures across the board. This year's funding level is roughly equivalent to last year's austerity budget, amounting to a suspension of most new maintenance and construction as well as some staff reductions [DPI/NGO/SB/10, A/40/13].

As in past years, anarchy and violence in Lebanon have imperiled both UNRWA clients and personnel, making the agency's work extremely difficult and dangerous. UNRWA was particularly alarmed when 1,500 Palestinian refugees were trapped in Tripoli in northern Lebanon for several weeks in the fall of 1985 when fighting broke out between the Syrian Army and a local Sunni militia led by Sheikh Shaaban. The equally violent "war of the camps" waged by the Shiite Amal militia against Palestinian refugee settlements in

Beirut, and the chronic conflict in southern Lebanon, have also impeded and imperiled the discharge of the agency's duties [PAL/1597].

3. Africa

African issues, perennially before the General Assembly, will claim especially high priority in the 41st Session. Two such issues, African development stagnation and Southern Africa, have reached crisis proportions in recent months and will be prominent on a crowded Assembly agenda. Each poses a direct challenge to the Assembly to advance a fundamental principle of the United Nations, "the dignity and worth of the human person, . . . the equal rights of men and women and of nations large and small" (Charter preamble).

The General Assembly has long been the major global forum to search for answers to the **chronic poverty and underdevelopment** suffered by many of its members. Nowhere have these problems proved more intractable than in Africa, a majority of whose nations have for many years lagged well behind even other low-income countries in the quest for development. At the start of the decade, the World Bank and the International Monetary Fund (IMF) began to demand fundamental policy reform and structural transformation in African states as the key to their escape from economic malaise. The Organization of African Unity (OAU), while recognizing domestic causes of continued underdevelopment, emphasized the contribution of world economic conditions to their plight and the importance of continental cooperation in achieving greater economic strength.

Years of continued economic decline, exacerbated by recurrent drought and famine over much of the continent, have left African countries little alternative but to follow donors' prescriptions for recovery. Meanwhile, the World Bank and other donors have recognized that sharply increased international aid and investment are required if African countries are to implement, and realize the benefits of, the indicated reforms [e.g., World Bank, *Financing Adjustment with Growth in Sub-Saharan Africa 1986–90*]. Thus was the stage set for a special session of the United Nations General Assembly in May 1986 to consider the African development crisis, the first such session ever devoted solely to the concerns of a single region. The African states took collective initiative through the OAU in proposing their own reform agenda, not unlike those demanded by the World Bank and the IMF, and sought in the special session specific international commitments to the required levels of external aid and investment.

The long-standing struggle for political freedom and social justice in **South Africa** has engaged the interests and energies of nations beyond the region and the continent to an unusual degree during the last two years. The economies of more developed nations have been affected by private investors' and bankers' unprecedented reconsideration of the prudence of maintaining their holdings in South Africa. Meanwhile, pressures have grown for governments to impose economic sanctions against South Africa to force political change. Unprecedented violence and instability within South Africa have had serious adverse consequences for the political and economic fortunes of vulnerable neighbors such as Mozambique, Lesotho, and Botswana, and may in fact fundamentally affect the course of on-going struggles for Namibia and Angola. The General Assembly may well be called upon to enact new measures, reinforcing those adopted in previous sessions, to hasten majority rule both in South Africa and in Namibia.

These two issues have been thrust with new urgency upon the global community represented in the General Assembly against the background of political turbulence, conflict over cultural identity, and economic struggle that have characterized independent Africa for more than a quarter of a century. Many issues born of such circumstances have found their way to the General Assembly in previous years, and may be expected to do so in the future. In recent months, however, they have remained to a relatively greater extent within the purview of the OAU, with the United Nations playing more a supporting but still consequential role. In this category are to be found those issues unsettling the Horn of Africa: **civil war** between Ethiopia and secessionists in Eritrea and Tigrai, and **border conflicts** between Ethiopia and Sudan and Ethiopia and Somalia. Of special importance, however, is Djibouti's initial success in promoting dialogue between Somalia and Ethiopia on their long-standing border dispute.

Large-scale refugee populations in the Horn of Africa and Southern Africa, to which United Nations and bilateral relief agencies seek to minister, symbolize the continent's pervasive political rootlessness, economic drift, and human tragedy. Political and economic crises in two of the continent's largest states, Zaire and Nigeria, which much earlier were projected onto the Assembly's agenda, attest to the continent's failure to capitalize upon its potential strengths. In contrast, Zimbabwe in 1986, once seriously threatened by drought, is producing an agricultural surplus and is a potential food exporter even to South Africa. Once a subject of General Assembly concern as a land in the grip of minority rule and racial oppression, and more recently tested by bitter internal conflict, Zimbabwe in 1986 shows promise of new domestic political harmony and strength.

Conflicts in **Western Sahara and Chad**, recently on the Assembly's docket, may again be found there in the 1986 session. These issues appear to have lost prominence, however, partly because each military conflict has stabilized to produce something approaching a tenable status quo, and partly because of the more urgent claims for the Assembly's attention of Southern Africa and the development crisis. Nonetheless, in April the Secretary-General, acting on the basis of General Assembly resolution 40/50, initiated a series of contacts to seek resolution of the conflict between Morocco and the Frente Polisario in the Western Sahara. Other disputes, many involving borders, appear to be quiescent for the moment and/or unlikely to find a place on the 41st General Assembly agenda. However, the border clash between Burkina Faso and Mali has now been brought within the jurisdiction of the International Court of Justice (World Court).

International issues of potential importance to the General Assembly are often treated in other multinational forums. **The July 1985 conference in Nairobi concluding the United Nations Decade for Women** is likely to overshadow any attention given to women's issues by the General Assembly. Nowhere are the issues addressed by the conference of greater significance than on the African continent, where women remain responsible for perhaps 60 to 80 percent of the agricultural production that provides a livelihood for more than 70 percent of the African people. Meanwhile, officially sponsored development projects often continue to overlook the significance of this reality for the strengthening of the agricultural sector and the restoration of healthy growth in African economies. Moreover, women's participation in government, trade unions, and political parties remains limited throughout the continent. Changes in inherited civil and customary law have been slow. On the other hand, many have spoken out in support of sexual equality and specific programs to promote women's participation in development processes.

The African Development Crisis

The stagnation of most African economies relative even to other low-income countries has been unmistakable in recent years. On balance, many African countries are poorer than they were when most achieved independence circa 1960. Growth in per capita income from 1965 to 1984 has been a mere 1.8 percent, only two-thirds that for all low-income countries as a group [World Bank, *Financing Adjustment with Growth*, 1986]. Annual growth in gross domestic product for low-income countries as a group has averaged 4.5 percent since 1960, whereas the African rate has declined from 3.8 percent in the 1960s to 3.0 percent in the 1970s. Some of the economic stagnation is attributable to rampant population expansion: 2.9 percent for the continent from 1973 to 1983 in comparison to 2.0 percent for all poor countries. In addition, much potential arable land remains uncultivated because of tsetse fly infestations, average per capita agriculture growth has actually been negative since 1982, and crop yields have declined.

Inappropriate cultivation methods, overcultivation and overgrazing of fragile lands in the Sahel and elsewhere, and rapid deforestation for lack of alternative fuel sources have mortgaged the ecological future of the continent and rendered many nations more vulnerable to devastating drought and fa-

mine. Increased dependence on food aid and more precarious African economies have been the inevitable result. To date, a majority of African countries
have been unable to develop human resources effectively enough to overcome
economic stagnation.

The World Bank's *Accelerated Development* (1981) found misconceived
policies and flawed domestic economic and political structures (for which
international development agencies themselves bear some responsibility) to
be more important in explaining African economic malaise than vagaries of
the international economy or shortage of development assistance. Thereafter,
the World Bank and the IMF have jointly led the way in subjecting African
governments' domestic policies to an unprecedented degree of international
review. The resulting document, known as the **Berg Report** (after principal
author Elliot Berg), became the basis for a new development policy ortho-
doxy among donors, which has called not only for more market-oriented
economies and greater support for smallholder agriculture, but also for increased reliance upon export earnings at the expense of import-substituting
infant industries. Subsequent World Bank reviews [*Toward Sustained Development in
Sub-Saharan Africa*, 1984, and *Financing Adjustment with Growth*, 1986] recognized that African economies can only accomplish such policy and structural transforma-
tion on the basis of increased development assistance from multilateral and
bilateral agencies, as well as increased private international investment. Massive infusions of international relief for African drought and famine victims
were, thus, to be matched by corresponding international investment in the
rehabilitation of African development processes.

United States Treasury Secretary James Baker underscored this premise
when, at a Seoul meeting of finance ministers in July, he proposed a **three-
point plan to relieve debt problems** of African and other nations by a $20
billion increase in commercial bank loans and a $9 billion increase in multi-
lateral development assistance for those countries undertaking the required
policy reforms. Simultaneously, the World Bank initiated a special Sub-Saharan Development Facility for countries prepared to accept the World
Bank's diagnoses and prescriptions for economic recovery. Bilateral donors
have followed suit by increasing funds available for development as well as
for famine relief. Fourteen nations subscribed $1.1 billion for the new fund,
and the United States earmarked additional funds for the same purpose to be
administered independently. However, a January 1986 Geneva pledging conference of food donor nations produced commitments for only 70 percent of
estimated food grain import requirements for the coming year.

The United Nations Food and Agricultural Organization announced in
December that all but six of more than 20 food-short African countries were
off the immediate danger list. Meanwhile Mozambique and Angola were
prominent among African countries indicating new willingness to accept at
least cautiously many of the World Bank and IMF policy prescriptions. To-

gether these trends may appear to support the proposition that coordinated international development assistance, combined with policy reform, will hasten economic recovery.

Two features of the new international initiative for African economic renewal deserve special note. First, African economic stagnation has not taken place in a political vacuum. Acquisition of arms by African countries absorbed with regional and sometimes domestic conflicts has increasingly diverted both human and material resources from the tasks of economic recovery. Soaring military expenditures in the midst of endemic poverty bring home the point. The U.S. Arms Control and Disarmament Agency estimates that between 1972 and 1982 **military expenditures in Africa** rose by an average of 8 percent a year, four times the rate of the North Atlantic Treaty Organization and almost twice that for Latin America and South Asia. In 1982, the African market accounted for 15 percent of the total world trade in arms, up from only about 5 percent a decade earlier.

Second, the special General Assembly session represents one of the first opportunities for African and other less developed countries to debate strategies for reversing development stagnation with industrialized countries as well as with each other. To date, the campaigns for policy reform have been initiated by the World Bank, the IMF, and donor countries—sometimes in concert with each other—in bilateral negotiations with individual African countries. Recipient African countries have been in a weak position to debate the merits of prescriptions for economic reform upon which there is growing donor consensus. Documentation for the session, however, has been provided at least in part by the Organization of African Unity.

How do African states diagnose the causes of their collective crisis, and what remedies do they prescribe? How do these analyses depart from the prescriptions of multilateral and many bilateral donors? The 15th Extraordinary Session of the OAU Council of Ministers reached a consensus that the economies of many of its members are verging on collapse. The ministers agreed that "lack of structural transformation and the widespread low level of productivity of the African economies are the fundamental causes of their continued underdevelopment and persistent economic crisis" [OAU/ECM/2XV/ Rev.2]. They recognized, too, that a "radical change in development priorities" would be required if sustained and self-reliant development were to be achieved.

Subtle but important differences appear to remain between African governments and donors on the **domestic causes** of their persistent underdevelopment. The ministers cite the "sharp contrasts" between urban development and rural poverty but do not focus specifically on low producer prices and urban consumer subsidies as have the donors. They recognize the "inadequacy and/or misdirection of human and financial resources" without referring to donor concerns about the size of the public sector, the absence of decentralization, and shortcomings in planning and priority-setting processes. The ministers agree with donors on the obstacle to increased standards of living posed by rampant population growth. They also share the donors' objections to the importation of substitution-based industrial development. The OAU has gone beyond the donors to recognize as culprits not only economic policies but also the political instability that has produced large numbers of refugees and "the persistence of social values, attitudes and practices that are not always conducive to development."

In the realm of external causes, the OAU centers on debt burden as the cause of continuing underdevelopment, where the donors have tended to emphasize debt ratios as a symptom of those causes. Thus, the General Assembly may be expected to debate the merits of major debt rescheduling and/or debt cancellation.

The OAU's **Africa Priority Programme for Economic Recovery 1986–2000 (APPER)** also differs from the evolving donor consensus in its estimate of how economic recovery is to be realized. First, it demands that reform measures take full account of the peculiar characteristics of individual countries and regions, whereas donor prescriptions have been more universalistic. The OAU agrees with donors on the priority of agricultural development, but does not emphasize the importance of the small producers who predominate in African agricultural sectors. Where donors emphasize price incentives and less intrusive government as the key to agricultural regeneration, the APPER list includes credit and input delivery systems, rural transport, special encouragement for women producers, and development of appropriate technologies—all implying little reduction in the scope of government.

The APPER appears to emphasize self-reliance to a greater degree than do the donors, notably in its call for the development and rehabilitation of agro-industries to support agricultural production: irrigation equipment, raw materials processing, renewable energy sources, and spare parts manufacturing. For the OAU ministers, moreover, governments appear to retain primary responsibility for achieving such self-reliance. The APPER calls for better public management of scarce resources, not less public sector management of the economy, and it suggests the importance of public mobilization of domestic savings. For the OAU the private sector is "to be encouraged through well-defined and consistent policies," not to be left free to seek its own ends. Finally, the APPER reiterates the **Lagos Plan of Action**'s call for inter-African cooperation—what Julius Nyerere of Tanzania has termed "south-south" cooperation. Donor manifestos have been mute on this point.

The Special Session forged a consensus on principles of a United Nations program for African economic recovery but failed to do so on important aspects of implementation. African nations sought specific aid commitments, which the industrialized countries were generally unwilling to make, insisting that the General Assembly session should not be a pledging conference. Some donor nations appeared to be more comfortable with bilateral negotiations with individual African countries, perhaps in the context of coordinated donor strategies, than with multilateral negotiations in the setting of the U.N. General Assembly.

Southern Africa

South Africa. Central to the crisis of Southern Africa is the persistence of white minority rule based upon apartheid within the Republic of South Africa. The South African Government has imposed an apartheid regime on Namibia (or South West Africa) in defiance of the United Nations, which long since withdrew South Africa's mandate to govern the territory; and it has sought to coopt, militarily attack, or overturn the governments of neighboring countries to prevent their being employed as bases for attacks on its racist rule within the Republic.

The central issue before the General Assembly in 1986 may no longer be primarily how to isolate and bring additional pressure to bear on the apartheid regime in South Africa but, rather, to what extent and in what ways to **support African resistance movements**, which have grown greatly in strength over the last year. In addition, the South African regime has taken unusual steps to create at least the appearance of commitment to change. The General Assembly is likely to debate the significance of these gestures by the South African Government, though South Africa's recent raids into Zambia, Zimbabwe, and Botswana caused an Eminent Persons Group, composed of Commonwealth diplomats, to conclude that the window of opportunity for a negotiated settlement had closed.

Since 1960, the General Assembly and the Security Council have repeatedly censured the South African regime for its apartheid policies. In 1985, the United Nations pension fund accelerated its eleven-year policy of selling holdings in companies doing business in South Africa. The Security Council urged voluntary economic sanctions against South Africa and the suspension of new investments in the country in response to the regime's declaration of a state of emergency in July. The 40th General Assembly overwhelmingly passed a series of resolutions condemning racial oppression in South Africa, calling for a tightening of the arms embargo and a banning of nuclear collaboration with South Africa, and a prohibition of all loans, credits, and investments in the country. The General Assembly may be expected to debate how far these moves portend real and not illusory or merely symbolic change. Turmoil in South Africa, moreover, may significantly affect regional balances of power and, thereby, the prospects for the independence of Namibia and resolution of conflicts within Mozambique and Angola.

Whereas racially based segregation, political subjugation, and economic exploitation date almost from the beginning of a European presence in South Africa in the mid-17th century, the systematic apartheid which characterizes South Africa today dates from the coming to power of the Afrikaaner-based National Party in 1948. For blacks, and to a large extent for Asians and mixed-race coloreds as well, apartheid has meant loss of all rights to participation in the central government, banning of interracial marriage; comprehensive restrictions on black movement within the country; "influx control" through enforcement of pass laws; heavy limits on the ability of blacks to own or occupy urban property for either business or residential purposes, exclusion of blacks in rural areas from large areas of good land reserved for white farming; onerous limits on the rights of blacks to seek and retain urban employment; denial to black unions of power to bargain collectively; refusal to permit many blacks to have their rural-based families join them in the cities where they struggle to find employment; limited and underfunded as well as noncompulsory public education; strict segregation of public facilities by race; and comprehensive assaults on rights of blacks to assemble, express themselves politically, and receive due process of law. From the early 1960s, much of the African political leadership was in prison, and African parties were unable to function internally until at least the late 1970s. The government also undermined traditional local African institutions, resulting in their atrophy.

The ultimate goal of the National Party regime has been to deny all but a handful of blacks their South African citizenship, assigning them instead to citizenship in one of several **ethnically based homelands**, or *bantustans*. Thus, most blacks became by official fiat "foreigners" in the cities of their own country, little differentiated from citizens of Botswana, Lesotho, and Swaziland who work in the Republic in great numbers. The homelands policy has reflected not only official racism, and an attempt not to appear racist before world opinion, but white fear of having the cities inundated by blacks who are unable to make ends meet in the rural areas. Ironically, the structure of the homelands has helped to produce that very result. Eighty-seven percent of the people of the country are assigned to *bantustans,* which represent only 13 percent of the land, and not the best land. The homelands, with Transkei's possible exception, have totally lacked the resources to establish even the impression of political autonomy and economic viability. They are rarely as ethnically homogeneous as they were designed to be, creating still further social insecurity, while individualization of landholdings in some has helped to crystallize enlarged rural unemployed classes.

Since the 1961 massacre at Sharpeville, South Africa has been the scene of an escalating struggle between the major African resistance movements [the African National Congress (ANC) and the Pan African Congress (PAC)] and the regime. Denied peaceful outlets for political expression, African resistance to apartheid has become increasingly militant, confrontational, and violent as the regime has become increasingly repressive in seeking to extinguish such protest.

The cycle of violence has been enlarged exponentially since the Botha regime began to undertake to "reform" apartheid in 1982. The government introduced a new constitution featuring a tricameral parliament with one house each for white, Indian, and colored populations. The new constitution established a president to be elected by a multiracial electoral college and advised by representatives of all three parliamentary chambers. The system preserved white dominance throughout the new structure while increasing the executive power of the state president. Whites alone were asked to approve the new constitution, which they did in November 1983 by a substantial majority, over objections that such changes implied too many concessions to other races.

The regime's attempt to coopt the Indian and colored communities failed, for 80 percent of both groups boycotted elections for the new parliaments. Blacks immediately greeted their renewed exclusion from the government with widespread and violent protests, which have increased in the ensuing months. Since the beginning of 1985, the Botha regime has been almost continuously engaged in making it appear that blacks, too, stand to gain in the new constitutional order. Increasingly it has been obliged to persuade not only blacks but also overseas investors, who have begun to limit their exposure in South Africa in the wake of escalating violence in which many hundreds of blacks have been killed and thousands more imprisoned. The violence of the Government's response to militant African resistance has undercut the Government's claims to be "abolishing" apartheid. It has periodically hinted that it might be prepared to release jailed African leader Nelson Mandela but has not followed through. Nevertheless, the removal of several pillars of the apartheid structure in combination with the absence of any new measures to permit black political participation suggest that the Botha regime is, at a minimum, seeking to maintain white minority rule on a new basis. It remains very unclear what the Government ultimately intends and whether the events of 1985 and 1986 will lead to the strengthening or to the demise of white rule in South Africa.

The changes introduced by the regime have raised more questions than they have answered. In February 1985, the Government announced it would grant some blacks the right to acquire 99-year leases on their urban homes, reversing previous insistence that they relocate in satellite townships. But it was not clear who would qualify and under what conditions. Two months later, it abolished the legislation prohibiting mixed marriages and sexual contact across racial lines without clarifying where racially mixed households would be able to live. In May, the Government determined not to uproot 700,000 blacks in 52 townships for deportation to various homelands, though all were still potentially subject to eviction based on other official policies. In the same month, the Government lifted a 17-year ban on multi-racial political parties, though there was no indication that the National Party would seek to broaden its base, nor was there any indication of how effectively such parties might be allowed to function in practice, given emergency measures in force. This change spoke to a long-standing policy difference within the African resistance movements over how broadly to cooperate with Indian and colored communities. In the fall, the Botha Government hinted that it might create a common citizenship for all members of all races without officially abandoning the homelands policy. The Government proposed to increase by 19 percent its expenditure on African education, but the total outlays still amount to only 20 percent of the overall education budget for African pupils making up two-thirds of the school-age population. Also in the fall, a Government panel recommended the abolition of the pass laws by which influx control had been maintained, a recommendation accepted by the Government in April 1986.

In July 1985, the Government assumed sweeping emergency powers to deal with escalating unrest. While periodically lifting restrictions in some districts and imposing them in others, Government forces have shot many protesting Africans and have continued to arrest and detain hundreds of others. Broad restrictions have been imposed on the outdoor conduct of funerals for African victims of the conflict, previously the principal legitimate avenue for Africans to assemble and protest. In September, 16 prominent activists of the United Democratic Front were arrested and brought to trial on charges of treason, though the cases were subsequently dropped in December. The Government has detained activists Allan Boesak and Winnie Mandela, then issued both provisional and conditional releases.

The official violence has failed to arrest the growing strength of domestic opposition to apartheid and overseas pressure on the regime to change its ways. Racial violence, previously confined largely to the African townships, began to spill over periodically into white areas for the first time. The outlawed African National Congress (ANC) has demonstrated its intention to step up guerrilla war against the Government. School boycotts became a common occurrence. African unions also flexed their political muscle. In September the National Union of Mine Workers briefly went on strike, affecting 10 percent of the country's half a million black miners. In December, South Africa's black union leaders joined forces to create the Congress of South African Trade Unions, embracing over half a million black workers. Opposition white politicians, clergy, and leading businessmen have journeyed to Lusaka, Zambia, to meet with representatives of the outlawed ANC. Consumer boycotts exposed the vulnerability of white businesses to African economic power, and many began to make overtures to the African communities.

The refusal of major international banks to renew loans to the country's large borrowers prompted the regime to suspend trading on its stock market briefly in late August 1985 as the rand plunged to its lowest level ever. Pressure for economic sanctions against the regime has grown in the United States and other industrialized countries, even as many firms have begun to reduce their holdings in South Africa. Later in September the Government felt obliged to freeze repayment of principal on its foreign debt for the balance of the year, and did not resume payment until March 1986. In November, a group of 186 American-based companies in South Africa called upon the Botha Government to lower tensions by effecting significant political change. Also in November, a United Nations panel recommended that transnational firms disengage from the Republic.

Namibia. The history of Namibia remained a troubled one in 1985 and 1986. A German colony before World War I, the territory known as South West Africa was captured by South African troops in the course of the war, and afterwards South Africa gained a League of Nations mandate to advance the interests of the colony. After World War II, the United Nations refused a South African request to annex the territory and proposed instead trusteeship status for Namibia, with South Africa as the administrator, which, unlike the mandate, more specifically implied steps toward self-rule. The International Court of Justice endorsed this step.

In defiance of the United Nations, South Africa has in effect annexed the territory, imposing apartheid policies and proposing to treat it as yet another homeland. The United Nations created the **United Nations Council for Namibia** in 1967 to administer the territory, but it has had to do so in exile, since South Africa would not admit its emissaries into the territory. In 1973, the United Nations reinforced its withdrawal of the League of Nations mandate by recognizing the **South West Africa People's Organization (SWAPO)** as the "authentic representative of the Namibian people." In response to South African attempts to formulate alternatives to a SWAPO-led independent Namibia, the United Nations has treated **resolution 435** of 1978 as the basis for a truly independent Namibia. The resolution calls for a cease-fire, South African military withdrawal, and free elections, all under U.N. supervision. Since 1978, complex negotiations have ensued to persuade South Africa to accept this resolution as the basis for the transfer of power to an independent Namibian government. These negotiations through mid-1985 have been summarized in *Issues Before the 40th General Assembly of the United Nations*.

The independence of Namibia remained elusive in 1985 and the early months of 1986. South Africa has made the withdrawal of **Cuban troops** from neighboring **Angola** a condition for permitting implementation of resolution 435. In this course, South Africa has gained encouragement from the Reagan Administration's policy of "constructive engagement," which has held that Cuban withdrawal is a legitimate quid pro quo for the Pretoria regime's retirement from Namibia. However, as long as the Angolan Government faces a serious military challenge from the forces of the National Union for the Total Independence of Angola (UNITA), which has derived military support from South Africa and more recently from the United States, Cuban withdrawal remains unlikely.

South Africa has made it clear that while international negotiations continue in search of a way out of this impasse, it will continue to engineer its own "solution" to the Namibian problem. South Africa's "solution" has been to devolve some power upon a coalition government of parties which excludes SWAPO. From an African perspective this strategy bears more than a slight resemblance to the internal settlement constructed by the Smith regime in Zimbabwe (then Rhodesia) and to the cultivation of "homeland" political leaders in the Republic, while many legitimate African leaders remain in exile, prison, or under other restraints. The South African strategy remains unacceptable to all nations, including the United States, which termed the maneuver "null and void" [*The Washington Post*, 4/18/86].

The 40th General Assembly in a series of resolutions condemned South Africa for its failure to honor the terms of resolution 435, in effect refusing to concede that any progress has been made in the long history of intermittently hopeful negotiations for South African withdrawal [A/Res/40/97]. The resolutions passed unanimously but for the abstentions of the United States and many European nations. Among the abstainees were the members of the Western Contact Group—Canada, France, the United Kingdom, the United States, and West Germany—which, because of their extensive economic interests in the region, have taken a leadership role in seeking to negotiate with South Africa for its withdrawal.

Noting that 1985 marked the 25th anniversary of the founding of SWAPO, the General Assembly reaffirmed its support for the party's armed struggle and condemned South Africa for its continued illegal occupation of the territory for which the United Nations has assumed direct responsibility prior to its independence, specifically condemning the "so-called interim government" imposed by the Pretoria Government and "all other fraudulent constitutional and political schemes by which the racist regime of South Africa attempts to perpetuate its colonial domination of Namibia." The General Assembly, further, rejected the linkage of Namibian independence to Cuban troop withdrawal from Namibia, and it endorsed what it recognized as "the world-wide and justified condemnation of the policy of constructive engagement," which it considered a failure and supportive of South African resistance to Namibian independence.

An often overlooked aspect of the Namibian issue has been the disposition of **Walvis Bay and the offshore islands**, source of important oil reserves, which South Africa has sought to rule independently of Namibia and, thus, to exclude from the negotiations over its independence. The 40th General Assembly reiterated the position it took in resolution 432 of 1978 that Walvis Bay and the offshore islands are integral parts of Namibia and cannot be detached by South African fiat. Although South Africa has occasionally indicated that Cuban withdrawal is the only issue standing in the way of Namibian independence, it is certainly possible that the matter of Walvis Bay will surface as a new obstacle to progress once the Cubans have departed.

The 41st General Assembly may well again consider the Namibian question. South Africa has not departed from its course of threatening to substitute its own "solution" for the U.N.-sponsored plan, in spite of the condemnation of the 40th General Assembly. Perhaps more important, a new form of linkage may have emerged, this time between Namibian independence and events within South Africa itself. To the extent that the Botha regime finds itself obliged to make significant concessions to African peoples within the Republic, it may be hard pressed to deny similar concessions to the people of Namibia. In particular the apparent abandonment of the influx and pass laws suggests the regime's recognition that the homeland strategy has failed. Can South Africa, through its attempted internal settlements, then continue to govern Namibia as though it were an extension of an increasingly discredited homelands policy?

South Africa and the Region. An issue of growing importance in 1985 and 1986 has been South Africa's use of military and economic power to prevent its neighbors from becoming bases for opposition to the apartheid regime. South Africa has supported UNITA's military challenge to the Dos Santos Government in Angola, and direct military action has included air raids and clashes on the ground with SWAPO partisans. South Africa has undermined the 1984 Nkomati Accord with Mozambique, under which South Africa was to withdraw its support from rebels opposed to the government of Samora Machel in return for Mozambique's denial of sanctuary for those planning military action against the apartheid regime. Its continued support for the Mozambique insurgents has become clear. Botswana has also felt the wrath of the Botha regime for its alleged support of militant liberation groups. Finally, South African economic pressure on Lesotho contributed to the fall of Chief Leabua Jonathan's government and its replacement by a military regime under General Justin Lekhanya, which promptly airlifted African National Congress partisans to Zambia.

In October, the Security Council unanimously condemned the raids on Angola. The underlying question, however, is whether the General Assembly or the Security Council will find it appropriate to take additional measures to support the territorial integrity of South Africa's neighbors. The possibility exists that if South African military and economic pressure on her neighbors continues, the General Assembly may declare South Africa a threat to the entire Southern Africa region and support regional defense efforts rather than simply assert the claims of individual countries against the Republic of South Africa.

4. Central America

The clash of wills between the Reagan Administration and the Sandinista Government of **Nicaragua** remains in 1986 the focal point of the crisis in Central America and has become a bitterly fought domestic issue in Washington. The White House successfully pressed Congress for a resumption of military aid to the "contra" guerrilla groups operating out of Honduras and Costa Rica, which had been cut off in mid-1984. The United States maintained economic pressure on Managua through a trade embargo and there were no bilateral negotiations. Although President Reagan stopped short of demanding the overthrow of the Sandinistas, he insisted that Nicaragua's "structure" must change through negotiations with the insurgents, new elections, and the establishment of a pluralistic political system that would include the rebel factions.

Efforts by four regional powers on the periphery of the dispute—Colombia, Mexico, Panama, and Venezuela, known as the "Contadora Group"—to win approval of a draft peace treaty covering all five Central American nations (Costa Rica, El Salvador, Guatemala, Honduras, and Nicaragua) have remained stalemated. Various U.N. bodies—the Security Council, the International Court of Justice (or World Court), the General Assembly, and the Commission on Human Rights—have continued to serve as political battlegrounds, without having a major impact on the crisis.

The contras, suffering from lack of arms and poor training, were said to number some 13,000 fighters, but only a few thousand were able to take the field [*Newsweek*, 3/17/86] against the Nicaraguan regular armed forces, whose strength was put at 62,850 by the International Institute for Strategic Studies in London [*The New York Times*, 3/16/86]. Nicaraguan troops scored major victories over the anti-Government guerrillas through the increasing use of a half dozen or more helicopter gunships in their possession. The rebels scored limited successes against the gunships with SAM-7 ground-to-air missiles, and the United States planned using part of the aid package—$70 million in military assistance and $30 million in nonlethal supplies—to provide them with more sophisticated Stinger missiles [*The New York Times*, 4/4/86]. Some 15 more Soviet-made combat helicopters arrived in Nicaragua in July, several weeks after the U.S. Congress approved the aid package.

The rancorous debate over aid in Washington centered on whether the United States had the right, the need, or the ability to forcibly stem the spread of "pro-Soviet" regimes in the region and whether the effort could lead to the use of American soldiers in combat in Central America. "If we don't want to see the map of Central America covered in a sea of red, eventually lapping at our own borders, we must act now," President Reagan warned. "Nothing less than the security of the United States is at stake." According to Administration officials, the imposition by the Sandinistas on October 15, 1985, of a state of emergency involving curbs on civil liberties was not the regime's response to the threat of insurgency but, rather, evidence of its Marxist and totalitarian nature.

Few congressional opponents of the aid defended the Nicaraguan Government, but they questioned the Sandinistas' capacity to export their revolution. They also questioned the abilities and intentions of the rebels, whose leaders range from disaffected Sandinistas, who opposed the Marxist tilt of the government and lost out in internal power struggles, to officers who served under Anastasio Somoza Debayle, the right-wing dictator overthrown by the Sandinista revolutionaries in 1979. And despite the Nicaraguan Government's strictures and economic woes, there was little evidence of broad popular support for the rebels inside Nicaragua. Human rights watchdog groups, such as the Americas Watch Committee and Amnesty International, have reported atrocities by both sides in the fighting.

Reagan lost an initial vote in the House of Representatives on March 20, by 222 to 210, but the following week Administration officials publicized a cross-border raid by some 800 to 1,000 Nicaraguan Government troops against rebel camps well inside Honduras. The Hondurans, who had sought to ignore the contra presence in their territory, finally protested the incursion at U.S. urging, and Nicaragua was obliged to admit the action. The second House vote on the aid package provided a victory for Reagan on June 26.

Just two days after the House acted, the World Court handed down its ruling that the U.S. support for the rebels was illegal. It called on the U.S. to end its support of the contras and to compensate Nicaragua for damages. The Court heard oral arguments in September 1985 on the case brought by Nicaragua following United States involvement in the mining of Nicaraguan ports by the contras. Washington said it would not accept the jurisdiction of the Court and boycotted the proceedings.

The international spotlight has veered away from **El Salvador**, where the six-year civil war between leftist guerrillas of the Farabundo Martí National Liberation Front and the government of Christian Democratic President José Napoleón Duarte continues at a lower level of intensity but with no end in sight. El Salvador's Minister of Culture met with a high-ranking representative of the guerrilla coalition on April 18 at the home of Peru's President Alan García with the purpose of negotiating an end to the conflict. In early June, President Duarte made an unexpected offer to the rebels to hold a new round of peace talks inside El Salvador in late July or August, and the leftist coalition replied on July 10 by offering to link a ceasefire to the start of negotiations [*The New York Times*, 6/3/86].

On the broader diplomatic front, the **Contadora Group**, named for the island off the coast of Panama where the four countries first launched their initiative, put forward the latest text of their peace treaty in September 1985. They received formal support from the newly elected democratic governments in Argentina, Brazil, Peru, and Uruguay. The treaty calls for an end to foreign support of insurgents, for "internal reconciliation" within each Central American signatory, and for the formation of democratic governments. President Reagan's special Central American envoy, Philip C. Habib, has said that the United States would "abide" by the treaty terms if all five countries sign it but that it would not sign the attached protocol. The protocol would legally bind Washington to comply with its requirements, limiting the U.S. military maneuvers in the area and ending U.S. aid to the contras. Nicaragua has said it would sign the text if U.S. aid to the rebels stops at the time of signing [*The New York Times*, 4/27/86]. But the Sandinistas fear that the Habib statement has a loophole that permits the United States to interpret "internal reconciliation" as requiring new elections in Nicaragua and a national government that includes the contras. They have also raised objections to the treaty's demand for the reduction of military forces. The Contadora Group set June 6 as the deadline for signing, but the deadline passed without an agreement being reached.

In the United Nations Security Council, to which Nicaragua appealed in December 1985 after a Nicaraguan helicopter was shot down by a SAM-7 missile, debate was inconclusive. A week later, the General Assembly adopted a resolution [A/Res/40/188; vote: 91–6, with 49 abstentions] regretting the imposition of a United States trade embargo on Nicaragua on May 1, 1985, and asking that it be revoked. A resolution sponsored by the Contadora Group—endorsing their treaty text, urging an end to United States military maneuvers in the region, and calling for the resumption of negotiations between the United States and Nicaragua—was not put to the vote when Nicaragua, Honduras, El Salvador, and Costa Rica each raised varying objections to it. The Council met again in July at Nicaragua's request to debate the American arms flow to the contras, but no resolution was presented.

The Assembly adopted two resolutions in December on **human rights violations in El Salvador and Guatemala**. The text on El Salvador [A/Res/40/139; vote: 100–2, with 42 abstentions] recognized improvements in the human rights situation there but criticized both the government and the insurgent forces for numerous and continuing violations. It urged the resumption of negotiations between the two sides. The resolution on Guatemala [A/Res/40/140; 91–8, with 47 abstentions] expressed concern at the continuing grave and widespread violations but noted with satisfaction that a new government and a new constitution—with human rights safeguards—would be installed in the country in January 1986. At its meeting on March 13, 1986, the Commission on Human Rights "welcome[d] with satisfaction the establishment, in accordance with the provisions of the Constitution of the Republic of Guatemala, of the National Human Rights Commission and the office of the Attorney for Human Rights [CHR resolution 1986/62].

The 41st General Assembly will consider human rights issues as well as the broader situation in Central America [A/41/50, item 43].

5. Afghanistan

The four-year-long U.N.-sponsored negotiations on an end to the Soviet occupation of Afghanistan reached a critical juncture in the months preceding the 41st General Assembly. Fighting intensified within the country and along the Afghan-Pakistani border, and Moscow in May replaced Babrak Karmal as head of the government it installed in Kabul in 1979. The new leader, Najibullah, offered in July to open talks with at least some rebel leaders, offering "reasonable compromises."

The issue of Afghanistan was one of the few direct confrontations between the superpowers in which both the General Assembly and the Secretary-General were directly engaged. On the basis of past Assembly resolutions, Diego Cordovez, the **Secretary-General's Personal Representative on Afghanistan,** held the fifth, sixth, and seventh rounds of indirect "proximity talks" between the Afghan and Pakistani foreign ministers in Geneva in August and December of 1985 and in May of 1986. Cordovez also met informally with Soviet and American representatives and conferred with the Iranians and the Chinese on the progress of the talks. Afghanistan was among the subjects discussed at the Soviet-American summit meeting in Geneva in November 1985.

Reports on the fighting came largely from the rebel side, through Western diplomats or through reporters who traveled with the *mojahedin* units. Their consensus was that both sides operated more aggressively and more widely over the past year, but the net result was to sustain the pattern of **hit-and-run actions** on both sides, along with the **deadlock** it has produced. The Institute of Strategic Studies in Pakistan estimates that 5,000 rebels are killed each year, as well as 2,500 Afghan Government troops and an equal number of Soviet soldiers [*The New York Times,* 12/27/85]. The Soviet troop strength in the country is believed to be 118,000, supported by some 45,000 to 60,000 Afghan army soldiers, facing some 35,000 rebels in almost 100 quasi-independent bands, but with a growing degree of coordination.

In his most recent report, prepared for the March session of the United Nations Commission on Human Rights, the United Nations' Special Rapporteur on human rights violations in Afghanistan, Felix Ermacora of Austria, accused Soviet and Afghan troops of killing more than 35,000 civilians in 1985. He alleged a campaign of "systematic brutality," involving the use against civilian targets of canisters of "liquid fire" dropped from planes, bombs that explode 24 hours after impact, and booby-trapped toys [*The New York Times*, 2/27/86].

The **rebel efforts** are financed in large part by a massive flow of U.S. covert aid, estimated at $250 to $280 million in fiscal 1985, and at as much as $480 million for fiscal 1986 [*The Wall Street Journal*, 10/8/85]. In addition, some $200 million more in arms flows were reported from China, Saudi Arabia, Egypt, Israel, and Iran during 1985. However, there have been charges that only a small portion of the aid flow reaches the *mojahedin* in arms and provisions, after passing through the hands of Pakistani authorities and the political leaders of the rebel factions, most of them based in Peshawar. (Pakistan, however, seeks to maintain the diplomatic fiction that it is not involved in rebel activities and that no guerrilla groups operate from its territory.) Some of the supplemental U.S. aid is believed to have gone for the British-made "Blowpipe" surface-to-air missiles, a highly portable system suitable for use against Soviet planes and helicopter gunships. American officials maintained that the use of more effective surface-to-air missiles by the rebels had limited the use of Soviet air power during antiguerrilla sweeps [*Dept. of State Bull.*, 12/85]. Nevertheless, the guerrilla groups continued to complain of the limited quantities of sophisticated arms, and maintained that they could put more troops in the field if they had more weapons [*The New York Times*, 12/27/85].

The **diplomatic process**, which has always moved by fits and starts, got some impetus in the fall of 1985. First the General Assembly adopted in November—by its largedst margin ever—a resolution calling for the immediate withdrawal of the foreign troops from Afghanistan, and endorsing the Cordovez negotiating effort [A/Res/40/12; vote: 122–19, with 12 abstentions]. In mid-December, the Assembly for the first time adopted a resolution expressing deep concern over the "gross and systematic" violations of human rights by the Afghan Government "with heavy support from foreign troops" [A/Res/40/137; vote: 80–22, with 40 abstentions].

At the same time, the United States removed one major obstacle to a negotiated agreement. It committed itself in writing, for the first time, to play (along with the Soviet Union) the role of guarantor for any agreement "provided that the central issue of Soviet troop withdrawal and its interrelationship to the other" elements of the agreement were "adequately addressed and resolved" [*Dept. of State Bull.*, 2/86]. This pledge was tantamount to a commitment to nonintervention, including a cutoff of arms aid to the Afghan rebels in tandem with, rather that after, a Soviet troop withdrawal. It evoked protests from Congress and factions in the Pentagon and the political right that opposed any "sellout" of the *mojahedin*.

In fact, however, the unspoken assumption of all parties is that any agreement, if it is to be fruitful, depends upon a development that cannot be encompassed in the formal U.N. negotiations: that is, the evolution of a more stable Afghan government that can survive the departure of the Soviet troops and prove acceptable to the major *mojahedin* factions, yet remain on friendly terms with Moscow. (In early May, following Karmal's mysterious month-long absence from Afghanistan, word came of his resignation from the top leadership post. This announcement on the very eve of negotiations could be a signal that the Soviets are moving to broaden the Afghan Government in a way that will satisfy the rebel factions.)

The talks involve four documents: an Afghan-Pakistani agreement on noninterference; the Soviet-American guarantee of Afghan security; an Afghan-Pakistani agreement on the return of some 3.5 million Afghan refugees, most of whom are in Pakistan; and a document linking Soviet troop withdrawal to the operation of the other three undertakings. The fourth document would also establish procedures for monitoring and adjudicating potential violations of the accords.

With the Americans on board, agreement on the first three texts was virtually completed at the December meeting in Geneva. But an impasse developed on the fourth document when Afghanistan insisted on face-to-face negotiations. Pakistan objected, contending that that would constitute de facto recognition of the Karmal regime. The impasse was broken in March, when Cordovez visited Kabul and Islamabad, and returned with an Afghan agreement to resume the talks on an indirect basis—and the first Soviet-Afghan draft of a **timetable for troop withdrawal.** While Pakistani officials raised the objection that the proposed withdrawal sequence is too lengthy [*The New York Times*, 4/4/86], Cordovez called the overcoming of the impasse "a very great step forward," because it "will allow the negotiations for the first time to focus on the crucial issue of the interrelationship between noninterference and withdrawal of Soviet troops."

The three-week Geneva round was suspended on May 23, and Cordovez said that both sides considered they had made substantial progress in the discussions that focused entirely on substantive issues—specifically on the fourth document. A number of important issues had been settled, including the binding legal status of the fourth document. The timetable for withdrawal—about which disagreement remained great—was the one main issue left outstanding and that needed to be tackled when the talks resumed on July 30. As that date approached, Pérez de Cuéllar called on both sides to stop dragging their feet on the draft accord presented by Cordovez.

However, officials involved in the negotiations said that the "real" timetable would emerge from the "political logic of the situation," and that the timetable is not the major obstacle remaining. Rather, it is the *sequence* of withdrawal, nonintervention, and the detailing of measures—including U.N. observers—to monitor compliance with the pact and to deal with alleged violations [Interviews with *Issues Before the 41st General Assembly*]. These officials cautioned that even if a final textual agreement were to be reached, the question of political will to put it into effect would remain unclear. The possibility remained, they said, that the entire negotiating process may be viewed by the superpowers as a purely tactical exercise, and one or both might be unwilling at present to end the armed struggle.

6. Indochina

The seven-year struggle between guerrilla groups and Vietnamese occupation forces in **Democratic Kampuchea (Cambodia)** settled quietly into an impasse in the months preceding the 41st General Assembly, with no major dry-season offensive launched by the Vietnamese, no immediate prospect of negotiation, and limited—but growing—guerrilla operations within Cambodia. Diplomatic reports from Hanoi suggested that the Vietnamese were focusing on preparations for their Communist Party congress toward the end of 1986, and would not be ready to come to grips with the Cambodia problem until the end of the year. The death of Vietnamese party chief Le Duan in July, and his prompt replacement by hardliner Truang Chinh, 79, was not viewed as a development that would break the stalemate.

Within a month of their invasion in December 1978, the Vietnamese easily ousted the Khmer Rouge regime of Pol Pot, which the international community recognizes as responsible for the deaths of some two million Kampucheans from 1975 through 1978. Hanoi installed in Phnom Penh the People's Republic of Kampuchea (PRK) under the leadership of Heng Samrin. That government has not won broad recognition, and the country's U.N. seat remains occupied by the **Coalition Government of Democratic Kampuchea (CGDK)**, an amalgam of three resistance groups, among them the Khmer Rouge. The other two factions are the Khmer People's National Liberation Front (KPNLF), headed by former Prime Minister Son Sann, and a smaller group, the Sihanoukist National Army (SNA), led by Prince Norodom Sihanouk, former hereditary ruler of Cambodia, who serves as titular president of the coalition and remains a respected figure within the country and the international community.

These strange bedfellows are backed by the United States, China, the Association of South East Asian Nations (ASEAN)—composed of Brunei, Indonesia, Malaysia, the Philippines, Singapore, and Thailand—and most members of the nonaligned movement, who view the occupation of any small nation by its larger neighbor as a potential threat to each of them.

When the 40th General Assembly convened, the Vietnamese had just completed a major dry-season offensive that had forced more than 200,000 Khmers—most of them anti-Vietnamese guerrillas and their families—into camps in Thailand. Vietnam used Khmer laborers to build a 50-mile-long barrier near the border in an attempt to prevent future incursions and the reestablishment of guerrilla camps in Cambodian territory.

Despite this setback, the CGDK and its allies were able to increase by four their vote total in the annual Assembly resolution calling for the withdrawal of all foreign forces from Kampuchea [A/Res/40/7; vote: 114–21, with 16 abstentions]. Hanoi submits its own rival item each year, entitled "Question of peace, stability and cooperation in South-East Asia," [A/41/50, item 39], but it has never had sufficient backing to put any resolution to the vote or even table a resolution on the item. Nor has it challenged the credentials of the CGDK delegation since 1982.

In the field, the most effective of the guerrilla groups has been the Khmer Rouge, equipped by China and mustering an estimated 35,000 troops. The KPNLF forces, estimated at 17,000, were hampered by a leadership struggle between Son Sann and his military commanders. The Sihanoukist forces are said to number about 8,000. The latter two groups get some arms from China, but their main sources of supply have been Singapore and Thailand, as well as covert cash grants from the CIA, channeled through the Thai Government, which are said to amount to $5 million a year [*The Washington Post,* 7/8/85]. Congress appropriated $5 million in overt military aid to the two factions for the first time in fiscal 1986.

In the spring of 1986, diplomats in Phnom Penh reported an increase in guerrilla activity throughout Kampuchea, including some joint operations by the KPNLF and the Sihanoukists, and by the Khmer Rouge and the Sihanoukists. These disruptions have added to Kampuchea's severe economic problems, and prompted the Soviet Union to double its economic aid to the country from the present level of $138.6 million [*The New York Times,* 4/6/86].

On the **diplomatic front,** quiet contacts between Hanoi and ASEAN have intensified, but with few tangible results. Vietnamese Foreign Minister Nguyen Co Thach met with Thai Foreign Minister Siddhi in Bangkok in April, their first meeting in three years. Hanoi has sustained its long dialogue with Indonesian Foreign Minister Mochtar Kusumaatmadja, who was selected to speak for ASEAN because of Indonesia's traditional tilt toward Hanoi and its long-term suspicion of Beijing. Vietnam has proposed direct negotiations with the ASEAN nations on the issue, and has long favored the convening of an international conference on Kampuchea that would include the major powers and India. It has also backed direct talks between the Heng Samrin regime and the Sihanouk and Son Sann factions—omitting the Khmer Rouge.

ASEAN officials dismiss these offers as tactical attempts to split the coalition and its allies. They have proposed negotiations between the CGDK and Vietnam, with the Samrin regime sitting in as part of the Vietnamese delegation. This plan was endorsed by President Reagan in May during his meeting with ASEAN leaders in Indonesia. "We are prepared to participate constructively in a regional settlement and call upon Vietnam to answer your reasonable proposals for negotiations," Reagan said. But the U.S. President stopped short of endorsing a new negotiating offer put forward by the CGDK in March [Reuters, 5/1/86].

The guerrilla coalition's eight-point plan also suggested talks between the CGDK and Vietnam (with the Samrin regime as part of the Vietnamese delegation), but for the first time it offered the creation of a coalition government that would include the Phnom Penh regime. It also put forward the idea of a two-phase withdrawal of the estimated 150,000 Vietnamese troops still in Kampuchea. After the initial Hanoi pullout and a cease-fire, negotiations between the Samrin regime and the CGDK could take place, as well as a larger international meeting on other aspects of the dispute. China and the ASEAN countries endorsed the proposal, but Vietnam rejected it immediately.

Hanoi also cut off talks with the United States in April on the search for remains of the 1,797 Americans still listed as missing in action (MIA) during the Vietnam war. Earlier that month, Vietnam had turned over the remains of 21 American MIAs. The Indonesians had helped to initiate the joint American-Vietnamese search operations, in the hope that a warming between Washington and Hanoi would eventually improve the prospects for a settlement in Kampuchea. But the Vietnamese were apparently upset when their gestures on MIAs failed to move them closer to diplomatic recognition by Washington. Hanoi cited the American air strike against Libya as the reason for the halt in the MIA program, and Vietnamese officials hinted that it could resume again in the future [Interviews with *Issues Before the 41st General Assembly*]. President Reagan, in Bali, called Hanoi's action "a great disappointment to us," and said that the resolution of the MIA issue would be in Vietnam's national interest.

The Secretary-General's 1985 Report on the Situation in Kampuchea declares that "a reasonable degree of convergence has emerged on the main elements of a comprehensive political settlement," and proposes "a limited international conference" with the participation of all parties directly concerned, the five permanent members of the Security Council, and other mutually acceptable countries [A/40/759].

7. Cyprus

The two-decade-long dispute between the Greek and Turkish communities on Cyprus is one of the few international issues in which the United Nations, and more specifically its Secretary-General, is the sole negotiating mechanism between the two sides. The United Nations has maintained a peacekeeping force on the island since 1964, when armed clashes erupted between the two sides. Javier Pérez de Cuéllar, who served as the chief U.N. representative on Cyprus from 1975 to 1977, has made the issue a personal priority ever since taking office as Secretary-General in 1982.

In the beginning of 1985, the Secretary-General brought the two sides close to an agreement that would provide the basis for reuniting the two communities in a bizonal federation. At a summit meeting in January 1985 in New York, the Turkish-Cypriot leader Rauf Denktash accepted the Secretary-General's draft, while the Greek-Cypriot President Spyros Kyprianou demanded further negotiations. A revised agreement, which took the Greek-Cypriot objections into consideration, failed in April 1985 over Denktash's objections. A third version of the "draft framework agreement" was submitted to both sides on March 29, 1986 [*The New York Times*, 3/30/86], and U.N. officials described it at the time as Pérez de Cuéllar's final attempt to find a common ground.

The March draft sets out a framework for negotiating an overall settlement of the Cyprus problem. It envisages a Greek-Cypriot president and a Turkish-Cypriot vice president, each with veto powers; a bicameral legislature in which one house would be equally divided and the other would provide the Greek Cypriots (who constitute 80 percent of the island's population) with a 70 to 30 margin; a cabinet with the same 70 to 30 ratio, but with one major ministry reserved for the Turkish Cypriots; and an evenly divided supreme court, with one non-Cypriot member who could break ties on disputes related to the division of functions between the federal and state governments. The Turkish Cypriots, who have controlled the northern 37 percent of the island since the invasion by Turkish troops in 1974, would be left with 29 percent of the land. The federal system would give each of the two federated states responsibility for local matters, while reserving sovereignty over the entire country for the federal government.

Under the U.N. plan, a transitional federal government could be established only after a final agreement was reached on all issues, including the three most fundamental ones: the timetable for the withdrawal of the 18,000 Turkish troops who still remain on the island, the nature of international guarantees, and the degree to which Cypriots from one state of the federation will be able to travel, own property, and reside in the other.

The Greek Cypriots maintain that the "three freedoms" must be absolute, that all Turkish troops must leave, and that Turkey can no longer serve as a guarantor, because that would provide it with an excuse for a renewed occupation. The Turkish Cypriots fear they will be overrun by the Greek Cypriot majority unless some restrictions are imposed on the "three freedoms." For the same reason, they require that a Turkish military presence remain and that Turkey retain its present role (with Greece and the United Kingdom) as guarantor of the pact.

Denktash accepted the March U.N. draft, but the Greek Cypriots raised some objections to its provisions. They wished to limit the veto power and feared that they would lose their bargaining leverage on the three unresolved issues if the rest of the pact were approved first. Rather than reject the Secretary-General's draft, however, Kyprianou proposed that the three outstanding issues be dealt with and resolved in advance, either at another summit session between the island's two leaders, or in an international conference, such as one proposed by the Soviet Union in April. Such a conference (with Soviet participation) would increase Greek-Cypriot leverage. The Greek-Cypriot stand was worked out with Prime Minister Papandreou of Greece [*The New York Times*, 1/17/86], who has long been blamed by American officials for blocking a negotiated settlement on Cyprus.

Pérez de Cuéllar, in a report to the Security Council on June 11 [S/18102/Add. 1], expressed regret at the Greek Cypriots' failure to accept his proposal, saying that this prevented negotiations on an overall solution, and raised concerns over "dangers inherent in the present situation." The nature of the dangers was made clear in July when Turkey's Prime Minister, Turgut Ozal, visited the Turkish-Cypriot sector in a show of support for Denktash. Greek-Cypriot demonstrators cut off the border crossings briefly, and Denktash responded by closing them for a week, isolating 650 U.N. troops based in an enclave in the Turkish-Cypriot zone. The crisis mood continued through the summer.

Most observers believe that unless the Secretary-General's plan is accepted, the status quo on the island will in due course become permanent and the Turkish Cypriots will gradually be recognized by a growing number of governments. The West fears that the Cyprus problem will contribute to a growing falling out between Greece and Turkey, which would damage the North Atlantic Treaty Organization (NATO); and Moscow fears that a partition of the strategically located island would end its nonaligned status and make it into a NATO base.

For the past 12 years, the peace has been kept in Cyprus by the **United Nations Peacekeeping Force in Cyprus (UNFICYP)**, which has some 2,300 troops and civilian police patrolling the 180-kilometer-long buffer zone between the two sides. But as of December 15, 1985, the force, which is financed solely by voluntary contributions, was $133.9 million in the red. This places a growing financial burden on the troop-contributing countries and raises questions about the future of UNFICYP—particularly if the Secretary-General's current effort does not succeed in moving the two sides toward an overall settlement.

The Security Council has consistently supported the Secretary-General's mission, including his most recent effort, and has called on the parties to cooperate with him in finding a solution. The "Question of Cyprus" is a perennial item on the General Assembly agenda [A/41/50, item 44], but has remained undebated since May 1983.

8. Other Colonial and Sovereignty Issues

One of the United Nations' historic achievements has been to stimulate the transition from colonialism to independence of almost half its present members, and this has virtually completed the task of decolonization. Aside from Namibia, and territories such as East Timor and Western Sahara, which have been annexed rather than gaining independence, most of the remaining handful of non-self-governing territories appear to be too small to be viable on their own.

The United Nations maintains a decolonization committee, formally entitled the Special Committee on the Situation with Regard to the Implementation of the Declaration on the Granting of Independence to Colonial Countries and Peoples, but informally known as the **Committee of 24**. This body, which celebrated its 25th anniversary during the 40th Assembly, monitors the status of the remaining territories and reports annually to the Assembly. In 1986, however, the United Kingdom (which administers most of the territories remaining on the U.N. list) announced that it would end its participation in the work of the committee, while continuing to submit annual reports on each territory to the Secretariat.

The 40th Assembly adopted resolutions on **six British territories** (Bermuda, the British Virgin Islands, the Cayman Islands, Montserrat, the Turks and Caicos Islands, and Anguilla) and **three American possessions** (American Samoa, Guam, and the U.S. Virgin Islands), generally assuming that independence would be their preferred destiny, and urging the colonial powers to pave the way for that future.

The most politically controversial among the remaining colonial questions involves the **Falkland Islands**, or **Malvinas**, in the South Atlantic, over which the United Kingdom and Argentina fought a brief but bloody war in 1982. London has ruled the islands for some 150 years, and the current inhabitants, virtually all of British descent, want its continued protection. Argentina's claim, never abandoned, has been on the U.N. agenda since 1965, and in November the 40th Assembly adopted an Argentine resolution calling for negotiations on all aspects of the dispute, using the "good offices" of the Secretary-General [A/Res/40/21; vote: 107–4, with 41 abstentions]. The text, far milder in tone than those of previous years, won 18 more votes than the previous resolution. But the United Kingdom remained opposed to discussing the sovereignty issue with Argentina, and there was no movement toward negotiations.

Differences between the United Kingdom and Spain on **Gibraltar,** which had been dealt with by the Assembly in the past, were the subject of a consensus decision [A/40/413] at the 40th Assembly and were expected to be handled the same way by the 41st, as talks between the two countries continued outside the United Nations.

The "**Question of East Timor**" remains on the Assembly agenda [A/41/50, item 111], but no resolutions have been adopted on the issue since 1982. Civil war broke out in the Portuguese territory in 1975 between a faction seeking independence, the *Frente Revolucionaria de Timor Leste Independente* (FRETILIN), and one seeking integration with Indonesia. Indonesia annexed the territory in 1976, and over the years the backing for the FRETILIN insurgency has waned, despite continuing reports of massive human rights violations, famine, and disease. Portugal and Indonesia hold periodic talks on the issue through U.N. Under-Secretary-General Rafeeuddin Ahmed, but there has been little movement.

There are two disputes involving **France** that stem from colonial situations. One is a **claim by Madagascar** to the islands of Juan de Nova, Europa, Bassas da India, and Glorieuses. Paris claims they were never part of Madagascar. No action was taken by the 40th Assembly, but the issue is on the agenda of the 41st Session [A/41/50, item 79]. The other deals with Mayotte, the fourth of the Comorian Islands, three of which achieved independence in 1975. The Christian residents of Mayotte, however, objected to linkage with the other three Moslem islands. The 40th Assembly adopted a resolution in December affirming the territorial integrity of the island group and the sovereignty of the Islamic Federal Republic of the Comoros over Mayotte [A/Res/ 40/62; vote: 117–1, with 22 abstentions].

The United Nations initially established a separate colonial category, the trust territory, and a Trusteeship Council to supervise the 11 areas involved. That system, and the Trusteeship Council itself, could expire in 1986, now that the United States has requested the termination of the last remaining territory, the **Trust Territory of the Pacific Islands,** also known as Micronesia. The vast area of 2,100 islands has 140,000 inhabitants, divided into four distinct districts: Palau, the Marshall Islands, the Federated States of Micronesia, and the Northern Marianas. The first three have chosen a "compact of free association" with the United States, which gives them autonomy but cedes defense arrangements to Washington. The Marianas opted in 1975 for commonwealth status.

Congress approved the package in December 1985, but action had been held up by a provision in the Palau constitution banning nuclear weapons from its territory. In January, the United States pledged not to use, test, store, or dispose of nuclear materials in Palau—a potential site for a major American naval base [*The Interdependent*, Jan./Feb., 1986]. And in February, 72 percent of the 15,000 Palauans voted for the agreement in a special plebiscite, observed by a Trusteeship Council visiting mission [Reuters, 4/1/86]. The termination of the mandate was proposed by the United States and approved at the summer session of the Trusteeship Council. But since Micronesia is a "strategic trust," the final decision belongs to the Security Council, rather than to the General Assembly, and there it could be blocked by a Soviet veto.

II
Arms Control and
Disarmament

I n 1985, the General Assembly tended to favor continuity over innovation in seeking consensus on matters that have long occupied its agenda. The 41st Assembly promises to continue in this spirit. But the consensus-building process will still have to overcome some of the serious conflicts of national interest, differing perceptions, and institutional rigidities that have stalled progress for so long.

At its 40th meeting, the General Assembly's First (Political and Security) Committee passed a total of 66 disarmament resolutions, a new record. These addressed virtually every aspect of disarmament, from the global to the country specific, from the political to the economic to the technological, from the visionary to the strictly administrative. Their wide range reflects the First Committee's position as the chief disarmament body in the United Nations system. To some observers this is also a sign of weakness, since the large number of resolutions indicates the Assembly's inability to agree on priorities among disarmament issues. Although 20 resolutions were adopted by consensus (another record), on most resolutions the General Assembly was unable to overcome the differences among the nations most involved.

Where consensus is impossible, the First Committee will often respond by passing several parallel resolutions on a single agenda item, each sponsored by a different voting bloc—usually socialist, Western, or nonaligned. There is growing recognition that parallel resolutions are themselves becoming part of the problem, and greater attention is being devoted to seeking single, consensus resolutions. A related problem is the tendency of the First Committee to adopt what amount to perennial resolutions. This situation is more difficult to address. Few delegations are willing to rule out any proposal that could facilitate progress toward disarmament or to admit that a particular disarmament cause is lost.

As a result, the General Assembly disarmament agenda is a highly ritualized one. Many items appear annually, with only slight modification. As a rule, the most reliable guide to this year's disarmament agenda is last year's. New items are usually introduced cautiously. Rather than take imprudent action, the Assembly may simply request reports from the Secretary-General.

Preparing these reports is a major responsibility of the United Nations Department for Disarmament Affairs, which is also well known for its annual *United Nations Disarmament Yearbook*. Many delegations are dissatisfied with the performance of the United Nations on disarmament matters. Their concern has led to several introspective resolutions initiating studies of the role of the United Nations on these issues in general and on the specific matter of U.N. disarmament studies [A/Res/40/94O, 152K].

The ritualization of the General Assembly disarmament agenda has the effect of concealing the importance of the United Nations in disarmament affairs. The fact remains that for most countries the First Committee is their primary disarmament forum, the one place in which they can count on being heard. France, India, and Mexico devote considerable energy to First Committee deliberations, as do such smaller nations as Denmark, Pakistan, Romania, and Sweden. The Soviet Union and its Warsaw Pact allies frequently use the General Assembly to present new disarmament proposals. The United States is very reticent by comparison, offering few initiatives and often relying on its North Atlantic Treaty Organization (NATO) allies to secure acceptable outcomes. Only recently has U.S. First Committee diplomacy shown signs of greater activism, introducing resolutions and pressing its positions.

Through its legislative activities, the General Assembly has developed its own approach to restraining armaments. The modest steps and elaborate rationales that characterize the superpowers' approach to arms control are not the style of the General Assembly, which favors sweeping measures, based on clear principles, to achieve outright disarmament. Some disarmament advocates go so far as to criticize arms control for legitimizing the role of armaments and the growth of arsenals. But there is also a cynical side to disarmament. As practiced in the General Assembly, disarmament commonly means disarming one's adversary. Proposals from the United States, for example, have a way of placing their greatest burdens on Moscow. The Soviet Union and its allies routinely present proposals that embarrass or divide the West. The nonaligned often seem more interested in restraining the great powers or their local opponents than in disarming themselves.

The 41st General Assembly faces an enormous disarmament agenda. Winnowing the wheat from the chaff will not always be easy; many disarmament proposals are intended for home consumption, as international propaganda, or scapegoating. But most initiatives represent genuine ideals and serious goals. One sign of this is the growing seriousness of First Committee deliberations. Many delegations have reacted to the superpowers' megaphone diplomacy by moderating their own rhetoric and intensifying their labors. Delegates from Europe and the nonaligned countries are more conciliatory and willing to focus on the nuts-and-bolts problems of disarming. The result of such an approach to disarmament issues may be a decrease in the quantity of disarmament resolutions and a corresponding increase in quality.

1. Weapons in Outer Space

As recently as the mid-1970s, outer space appeared to be safe from the specter of military confrontation. Three major treaties formed a bulwark against using space for testing or deploying nuclear weapons or defenses against nuclear attack: the 1963 Limited Nuclear Test Ban Treaty, the 1967 Outer Space Treaty, and the 1972 Anti-Ballistic Missile (ABM) Treaty. Since then, new technologies and military doctrines have brought outer space to the forefront of international security debates. The General Assembly has become preoccupied with the issue to a degree that has not been seen since the nuclear proliferation debates of the 1960s. The United Nations has established a framework for addressing the militarization of outer space, but much remains ambiguous, and several delegations are striving to pass more concrete resolutions. For many years, the Soviet Union and the nonaligned dominated the presentation of resolutions in the General Assembly. More recently, they have been joined by Eastern and Western Europe. Today the Assembly is engaged in a debate of truly global proportions.

At the time the existing treaties were completed, placing weapons in space was neither feasible nor appealing. Today, three emerging technologies threaten to make outer space an essential part of future world wars: improved communications and reconnaissance satellites, antisatellite weapons (ASAT), and space-based ballistic missile defenses.

Satellites have been used for military purposes since 1960. Their use in military communications is widely accepted. Satellites for early warning and reconnaissance promote stability and ease verification of compliance with strategic arms treaties. But the new types of satellites being deployed by the great powers are more worrisome. These could directly affect the course of a war by guiding strategic weapons as well as naval and land forces.

As satellites gain military importance, the superpowers have invested in **ASAT systems** designed to destroy their adversary's satellites. From 1978 to 1982, the Soviet Union tested an ASAT system that the United States claims is operational. A more sophisticated system is being developed in the United States. Testing and deployment of the U.S. system was halted by Congress in 1985 to facilitate negotiation of bilateral restraints. Both systems appear to be designed to attack targets in low-Earth orbit, where photoreconnaissance, electronic intelligence, and ocean surveillance satellites are concentrated. Bilateral negotiations on ASAT technologies were started in the 1970s but became a casualty of the Soviet intervention in Afghanistan. Today ASAT is on the agenda of the Soviet-U.S. talks in Geneva.

Space-based missile defenses (also known as Star Wars, the Strategic Defense Initiative, or Space Strike Weapons) still lie in the future, but they already weigh heavily in superpower negotiations and in the General Assembly. In theory, successful space-based defenses could dramatically alter the foundation of superpower security. Instead of relying solely on offensive missiles to deter war through threat of retaliation against cities, security would be maintained by defending against attack. The actual capabilities and implications of space-based defenses are impossible to assess; the technology is still too primitive and the doctrines that would justify procurement are very controversial. Both superpowers have research and development programs. The Soviet Union has funded a significant program since the mid-1970s. Most analysts believe the United States has gained a commanding lead in the field since 1983, when the White House massively expanded U.S. research under the Strategic Defense Initiative (SDI). Tests have demonstrated the feasibility of some of the technologies involved. But formidable obstacles remain and much is still unknown, including the basic architecture of a complete system, its costs, capabilities, and vulnerabilities.

Advanced testing and deployment of space-based defenses would violate the 1972 ABM treaty, necessitating its abrogation or renegotiation. But research and development, which need not violate the treaty, is acquiring momentum of its own. Other nations are getting involved as well. The United Kingdom, West Germany, and Israel are formally participating in U.S. research. Other U.S. allies are discussing participation. Some European leaders believe a European Defense Initiative may be the best long-range solution to Europe's security woes. France has its own program along these lines.

Since March 1985, the superpowers have been negotiating the future of space-based defenses and strategic offensive arms in Geneva. Little progress has been made. Moscow insists on extending the principles of the ABM treaty to prohibit all work on space-based defenses. Washington takes the opposite position and refuses to consider any limitations on SDI research. Neither side has been willing to make concessions on this issue so far. Arms control specialists note that a prohibition on research cannot be adequately verified without intrusive on-site inspection. Similar considerations may have led Soviet officials to suggest in mid-1985 that their government might tolerate continued research and to propose more recently a new commitment to the ABM treaty, which permits research.

While bilateral negotiations are deadlocked, the General Assembly has repeatedly iterated its goal of "preventing the militarization of outer space." At its 40th meeting, the First Committee started with five draft resolutions on the topic, representing all perspectives. In its most impressive accomplishment of the session, the Committee winnowed these down to a single compromise resolution accommodating all delegations except the United States and Grenada, both of which abstained. The resolution requests a study of the consequences of militarizing outer space and urges the Conference on Disarmament to start multilateral negotiations on the topic [A/Res/40/87].

The Conference on Disarmament, a 40-nation negotiating body in Geneva, has established its own *Ad Hoc* Committee on the Prevention of an Arms Race in Outer Space. The increasing role of the Conference on Disarmament is criticized by many nonaligned nations, which would rather hold such talks in the United Nations Committee on the Peaceful Uses of Outer Space, where they have a stronger voting majority. The socialist nations are pressing to accelerate work on an accord to prohibit weapons in space. Western governments argue that not enough is known about the weapons and their implications to justify speedy action. This pattern of disagreement has produced a standoff in which U.N. institutions devote great attention to space issues but can make only slow progress toward their formal resolution.

2. Nuclear Weapons and the Superpowers

The General Assembly's growing concern with outer space also reflects the prevailing frustration with terrestrial matters. Chief among these are the superpowers' nuclear arsenals. Because of the global implications of a potential superpower nuclear exchange, the majority of Assembly members insist that the issues involved are too important to be left to Moscow and Washington alone. Moreover, many governments are convinced that they cannot risk cutting their own forces until the superpowers significantly reduce their massive arsenals. The General Assembly endorses a variety of approaches to superpower disarmament. None of these approaches has been translated into an actual agreement, and most of them will be reiterated at the 41st Session.

Agreement on major new arms treaties would require significantly better superpower relations. Since the decline of détente in the mid-1970s, Soviet-U.S. relations have oscillated between bad and worse. While both sides have managed to prevent tensions from escalating uncontrollably, neither will make the concessions required for lasting improvement. Relations are not as bad today as they were in the fall of 1983, when the Korean airliner disaster, NATO missile deployments, and the collapse of bilateral negotiations brought tension to its worst point since the early 1960s. But there is also no consistent evidence of a warming trend. Contrary to the expectations of some, Soviet Communist Party General Secretary Mikhail Gorbachev has not abandoned the policies of his predecessors, although he has implemented them with greater imagination. The Reagan Administration also shows few signs of wavering from its established policies. Measures such as the Gramm-Rudman deficit reduction bill may cut U.S. defense spending unilaterally, but the international political climate appears to be beyond legislation.

Through 1985 there was modest hope for **superpower arms control**, but these hopes were confounded by subsequent events. A new negotiating forum was established in Geneva in January 1985 to replace the defunct Strategic Arms Reduction Talks. Known as the Nuclear and Space Arms Talks (NST), this is an umbrella for three separate negotiations on offensive strategic weapons, intermediate-range nuclear weapons, and weapons in space. These bilateral talks have the support of the General Assembly [A/Res/40/152B]. But the new talks were deadlocked from the start. Moscow insists that the United

States abandon its Strategic Defense Initiative before the Soviet Union will consider additional restraints on offensive weaponry. The White House continues to regard SDI research as nonnegotiable.

The Soviet Union has issued a flurry of arms control declarations and proposals in the last year. These include a halt to further deployments of intermediate-range nuclear weapons and a moratorium on all nuclear testing. The latter started on August 6, 1985, the 40th anniversary of the bombing of Hiroshima. Moscow encouraged the United States to join the moratorium and extended its declaration twice. Despite pressure at home, the White House refused to join, contending that any test moratorium would only preserve Soviet advantages. On another tack, Soviet Foreign Minister Shevardnadze proposed a 50 percent cut in nuclear arsenals if the United States would abandon the SDI. This proposal was incorporated into a sweeping plan for complete disarmament presented by General Secretary Gorbachev on January 15. The Gorbachev plan builds upon established Soviet positions, integrating them into a 15-year, three-stage program that includes strategic weapons, intermediate-range nuclear forces, weapons in space, a comprehensive nuclear test ban, and other measures. President Reagan has likewise called for radical reductions in nuclear arsenals.

At the time of the 40th General Assembly, superpower relations appeared to be moving in the direction required for successful arms control. At the center of these hopes was the first **Reagan-Gorbachev summit,** held in Geneva on November 19–21, 1985. The General Assembly rushed to pass a supportive resolution before the meeting [A/Res/40/18], but the summit failed to reconcile outstanding disputes, nor has it engendered a sustained dialogue. By early 1986, the Kremlin was not concealing its anger with the United States for failing to join its nuclear test moratorium or to respond enthusiastically to Gorbachev's disarmament plan. Efforts to schedule a second summit in 1986 have been unsuccessful, though hints from both capitals suggest that one still might be possible.

Despite these frustrations, the **arms control process** is far from dead. Even in this era of renewed confrontation, old treaties continue in force and new agreements have been concluded. Moscow and Washington continue consultations on accidents at sea, on nuclear proliferation, and in the Standing Consultative Commission. The Hot Line has been modernized. Understandings signed in June 1985 commit the superpowers to consult with each other on nuclear terrorism and nuclear threats or attacks by third parties. Following the Chernobyl nuclear incident, the two sides joined other countries in intensive discussions at the International Atomic Energy Agency on ways to improve warnings of and to limit collateral damage from nuclear accidents.

Even treaties that have expired or were never ratified—SALT I, the Threshold Test Ban, Peaceful Nuclear Explosions, and the SALT II treaties—continue to be observed. Both Moscow and Washington have accused each other of treaty violations, raising the issue of treaty verification. The socialist nations tend to underplay the importance of verification, stressing the principles of disarmament above all. Western nations usually contend that formal agreements are meaningless unless compliance can be verified effectively. In a possibly significant move, the two countries agreed to meet in late July to discuss verification issues related to limits on nuclear tests.

The Reagan Administration is concerned especially with the dangers of Soviet treaty violations, and issues regular reports charging the Soviet Union with noncompliance. Moscow has replied to these White House allegations with charges of its own. The most important U.S. charge concerns the Soviet radar facility at Abalakova (or Krasnoyarsk). Many Western analysts are convinced that this installation violates the 1972 ABM treaty. In order to discuss these charges and countercharges, the United States and the Soviet Union agreed to reconvene their Standing Consultative Commission in late July 1986, a step that some observers hope will help clear the air for arms control progress. Some U.S. officials urge **proportionate responses** to alleged Soviet violations, selectively abrogating treaty limitations to demonstrate U.S. resolve. President Reagan has avoided this path so far. Any future arms control treaty will have to address the verification problem, in many cases through on-site inspection. The 40th General Assembly supported Western resolutions encouraging cooperation on verification [A/Res/40/94L, 152O]. Moscow traditionally opposes rigorous verification procedures, but recent Soviet statements suggest greater willingness to accept on-site inspection.

A promising area for a major new arms control treaty may be **intermediate-range nuclear forces (INF)**. The bitter disputes over Soviet deployments of SS-20 missiles and U.S. Pershing II and ground-launched cruise missiles have abated now that these deployments near completion. Both superpowers have shown interest in proposals to reduce the levels of these weapon systems, possibly to zero. Secretary Gorbachev says that his government no longer demands that an INF agreement be linked to U.S. concessions on its Strategic Defense Initiative. Barriers to an agreement remain. The Soviet Union still maintains that an agreement must limit British and French nuclear forces. Washington, for its part, wants restraints on Soviet SS-20s in Asia, which it fears could be moved to Europe in time of crisis.

The United Nations supports bilateral negotiations but also has its own agenda for dealing with superpower nuclear weapons. In the United Nations, the proposed **Comprehensive Nuclear Test Ban (CTB)** attracts special attention. Advocates argue that a test ban would erode confidence in nuclear weapons and hinder modernization, thereby leading to reduced reliance on nuclear deterrence. It would also make it more difficult for additional countries to become nuclear powers. Currently, nuclear testing is restrained by the 1963 Partial Test Ban Treaty and the unratified 1974 Threshold Test Ban Treaty. The proposed CTB has been negotiated in several fora, most recently in the Geneva-based Conference on Disarmament.

Washington opposes a CTB in the near term on the grounds that it would confer advantages on the Soviet Union, complicate modernization, and cannot be adequately verified without the sort of intrusive on-site inspection that Moscow refuses. Critics also suggest that a CTB could be counterproductive, compelling the nuclear powers to expand their arsenals to compensate for their declining confidence in individual weapons. China and France have expressed reservations, noting that a CTB would put disproportionate burdens on smaller nuclear powers, although China now says it favors a CTB if it is part of a superpower disarmament process. The whole question received new emphasis following the Soviet Union's unilateral test moratorium (which ended in April 1986 and has been extended). At its 40th session, the First Committee passed four resolutions supporting a CTB [A/Res/40/80A, 80B, 81, 88]. These differ on how to achieve a treaty, the urgency, and verification. The 41st General Assembly will face stiff barriers as it tries to develop a single, consensus position.

In a similar spirit, the General Assembly continues to endorse a **nuclear freeze**. Proposals to halt the manufacture and deployment of nuclear weapons grew out of public protests in the West in the early 1980s. In the United Nations, support comes largely from socialist and nonaligned nations. Past resolutions call for negotiations in the Conference on Disarmament. Related proposals call for prohibiting production of fissile material for military purposes and prohibitions on new classes of nuclear weapons [A/Res/40/94G, 94H, 151C, 151E, 152P]. The United States and some other Western governments object that such proposals are at best misguided and at worst propaganda stunts that cannot be effectively verified.

The General Assembly also supports **measures designed to reduce the likelihood of nuclear war**. These proposals deal with the doctrines and attitudes regarding nuclear weapons. Chief among these are traditional resolutions urging nuclear weapons states not to initiate the use of nuclear weapons [A/Res/40/151F, 152A]. No-first-use is already the declared policy of the Soviet Union and China. It also has vigorous support from the nonaligned. The NATO alliance, on the other hand, relies on the threat of nuclear escalation as a deterrent to compensate for the weakness of its conventional forces. The NATO allies object to no-first-use resolutions and concomitant resolutions urging the Conference on Disarmament to promulgate a treaty to that effect. But NATO opinion is not monolithic. Many influential Western leaders criticize NATO's dependence on nuclear weapons as a political albatross; they would exchange it for greater investment in conventional forces. This sentiment has generated support within some NATO governments for less contentious resolutions on the special responsibilities of the nuclear powers to prevent nuclear war [A/Res/40/152G]. Other NATO governments are satisfied with the Alliance's standing declaration that it will not be the first to use *any* weapons.

A related theme emphasizes the horrors of nuclear war. This is manifested in resolutions on the climatic effects of nuclear war, including **nuclear winter** [A/Res/40/152G]. The nuclear winter hypothesis maintains that a war involving several hundred or more nuclear explosions could produce enough smoke and dust to block sunlight, cooling the Earth's temperature and triggering climatic disaster. A resolution initiated by the nonaligned requests a study by the Secretary-General of the climatic effects of nuclear war. The United States objects to having to pay for another study of the matter, noting that there is already a hefty literature.

Another approach to preventing nuclear war is to build confidence among the adversarial alliances. **Confidence-building measures (CBMs)** increase knowledge and communications to reduce the risk of misunderstandings that could provoke war. They can also reinforce stability by reducing opportunities for surprise attack. Among the most important CBMs are requirements for notification of troop movements and military exercises, provisions of the 1975 Helsinki Final Act. Talks are in progress to expand these limited measures in the 31-nation Conference on Confidence and Security Building Measures and Disarmament in Europe (CDE) in Stockholm. After a fast start in 1984, the Stockholm negotiations stalled on questions of verification, exchange of information, numerical limits, measurement procedures, and inclusion of naval and air forces. Negotiations on Mutual and Balanced Force Reductions (MBFR) in Vienna appear to be overcoming an older logjam on related issues, suggesting that progress toward agreement is still possible.

3. The Spread of Nuclear Weapons

Preventing the spread of nuclear weapons has never been as difficult as it is today. The basic technology is quite old and the costs are less than for many conventional weapons systems; some analysts believe a complete capability can be developed for about $200 million. Five nations have major nuclear arsenals: the United Kingdom, China, France, the Soviet Union, and the United States. Other nations are thought to be able to assemble bombs at will. India detonated a "peaceful nuclear explosion" in 1974. Israel is widely assumed to be "only a screwdriver away." Taiwan and Argentina have announced their ability to build nuclear weapons, and Pakistan and Brazil will probably have the same ability within a few years. Still other countries, South Africa among them, may be working surreptitiously on a "bomb in the basement." Increasingly, the question is one not of capability but of intention; how can nations with the ability to build nuclear weapons be convinced not to?

At the center of attention in proliferation questions is the 1968 Treaty on the Non-Proliferation of Nuclear Weapons (NPT). In August and September 1985, the future of the treaty was debated at the **Third Review Conference of the Parties to the Treaty on the Non-Proliferation of Nuclear Weapons** in Geneva. With 86 of 130 parties to the treaty present, there were expectations of success. Unlike its predecessors, the Third Review Conference was not dominated by threats to withdraw from the NPT or efforts to amend it.

Where the 1980 review conference broke up acrimoniously, the 1985 meeting adopted by consensus a Final Declaration reaffirming the NPT and the principles and policies it stands for. The degree of consensus surprised many observers but reassured very few. When the General Assembly subsequently endorsed the Final Declaration [A/Res/40/94M], it reaffirmed the basic goal of nonproliferation for the first time in many years. In December 1985, the NPT was strengthened further when North Korea, a holdout, became a signatory.

Nevertheless, the conference disappointed nonproliferation activists by failing to confront some of the most serious proliferation threats. For example, among the "problem countries" that refuse to sign the treaty, only Israel and South Africa—traditional U.N. whipping boys—are explicitly mentioned in the Final Declaration. Others, such as Argentina, Brazil, India, Pakistan, and Taiwan, were virtually ignored.

Strengthening the **International Atomic Energy Agency (IAEA)** also proved difficult. Under the NPT, treaty signatories submit their nuclear facilities to inspection by the IAEA to safeguard against diversion of nuclear materials for military uses. The Final Declaration strongly supports existing safeguards. But the conference failed to take measures to strengthen the IAEA, despite contentions that the IAEA lacks the authority and resources to do its job effectively. Only Israel and South Africa were singled out for refusing to cooperate with the IAEA. Many other potential proliferators oppose safeguards or restrict IAEA inspectors to selected facilities.

Supplier restraint is also essential to inhibiting proliferation. The most important form of supplier restraint is self-control through national export licensing. Unfortunately, self-control has repeatedly failed to stop transfers of critical technology. After India's "peaceful nuclear explosion" in 1974, a multilateral process, the London Nuclear Suppliers' Group, was established to monitor exports of nuclear technology. A major controversy surrounds U.S.-led proposals to extend London Group and IAEA authority to include all elements of nuclear technology. Such "full-scope safeguards" are opposed by some established nuclear exporters, including Belgium, Switzerland, and West Germany, and by such emerging exporters as Argentina, Brazil, China, and Israel. Another dimension of the problem is the illicit traffic in nuclear equipment and know-how, which the international community is only beginning to confront. More has been done to reduce the risks that terrorists or national separatists will acquire nuclear materials. With the latter problem in mind, the Final Declaration urges greater adherence to the new International Convention on the Physical Protection of Nuclear Materials. The convention still lacks sufficient signatures to go into effect.

The nonaligned countries are increasingly vocal in their demands for easier access to civilian nuclear technology. Article IV of the NPT and the IAEA Charter assure the nonnuclear weapon states access to civilian technology in exchange for safeguarding their facilities. The nonaligned routinely condemn export restrictions that hinder their nuclear programs. The London Group has been criticized as an economic cartel that violates the spirit of Article IV. To ease access to civilian nuclear technology (much of it with enormous military implications), these countries have called for a **United Nations Conference for the Promotion of International Cooperation in the Peaceful Uses of Nuclear Energy**; such a conference is now scheduled for November 18–28, 1986, in Geneva.

Another source of resentment is the failure of states with nuclear weapons to take steps to improve **the security of non-weapons states.** In the General Assembly this brings demands for an international treaty to assure the security of nonnuclear weapon states from nuclear attack [A/Res/40/85, 86].

There is also the problem of compliance with Article VI of the NPT, which commits the nuclear powers to pursue arms reductions. The frustrations with this aspect of the treaty—nuclear arsenals have tripled in numbers of warheads since the NPT was negotiated—have been cited by some third world leaders as their reason for repudiating the NPT altogether. These critics charge that the treaty has the effect of controlling horizontal proliferation (the spread of nuclear weapons to more countries) while doing nothing to discourage vertical proliferation (the growth of extant nuclear arsenals). One measure that would assuage many of these critics is a comprehensive nuclear test ban treaty (CTB). The Final Declaration emphasizes the need for a CTB agreement to help achieve "a balance of . . . mutual obligations," a point consistently supported by the General Assembly [A/Res/40/94N].

Proposals for **nuclear-weapons-free zones (NWFZs)** offer another way of restraining the spread of nuclear weapons. NWFZ treaties already in effect cover Antarctica, the ocean floors, the moon, and outer space. Extending the concept to inhabited areas has proven more difficult, given regional tensions and the desire of some countries to maintain the nuclear option. An example is the Treaty of Tlatelolco, which aims to establish a Latin American NWFZ. The treaty is not adhered to by the Latin American nations most likely to have such weapons in the future: Argentina, Brazil, Chile, and Cuba. Another problem arises when an outside power has—or reserves the right to have—nuclear weapons in the region. In the case of Tlatelolco, France reserves the right to base nuclear weapons in its territories in the region. The latter problem is emphasized by the General Assembly [A/Res/40/79]. The general problems of establishing NWFZs are discussed by the United Nations Group of Governmental Experts on Nuclear-Weapons-Free Zones [A/Res/40/94B].

NWFZ proposals have been put forward for virtually every region of the globe. The General Assembly has shown greatest interest in proposals for Africa, the Middle East, and South Asia. The main barrier to the denuclearization of Africa is South Africa, the only African nation capable of fabricating nuclear weapons in the foreseeable future [A/Res/40/89]. The Middle East NWFZ proposal is relatively noncontroversial but complex, since many countries in the region are known to be interested in acquiring nuclear weapons. Israel is specifically condemned by the General Assembly for refusing to renounce nuclear weapons. Israel is also condemned for its June 7, 1981, raid on Iraq's nuclear facilities, a nonproliferation policy to which the General Assembly takes exception [A/Res/40/82, 93]. The South Asian NWFZ proposal was initiated by Pakistan after India's nuclear test in 1974 [A/Res/40/83]. India opposes it on the grounds that her government cannot renounce nuclear weapons unless China, with whom India shares a long and contested border, does likewise. India is also concerned with balancing the superpower presence in the Indian Ocean. The General Assembly keeps the proposal alive, but without optimism.

Two newer NWFZ proposals concern the Balkans and the South Pacific. Greek Prime Minister Papandreou has called for a Balkan NWFZ after denouncing U.S. nuclear weapons in Greek bases. Turkey, which shares a long border with the Soviet Union, is less enthusiastic. Prospects are better for U.N. action on a South Pacific NWFZ. New Zealand took the leading role on the issue, banning U.S. warships from its harbors unless they are declared to be free of nuclear arms and demanding an end to French nuclear testing at Mururoa Atoll, 3,000 miles to the northeast. Following the sinking of a protest ship docked in New Zealand on July 10, 1985, later traced to French agents, a treaty prohibiting the manufacture, testing, or stationing of nuclear weapons was signed by eight South Pacific states—Australia, the Cook Islands, Fiji, Kiribati, New Zealand, Niue, Tuvalu, and Western Samoa.

4. Chemical, Conventional, and Other Weapons

The early months of 1986 saw modest progress in the **negotiations on a chemical weapons ban**. These talks have continued in the Conference on Disarmament (C.D.) in Geneva since 1968, striving to finish the job started by the 1925 Geneva Protocol. The Protocol, with 118 signatories, is the oldest multilateral arms control treaty still in effect. It prohibits the use of chemical weapons in war but does not ban their production. It is buttressed by the 1972 convention banning biological weapons, with 92 signatories. Compliance with both agreements is voluntary; they have no verification procedures and rely on good faith and enlightened self-interest to assure compliance. Rather than rely on the good will of their adversaries, many nations continue to prepare for chemical and biological warfare (CBW). France, the Soviet Union, and the United States maintain significant stockpiles of chemical weapons. The U.S. Department of Defense estimates that 14 to 16 other nations have smaller CBW stockpiles.

Events in recent years have kept the CBW issue controversial. Charges by the United States that Vietnam and the Soviet Union used toxic "yellow rain" in Kampuchea, Laos, and Afghanistan remain unconfirmed. Studies by the Secretary-General were unable to arrive at authoritative conclusions; but in May 1986 the British Ministry of Defense revealed that "its tests of 1983 had failed to detect trichothecenes [fungus-made toxins] in 'alleged chemical warfare' samples supplied by American authorities" and, further, that its studies "'neither support nor contradict'" the widely held thesis that yellow rain is bee excrement [*The New York Times, 6/16/86*]. Moscow steadfastly denies the allegations, while making an issue of United States plans to modernize its chemical weapons arsenal. The U.S. program calls for "binary" munitions designed for improved safety. Washington denies that the switch escalates the arms race.

The Geneva negotiations are dominated by the superpowers, but chemical weapons can be fabricated by virtually any country willing to make the investment. This was illustrated in the spring of 1984, when the world learned that Iraq was using chemical weapons in its war with Iran. Iraq is suspected of having used civilian fertilizer factories purchased from Europe to produce its chemical weapons. By using civilian technology to violate the 1925 Geneva Protocol, Iraq demonstrates the need for a comprehensive ban and the difficulties of verifying one.

In 1984, negotiations in the C.D. received a new impetus when Moscow accepted the principle of continuous on-site monitoring during the destruction of its chemical weapons stocks. The United States subsequently tabled a draft treaty stressing verification through inspection of all government-owned facilities. The White House sought in this way to prevent civilian chemical plants from being misused. Soviet spokesmen ridiculed the idea initially but appear to be growing more tractable. At the Geneva summit, Secretary Gorbachev and President Reagan pledged to accelerate the talks. Since then the negotiations have made progress on the key questions of the commercial chemicals to be covered and verification of the destruction of stockpiles. The big problem of verifying all possible production facilities remains and is unlikely to be overcome soon.

The disputes in the C.D. are mirrored in the General Assembly, which passed three resolutions last year on CBW [A/Res/40/92A, 92B, 92C]. These include a consensus resolution supporting the C.D. negotiations. Another resolution sponsored by the socialist nations was opposed by some Western delegations for criticizing U.S. resumption of chemical weapons production after a 15-year hiatus while, in their view, the Soviet Union continuously built up its chemical stockpile. Finally, a resolution initiated by the United States emphasizing verification was opposed by the socialist nations, ostensibly on legal grounds.

Another issue showing new signs of life is **conventional armaments**. Since 1945, some 20 million people have died in military conflicts, almost all the victims of conventional weapons. Most nations devote their entire military budget to conventional forces. Even the five nuclear powers invest 80 percent of their defense spending on nonnuclear forces, according to the United Nations Department of Disarmament Affairs. Nevertheless, conventional disarmament is traditionally near the bottom of the General Assembly's priorities. Only in the case of South Africa has the Assembly acted forthrightly to restrain arms sales, passing embargoes in 1963 and 1977. While several Western delegations believe that conventional and nuclear weapons should receive equal emphasis, the nonaligned majority insists that nuclear weapons pose the greatest threat to humanity and should be the exclusive priority of U.N. disarmament activities.

A Danish initiative in 1980 [A/Res/35/156A] won indifferent approval for a study of conventional disarmament. This is still being completed [A/Res/40/94C]. The 40th Session passed a resolution on conventional disarmament urging cuts in conventional arms spending and negotiations to facilitate limitations. But the document also "reaffirms the primary responsibility of the militarily significant states, especially the nuclear-weapon states, for halting and reversing the arms race" [A/Res/40/94A].

Another aspect of conventional weaponry on the General Assembly agenda is **naval disarmament**. Navies remain a basic tool of diplomacy and foreign intervention. Their significance is seen continuously in naval exercises and events like the 1982 South Atlantic War and U.S. naval activity off the coast of Libya. Since the 38th Session, Bulgaria has sponsored a resolution calling on the naval powers to restrict their naval activity to their own waters [A/Res/40/94I]. Aimed chiefly at NATO, this resolution is a controversial one (the vote at the 40th Session was 71–19–59). A Swedish proposal calling for a study by the Secretary-General [A/Res/40/94F] won stronger support (only the U.S. is opposed).

Finally, the General Assembly opposes the development or introduction of **new types of weapons**. These include weapons of mass destruction, radiological weapons, and excessively injurious conventional weapons [A/Res/40/ 84, 90, 94D]. Since the controversy in 1977 over enhanced radiation weapons, the Assembly has opposed production of the "neutron bomb" [A/Res/40/152H]. Growing numbers of delegations find this position obsolete now that at least two nations—France and the United States—have stockpiled such weapons. Others maintain that it exaggerates the significance of the weapon. At the 40th Session, this First Committee resolution passed by a vote of 70–11–65.

5. Comprehensive Disarmament

While the First Committee's agenda is dominated by proposals for partial disarmament, programs for comprehensive disarmament still receive vigorous support. Many of these are extremely ambitious, even though there is little expectation they will be implemented in the foreseeable future. For many delegations in the General Assembly, they remain a cherished long-range goal.

"**General and complete disarmament**" was first endorsed by the General Assembly in 1959. It is still on the agenda, but largely as a miscellaneous category for hard-to-classify proposals, such as the naval arms race and radiological weapons [A/Res/40/94A-O]. Its original role has been assumed by other initiatives. In Geneva, for example, the Conference on Disarmament continues to work on its Comprehensive Program of Disarmament [A/Res/40/152D]. Related work continues in the *Ad Hoc* Committee on the World Disarmament Conference, preparing for the world's first such meeting since the ill-fated disarmament conference of 1932-34 [A/Res/40/154].

Another approach to general disarmament emphasizes the **reduction of military spending**. With this goal in mind, the General Assembly supports studies that aim at determining the economic and social consequences of the arms race [A/Res/40/94O] and the relationship between disarmament and development [A/Res/40/155]. Plans for an International Conference on the Relationship Between Disarmament and Development are being considered by a Preparatory Committee established in 1984 [A/Res/39/160]. (France, which is the conference's host, requested its postponement from July 15-August 2, 1986, to sometime in 1987, citing continuing lack of agreement on the format and content of a draft final document of the conference among the participating countries [U.N. press release DC/1996, 6/2/86].) In its resolution on the reduction of military budgets, the 40th Session urged cuts and further study by the United Nations Group of Experts on the Reduction of Military Budgets. It also stressed that budget cuts must be led by "the most heavily armed states" [A/Res/40/91]. Comprehensive disarmament might also be achieved by isolating regions of the world from external sources of conflict. The leading regional proposal calls for implementing the 1971 **Declaration of the Indian Ocean as a Zone of Peace** [A/Res/40/153]. Efforts to convene an international conference on the Indian Ocean have been stymied by the Western concerns over the security of the Persian Gulf and the Soviet presence in Afghanistan. Some countries on the Indian Ocean littoral also fear that the withdrawal of outside forces could create a dangerous power vacuum. A conference has been discussed annually for many years, but is unlikely to take place in the near future.

In 1978 and 1982, the General Assembly tried to increase global pressure for disarmament through its two Special Sessions on Disarmament (SSOD I and II, also known as the Tenth and Twelfth Special Sessions of the General Assembly). SSOD I was the more successful of the two, producing a consensus document that set out priority items; at SSOD II no agreement was reached on a substantive statement. Among the legacies of these Special Sessions are the United Nations World Disarmament Campaign, Disarmament Week, and United Nations Disarmament Fellowships, now established components of the United Nations system [A/Res/40/151B, 151D, 151H, 152E], although some delegations question their utility. The 40th General Assembly Session added a similar measure by establishing the United Nations Regional Center for Peace and Disarmament in Africa [A/Res/40/151G]. The 41st General Assembly is expected to schedule a Third Special Session on Disarmament [A/Res/40/151I].

III
Economics and Development

1. The World Economy in 1986

World economic growth was disappointing in 1985 when compared with the strong recovery of 1984. Expansion among the advanced industrial states was more modest than anticipated and world trade slowed substantially. Exchange-rate misalignments, particularly between the dollar and the yen, contributed to huge balance of payments deficits in the United States and to heightened protectionist sentiment. Exports and growth of the less developed countries (LDCs) reflected the slowdown. Commodity prices slumped in 1985, developing-country terms of trade deteriorated slightly, and aggregate LDC growth fell to a little over 3 percent from its 1984 rate of 4 percent. Net lending to the 15 most heavily indebted countries was virtually zero, contributing to debt-servicing difficulties among a number of LDCs [International Monetary Fund, *World Economic Outlook* (Washington, D.C.: IMF, April 1986), p.4]. Developing countries are thus likely to continue to press for multilateral discussions of the interrelated problems of trade, debt, and structural adjustment.

On the other hand, there were important new developments that provide grounds for cautious optimism. The most dramatic has been the **sharp decline in oil prices.** Over the first half of 1985, Saudi Arabia cut production in an effort to stem the slide in prices. In the end, the pressure from oil producers not belonging to the Organization of Petroleum Exporting Countries (OPEC) and from poorer OPEC members exceeding their quotas proved too great. Saudi Arabia, and later OPEC as a whole, shifted to a strategy of expanding output and moving to a market-based pricing system in an effort to regain market share and put pressure on high-cost producers. In December 1985, oil prices stood at $28 a barrel, already down from the peak of over $34 in 1979. At their lowest point in the spring, prices dipped below $10. OPEC proved unable to reach a consensus on pricing and production that would allow it to regain control of the market [*The New York Times*, 4/22/86]. While creating obvious problems for oil exporters, particularly those with high levels of external indebtedness, the price decline came at a time when inflation and interest rates were already falling among the advanced industrial states. If cheaper oil is here to stay—and that is by no means certain—it will contribute to noninflationary growth in the advanced industrial states and provide relief for oil-importing LDCs.

The past year has also seen a flurry of important new cooperative efforts, led by the United States. Though it is unlikely there will be a move toward formal management of the exchange-rate system, such as a target zone, the advanced industrial countries have shown a greater willingness to coordinate exchange-market interventions on an ad hoc basis. At the joint meeting of the International Monetary Fund (IMF) and the International Bank for Reconstruction and Development (World Bank) in October 1985 in Seoul, U.S. Treasury Secretary James Baker unveiled an ambitious new plan for managing the debt crisis. In addition, the preparatory phase of a new round of General Agreement on Tariffs and Trade (GATT) talks has formally begun, providing a new forum for the multilateral discussion of trade conflicts. Important differences exist among the advanced industrial states as well as between North and South, and problems will surface in negotiating the details and in implementation. Nonetheless, the initiatives suggest a somewhat more cooperative stance, particularly from the United States.

A brief review of economic performance and prospects provides a background to the specific policy issues that will emerge during 1986 in the areas of finance and trade. Over 1985, the rate of growth among industrial countries dropped to 2.8 percent compared to the 4.7 percent of 1984. The main reason had to do with the sharp slowdown in growth in the United States from 6.5 percent in 1984 to 2.2 percent in 1985. Gross national product (GNP) growth also moderated slightly in Japan, from a rate of 5.1 percent in 1984 to 4.6 percent in 1985. European growth in 1985 was the same as in 1984—2.3 percent—which is particularly disappointing, given continued high levels of unemployment. There were variations among the major European countries: the German economy rebounded toward the end of the year; British growth was reasonably strong, Italian growth less so, and French economic performance more sluggish [*Ibid.*, p. 30]. The debate continues over Europe's long-term economic future. Many economists argue that unless strong economic measures are taken to boost research and development, free labor markets, and speed structural adjustment to new competitive conditions, the center of the world economy will continue to shift inexorably from the North Atlantic to the Pacific Basin. Overall, the IMF forecasts a 3 percent growth rate among the advanced industrial states in 1986, a fairly modest gain from 1985, given the substantial savings—three-fourths of 1 percent of advanced industrial states' GNP—associated with lower oil prices [*Ibid.*, pp. 25–26].

The consistent anti-inflationary stance of government policies among the advanced industrial states has led to a slowing of price increases, with Japan and Germany once again achieving the lowest levels of inflation. In 1985, the weighted average of inflation rates in industrial countries fell to 3.9 percent, the lowest rate of increase since the late sixties. Assuming a continuation of past policies, and a successful attack on the budget deficit in the United States, **rates of inflation** will continue to decline. The passage of the Gramm-Rudman-Hollings deficit reduction bill in December signals heightened U.S. concern with the deficit, but both its constitutionality and the policies of its implementation have yet to be worked out.

After four years of seemingly interminable ascent, the U.S. dollar finally began to depreciate beginning in March 1985. Through March 1986, the depreciation amounted to almost 25 percent, with the rise of the yen particularly sharp. A number of economic factors, including slowed growth and monetary expansion in late 1984 and early 1985, helped to break the dollar's rise. This trend was assisted by a series of joint actions following a meeting of central bankers and finance ministers of the Group of Five countries—the United States, Japan, Germany, the United Kingdom, and France—in September [*Ibid.*, p. 35]. It was agreed that a further rise of the dollar would be undesirable, and throughout the rest of 1985, the Group of Five undertook sizable coordinated interventions in the foreign exchange markets. This contributed to the dollar's continued decline and even gave rise to an expression of concern from the head of the Federal Reserve, Paul Volcker, that the dollar had fallen enough [*The Wall Street Journal*, 2/20/86]. These exchange-rate developments would not begin to be reflected in the distribution of current account surpluses and deficits until the summer, however, meaning that protectionist pressures in the U.S. are likely to persist. Despite a declining dollar, the U.S. trade deficit grew to a record $148.5 billion in 1985 [*The New York Times*, 1/30/86]. Protectionist pressures in Europe and Japan will probably increase if the dollar, and the relative competitiveness of their products, continues to fall.

Though **the advanced industrial states** made an effort to present a self-congratulatory front at the Tokyo summit, important differences persist on a range of issues from trade to macroeconomic policy. The United States believes that the Japanese are not moving quickly enough to liberalize imports and provide a stimulus to world recovery through domestic expansion, despite continuing moves by Prime Minister Yasuhiro Nakasone to convince the United States otherwise. For their part, Japanese business and political leaders are beginning to reevaluate the costs of cooperation. Before the September meeting of the Group of Five, the yen was trading at 242 to the dollar; by mid-May it had strengthened to about 165 to the dollar. This has meant a decline in Japanese exports, a slowing of growth, and narrower profit margins [*The New York Times*, 4/28/86]. The United States has also urged Germany to pursue a more expansionist line, arguing that the Germans are "excessively preoccupied with deficit reduction and inflation." German leaders argue that their policy mix is appropriate and is contributing to a renewal of noninflationary growth [*The Wall Street Journal*, 4/29/86].

//   **The developing countries** present a varied picture, though on the whole, their performance in 1985 was disappointing, reflecting slower growth among the advanced industrial states. Aggregate growth of output, which hit 4 percent in 1984, dropped back to 3.25 percent in 1985 [*World Economic Outlook*, (Washington, D.C.: IMF, 1986) p. 48]. The oil-exporting countries were, of course, the most severely affected. In 1985, these countries' real export earnings fell 8 percent, with aggregate gross domestic product (GDP) unchanged from the year before and expected to drop slightly in 1986. Among the oil exporters a further distinction can be made between those that have been capital exporters and those that have been borrowers, though neither group faces particularly good prospects. The capital exporters have accumulated assets that can act as a cushion during the transition to a period of lower oil prices. On the other hand, the capital-surplus oil exporters tend to be highly dependent on oil and thus will have more difficulties adjusting. The heavily indebted oil exporters, including Mexico, Nigeria, Venezuela, Algeria, and Indonesia, have more diversified economies but face an equally daunting set of problems. The decline in export revenues has created new debt-servicing problems. According to one calculation, $15-a-barrel oil will mean a $26 billion deterioration in the current accounts of 11 major oil exporters, even after allowing for a 1.5 percent drop in interest rates [*South*, 4/86].

    It is possible that if oil prices continued to fall—below $10 a barrel, for example—pressures for collective management could grow both inside and outside of OPEC. A number of factors count against this development, however. First, the transition from a system based on fixed prices to one of market-based pricing was swift and will be difficult to reverse. The oil market is coming to look more and more like a traditional commodities market. Second, there are a number of political barriers to collective action. Everyone agrees on restraint in principle; no one wants to be the first to act. The oil-exporting debtors are pulled in two directions. Collective restraint would raise export earnings, particularly for those with spare capacity. In the short run, balance of payments pressures push them to produce flat out. At this point, the United Kingdom and the United States remain ideologically opposed to a managed market.

    As a group, the oil-importing countries have done better over the last two years than the oil-exporters and stand to benefit materially from the latter's misfortune. Output growth accelerated to 5.5 percent in 1984 in response to the recovery in the United States, dropping back to 4.75 percent in 1985 [*World Economic Outlook*, 1986, p. 51]. The oil-importing LDCs must also be divided into two groups, however: commodity exporters and exporters of manufactures. Though some commodities, such as coffee, fared better than others, primary commodity exporters on the whole had a bad year in 1985, sustaining price declines of 12 percent in U.S. dollar terms and significant terms-of-trade losses that contributed to existing debt problems [*Ibid.*, p. 61].

Exporters of manufactures have not experienced similar terms-of-trade losses. On the whole, this group has experienced extremely high levels of growth—8.25 percent in 1984 and 6.5 percent in 1985—even during times of international economic turbulence. Countries that have managed to expand their exports of manufactures rapidly have, on the whole, avoided debt-servicing problems and fared better in terms of GDP growth.

Many of these **"newly industrializing countries," or "NICs,"** are located in Asia, which has become the most economically dynamic region in the world. This can be seen in surprising statistics on the growth of per capita GDP between 1980 and 1985 [*Ibid.*, p. 54]. While per capita GDP grew 9 percent during this period in the advanced industrial states, it did not grow at all in the developing countries as a whole. Yet there were sharp regional variations. Africa's per capita GDP declined 11 percent over the period, the Middle East's 20 percent, and the developing Western Hemisphere's 7 percent, while Asia's grew 19 percent. The lessons of East Asia's growth have not been fully absorbed, though even China is undergoing deep-reaching, and possibly irreversible, reforms.

In sum, the economic outlook is a mixed one. Despite their differences, the advanced industrial states can claim a moderately better performance this year than last. In this, the industrial nations have been aided at least in part by greater cooperation among themselves, though generally outside multilateral forums. The picture for the LDCs is more uneven. Although some continue to prosper and all will benefit from increased growth in the North, the debt crisis lingers and the sharp decline in oil prices, and commodity prices more generally, presents continuing problems. These problems are best explored through a more detailed examination of specific issues.

2. Money and Finance

Three developments will shape the international financial and monetary system through the end of the decade. First, the **financial markets** themselves are changing rapidly [International Monetary Fund, *International Capital Markets: Developments and Prospects* (Washington, D.C.: IMF, 1986), ch. 2; Supplement to *Euromoney*, Jan. 1986]. High and variable rates of inflation and fluctuating interest rates have spurred the development of new financial instruments. Deregulation, liberalization of the financial sector in a number of countries, including Japan, and the blurring of the line between banking and the securities business have accelerated the integration of the world's capital markets. Although these changes promise greater efficiency and a diversification of risk, they also pose new challenges to the formulation of national regulatory and macroeconomic policies and to international efforts to coordinate supervision.

Second, the **debt crisis** persists. Techniques for restructuring debt continued to evolve over 1985. By the beginning of 1986, however, the steep drop in oil prices, the specter of a second Mexican debt crisis, and growing recognition of the political limitations of continued austerity raised doubts about the current ad hoc structure of crisis management. Broader reforms, such as a cap on interest payments, were once again being discussed.

Changing financial markets, the lingering debt crisis, mounting trade tensions, and a changed attitude on the part of the United States produced a third development, however: the quest for **greater international cooperation** in financial and monetary matters. In September 1985, central bank presidents and finance ministers from the major industrialized nations met to coordinate intervention in the foreign exchange markets to decrease the dollar's value. The American "Baker Plan," unveiled in Seoul in October 1985, sought new commercial bank lending and an expanded role for the World Bank in the management of the debt crisis in return for structural reforms in the LDCs. In March, Japan, West Germany, and the United States acted in concert to lower interest rates. Cooperation on trade, exchange rates, and macroeconomic policy headed the economic agenda of the Tokyo summit in early May. These initiatives took place outside of the United Nations, however, reflecting the continued ambivalence of the major industrial states toward multilateral fora.

The Debt Crisis

A number of developing countries, particularly in Asia, continue to have access to commercial bank lending; a few LDCs have even tapped the Eurobond market. In Latin America and Africa, however, the debt crisis continues. The largest share of total bank lending to LDCs continues to come in the form of "involuntary" lending associated with rescheduling efforts, though the value of this new financing dropped in 1985. For the fourth year in a row, the net amount of foreign loans and investments to Latin America was less than net remittances of interests and profits. Countries in the region transferred $30 billion abroad in 1985. Capital flight represents an increasingly controversial portion of these transfers. Recent estimates indicate that capital flight from Latin America is declining, but an unknown amount of total Latin American capital stock that might be used to stimulate domestic production remains overseas [Morgan Guaranty, *World Financial Markets* (New York: Morgan Guaranty, 1986), pp. 13–15]. Owing to the smaller total debt involved, Africa's problems have not attracted the same attention as Latin America's, though they are more severe. By mid-1985, a number of African countries were in arrears to the IMF itself [*The Wall Street Journal*, 7/25/85].

Since 1982, the management of the debt crisis has centered on three sets of actions: the provision of new financing, adjustment—and particularly import cuts—by the borrowing countries, and debt rescheduling and restructuring. Between 1983 and 1985, 31 countries reached agreements with their commercial bank creditors covering $140 billion in external debt [*World Economic Outlook*, 1986, p. 92]. The most significant recent innovation has been the negotiation of multiyear restructuring agreements, or MYRAs, pioneered by Mexico in the fall of 1984. MYRAs avoid the burden of repeated annual reschedulings, while providing a clear planning horizon to both debtors and creditors. As with previous reschedulings, the IMF plays a central role in monitoring the debtors' economic performance. MYRAs are accompanied by "enhanced surveillance," a process that includes closer monitoring of financial programs and the release of IMF reports to creditors. Co-financing between the World Bank and private creditors is another innovation. Swaps and even outright sales of loan claims among banks have increased as well. The development of a market in developing-country debt signals a willingness on the part of the banks to recognize losses but raises troublesome regulatory issues. How does the sale of some debt at a discount affect the value of other debt of the same country? [IMF, *International Capital Markets*, p. 57].

Despite these innovations, pressures for more comprehensive action surfaced over the course of 1985 and 1986, due, in part, to a sagging oil market, in part to resistance to continued austerity, and in part to the failure of ad hoc management to improve growth or creditworthiness. Speaking for the Group of 77 before the Trade and Development Board meeting in March, Jayantha Dhanapala of Sri Lanka argued that "far too much emphasis continues to be placed on changing domestic policies and on conditionality and there is far too little awareness of the need to improve external variables" [U.N. Press Release, TAD/1412].

Some countries have taken a tougher unilateral stance. In July 1985, Peru announced that it would unilaterally limit payments on its foreign debt to 10 percent of export earnings and ended the year owing $1.1 billion in overdue servicing [*Latin America Weekly Report*, 1/24/86]. Peru refused to negotiate with commercial banks and even accumulated arrears to the IMF. As a result, Peru joined Poland, Zaire, Sudan, Nicaragua, and Bolivia on the list of particularly troubled debtors for which American banks are required to maintain special loan-loss reserves [*The Wall Street Journal*, 9/29/85]. Nonetheless, in April, the government of Peru unveiled a new rescheduling plan that involves repayment periods three times the present norm and interest rates a quarter of those now owed [*Latin America Weekly Report*, 4/18/86]. In January of this year, Nigeria also announced that it was limiting payments to creditors to 30 percent of export earnings [*The Wall Street Journal*, 1/3/86].

Meeting in Punta del Este, Uruguay, in late February, the Cartagena Group of Latin American debtors signalled its approval of such actions, announcing that "significant changes in the current loan agreements can't be delayed any longer, particularly with reference to interest rates" [*Ibid.*, 3/3/86]. Other solutions under discussion include interest capitalization and placing a cap on the rate of interest paid, capitalizing the remainder.

Even if such solutions were forthcoming, they would not eliminate the need for the borrowing countries to adjust through domestic reforms. The results of such efforts among the major debtors have been mixed. In March, Brazil's President Sarney gained wide popular support for an anti-inflation program that includes wage and price freezes and the introduction of a new currency. In 1985, Brazil achieved 7 percent growth, large trade surpluses, and a buildup of reserves. As a result, the country does not need new financing [*Latin America Weekly Report*, 1/10/86, 3/7/86]. Argentina has been hailed for its "Austral Plan" of June 1985, which introduced a new currency while bringing a virtual hyperinflation under control. By late 1985, however, discontent with continued austerity was growing. The effects of a "second phase" to the Austral Plan, launched in February, remain to be seen [*Ibid.*, 2/14/86].

Mexico presents the most difficult case. How Mexico is handled will affect the management of the other "oil shock debtors"—Venezuela, Nigeria, Ecuador, and Indonesia—and provide a concrete test of the Baker Plan (discussed in the next section), although the plan was not intended to deal with crises of the magnitude of the one now confronting Mexico. The collapse in oil prices, coming just as the country was beginning to emerge from three years of austerity and to rebuild what a devastating earthquake had destroyed, caught Mexico by surprise. Current discussions between Mexico, the IMF, and the banks continue to center on the details of Mexico's new financing needs. In February, President de la Madrid promised to continue economic reforms but asked for "an adjustment of the debt servicing to the country's capacity to pay" [*The Economist*, 4/12/86]. The United States responded by expressing a willingness to extend some special assistance. By March, Mexico was assuring both the United States and its creditors that declining interest rates and expanded oil exports would allow it to live within the financing needs announced before the slide in oil prices. Some combination of new lending and further rescheduling seems inevitable, however.

Given the political realities of the situation, official development assistance is unlikely to keep up with the needs of long-term development financing, and there is now wide agreement on the goal of reestablishing the debtors' creditworthiness, which would allow them to return to the private capital markets. Debate turns on two issues: the balance between new international initiatives and domestic reforms on the part of the debtors themselves; and the nature, extent, and pace of the reforms required. Both of these disputes can be seen in discussions of the Baker Plan.

The Role of International Institutions and Cooperation

A major shift in the U.S. posture toward the debt crisis was signaled in an initiative unveiled at the 40th annual convention of the IMF and the World Bank in Seoul in October 1985. The **Baker Plan** calls for a $9 billion increase in lending by the World Bank and the Inter-American Development Bank between 1986 and 1988, a 50 percent rise over anticipated lending. Over the same three-year period, the private banks would provide $20 billion in new loans, increasing their exposure to the LDCs by about 2.5 percent annually. This lending would be concentrated on 15 debtor countries. The list consists entirely of middle-income countries and includes all the major debtors in Latin America: Brazil, Argentina, Mexico, Venezuela, Colombia, Peru, Chile, Bolivia, Ecuador, and Uruguay. The other intended beneficiaries are Nigeria, the Philippines, the Ivory Coast, Morocco, and Yugoslavia. The loans would be contingent on the adoption of broad economic policy reforms that have as a primary objective the resumption of growth in the debtor countries.

The Baker Plan calls for greater collaboration between the IMF and the World Bank, but the spotlight placed on the **World Bank** suggests a subtle deemphasis on the role of the IMF and a growing convergence around the view that successful adjustment cannot be confined to standard therapy. The World Bank's lending programs, particularly its "structural" and "sectoral" adjustment loans, are supply-side oriented and hence geared toward the enhancement of productive capacity and growth rather than demand restraint. The World Bank has faced a leadership crisis over the last year, however. Among the major tasks confronting the new president, former Republican Congressman Barber B. Conable, Jr., is to shape the organization's response to the new demands that are being placed on it to cope with the debt crisis. Even as the World Bank was being urged to increase its financing to distressed borrowers, it was failing to meet its own lending targets. In fiscal year 1985, its volume of loan approvals declined by the astonishing amount of more than $1 billion over the level of the previous year [World Bank, *Annual Report 1985*].

The rise in lending anticipated under the Baker Plan could be achieved in two ways: an early increase in the World Bank's subscribed capital or an increase in its conservative 1:1 gearing ratio. The U.S. has yet to commit itself to the first method, which would require an increased capital commitment by donor countries. As with all initiatives involving new funds, this one is unlikely to make its way easily through a Congress pledged to fiscal austerity. The alternative, which would liberalize the gearing ratio of the World Bank, would decrease the Bank's working capital while increasing its capital base for loan dispersals. This initiative could increase the World Bank's official lending capacity by as much as 18 times at no cost to donor country taxpayers [Committee for Development Planning, *Doubling Development Finance: Meeting a Global Challenge* (New York: CDP, 1986) pp. 8, 42].

Although several countries were targeted for "Baker loans"—Argentina, the test case, is slated to receive up to $2 billion in World Bank loans in 1986 and 1987 as part of the increased financing associated with the plan [*Financial Times,* 12/9/85]—the initiative has yet to get off the ground. The commercial banks, the primary players in Baker's strategy, have responded with mixed signals, ranging from endorsements on the part of some of the larger banks in the United States to opposition on the part of many European and Japanese banks, which are being asked to shoulder a disproportionate share of the burden. Since the majority of private lenders are still uncertain about the fate of past loans, few are likely to embrace the open-ended commitment implied by the Baker Plan, particularly when the United States Government is committing none of its own resources.

Developing countries have welcomed the United States' abandonment of its previous "magic of the marketplace" posture but have warned that the plan falls short of offering a solution to the crisis. U.N. estimates of the capital needs of the developing countries differ sharply from those offered by the IMF [*Journal of Development Planning,* Sales No. E.85.II.A.12]. A special meeting of the Group of 24, representatives of the developing countries within the World Bank and the IMF, held in preparation for the spring meetings of the Bank-Fund Interim and Development Committees, cautioned against the "continuing renegotiation of debt from a purely accounting point of view." They also called for reductions in interest rates on old debt, a reversal of the decline in levels of development assistance, a new allocation of Special Drawing Rights (SDRs), and an expansion of the IMF's compensatory financing facility to include shortfalls in earnings from petroleum [*IMF Survey,* 3/17/86]. None of these proposals is likely to receive serious hearing.

Multilateral assistance to **the poorest countries**, however, has recently done marginally better. On July 1, 1985, the World Bank began operating a Special Facility for Sub-Saharan Africa consisting of some $1.2 billion. Lending from the facility will be made on the terms of the International Development Association (IDA), the soft-loan window of the World Bank. In March 1986, the IMF launched its own Structural Adjustment Facility with $3.1 billion in resources. It will provide loans to the world's 60 poorest countries, with the notable exceptions of China and India, which have both agreed not to avail themselves of its resources [*Ibid.,* 3/31/86; *The Economist,* 4/5/86]. The major test of multilateral assistance, however, will be the eighth replenishment of the IDA. Most of the advanced industrial countries have agreed to a replenishment of $12 billion, but this figure, while low by previous standards, is being resisted by the United States.

These initiatives do not necessarily mean an expanded role for the United Nations proper. The Group of 77 has decried the lack of progress on the New International Economic Order, issued new demands, and continued to call for wide-ranging international negotiations covering international trade, financial, and development issues [A/ 40/742]. A preparatory committee of the Group of 77 will seek to develop these views in a draft agenda for the United Nations Conference on Trade and Development (UNCTAD) VII. UNCTAD VII is scheduled to be held in 1987 in a Latin American country. Though Cuba has offered to host the meeting, a final decision on venue was not reached at the Trade and Development Board meetings in March. The developed countries resist the multilateral discussion of economic issues, particularly in any forum controlled by the developing countries.

Movement on more specific initiatives is also modest. A midterm review group found negligible progress in reaching the main goal of the **Substantial New Programme of Action for the 1980s for the Least Developed Countries**: to increase official development assistance (ODA) to the LDCs. Adopted in 1981, the target of the program was an increase of ODA to 1.5 percent of the developed countries' GNP, or double the target level of 0.7 percent set by the General Assembly in 1970. The likelihood of any such dramatic increase in ODA is slim, since only a handful of developed countries have met the original 0.7 percent target to date [OECD, *Development Cooperation: Efforts and Policies of the Members of the Development Assistance Committee*, 1982 Review (Paris: OECD, 1982), pp. 160, 182, 183]. The program also called for the cancellation of all ODA debt by all bilateral donors who had not yet done so, a measure that would provide annual relief of about $500 million a year for the rest of the decade. The program is of particular interest for the priority it accords to agricultural development measures to be undertaken by the developing countries themselves. Though seven of the least developed countries managed to meet the program's 4 percent growth target, aggregate agricultural production from 1980 to 1984 fell below growth levels achieved in the 1960s and 1970s [*U.N. Chronicle*, Nov.-Dec 1985; *UNCTAD Bulletin*, Nov. 1985]. Given rapid population growth, this slowdown means a per capita decline in food production, the most serious challenge facing the least developed countries over the next decade.

The dramatic changes in the world economy over the early eighties have also called into question the assumptions of the International Development Strategy for the Third United Nations Development Decade, adopted by the General Assembly in December of 1980. The strategy set a number of annual targets: 7 percent for GDP growth; 7.5 percent for export expansion; 8 percent for imports of goods and services; and 4 percent and 9 percent, respectively, for expansion of agricultural production and manufacturing output. After what its chairman called "difficult and protracted" negotiations, the committee established to review the strategy in September of 1985 could reach only the most general conclusions regarding further reform efforts [*U.N. Chronicle*, Sept. 1985; A/AC219/36]. In sum, with the possible exception of the United Nations General Assembly's Special Session on Africa, the North-South dialogue remains stalled, and major breakthroughs cannot be expected in the 41st Session.

3. Trade

Since the move toward floating exchange rates in 1971, trade and monetary questions have become tightly linked. This link is even more evident during periods of financial volatility. Exchange-rate misalignments, particularly the continued strength of the dollar through 1985, affect the prospects of commodity exporters and have been an important source of protectionist pressure in the United States. Though the dollar has since weakened, some countries argue that trade and monetary reform must be undertaken together if either is to be effective. International trade politics have also been affected by the debt crisis, and vice versa. Balance of payments difficulties reduce the LDCs' ability to import, and trade restrictions make it more difficult to service debts. Despite these difficulties, the common picture of a relentless trend toward increasing protectionism is misleading. Selective protection and "managed trade" coexist with new liberalization efforts. These include sectoral arrangements, regional and bilateral accords, as well as the launching of a GATT round that will tackle a number of new issues. The success of multilateral efforts will hinge on finding appropriate tradeoffs among different groups of countries, and ultimately on the political ability of states to adjust to rapid structural changes in the international division of labor [UNCTAD, "Restrictions on trade and structural adjustment," TD/B/1081, Part 1].

Oil, Commodities, and Agricultural Products

The most dramatic change in the international trading system in the mid-1980s is the "third oil shock": **the decline in the price of oil** that began in mid-1985 and accelerated rapidly over the early months of 1986. In December, oil prices were at $20 a barrel; at their lowest point in the spring, they had dropped below $13 [*The Wall Street Journal*, 4/15/86]. The causes have been both economic and political. The difficulties confronting OPEC stem in the first instance from changes in the structure of the world oil market, especially the general decline in demand for oil and the rapid increase in production from non-OPEC sources, including Mexico, the United Kingdom, Norway, and Canada. The price slide also stems from conflicts within OPEC and between OPEC and non-OPEC producers. Saudi Arabia has historically played the role of swing producer within the cartel, adjusting its production to defend prices. Over the course of 1985, poorer cartel members exceeded the quotas negotiated in 1984. Saudi Arabia acted on its threat to raise production to the full amount of its quota unless its demands for an end to underpricing and overproducing were met. The strategy was also aimed at eliciting greater cooperation from non-OPEC producers who benefited from OPEC prices without having to limit their own production.

In December 1985, the new OPEC strategy was announced. OPEC

would seek to defend its share of the market by increasing production and allowing prices to fall. By the end of January, crude had fallen to under $20 a barrel [*The New York Times*, 1/21/86]. U.S. Vice President George Bush became embroiled in a public controversy when he suggested in April that oil prices should be stabilized, reflecting the damage the price drop was doing to Northern producers. OPEC seemed incapable of stabilizing the market, however, due to internal divisions over how production cuts should be shared. Meetings in March and April failed to establish a consensus on prices and production [*The Wall Street Journal*, 4/22/86].

Oil is not the only commodity to have witnessed sharp price declines. The upward trend in nominal prices of **commodities** over the seventies reversed itself in the early eighties, reaching a low in the fourth quarter of 1982. A minor recovery followed, but non-oil commodity prices dropped an unexpected 12 percent in U.S. dollar terms over 1985 [*World Economic Outlook*, 1986, pp. 61, 63]. Problems in particular markets have adversely affected the foreign exchange earnings of producers, while making efforts at international cooperation more difficult.

In October 1985, the buffer stock manager for the International Tin Council suspended operations, throwing the tin market into crisis. The immediate cause for the collapse was the purchase of large amounts of forward tin contracts on margin. When prices declined, these contracts could not be honored. The more fundamental causes are open to dispute. UNCTAD notes the inadequate financing available to the buffer stock manager, currency realignments, and declining trends in world demand [*UNCTAD Bulletin*, Jan. 1986]. Northern observers blame the effort to hold prices artificially high [*The Wall Street Journal*, 4/7/86]. This debate has been replayed in the efforts to negotiate particular International Commodity Agreements (ICAs) and to revive the Integrated Program for Commodities. Consumers and producers failed to reach agreement on the renegotiation of ICAs covering cocoa and natural rubber due to differences over prices. Discussions on a number of commodities not yet covered by ICAs are in abeyance.

Six years after the adoption of the agreement establishing the **Common Fund for Commodities**, progress in implementation remains small. In January 1986, the agreement was ratified by the 90th country, fulfilling one condition for its entry into force. A further requirement—that the countries having ratified the agreement represent two-thirds of the Common Fund's directly contributed capital of $470 million—has not been met. The United States has signed, but not ratified, the agreement, while the socialist countries have not taken any action on it. Even if the agreement were to enter into force, the size of the Common Fund would be too small to stabilize large and volatile markets. In the aggregate, commodity prices are expected to revive in 1986, but much of the increase is expected to come from sharply increasing coffee prices [*World Economic Outlook*, 1986, p. 63]. On the other hand, prospects for commodity producers will improve with lower interest rates and any easing of exchange-rate volatility.

Though commodity trade is frequently seen as a North-South issue, trade in **agricultural products** has generated significant political conflict among the advanced industrial states. In June of 1985, the United States raised duties on European Economic Community (EEC) pasta in response to the EEC's creation of a preferential scheme for Mediterranean citrus. A "pasta war" ensued, escalating in November with additional retaliation. The United States and the EEC have also been undercutting one another in a costly subsidies battle aimed at securing and defending cereals markets. The United States continues to press Japan to liberalize imports of citrus, beef, and tobacco. Finally, in April of this year, a potentially more serious agricultural trade dispute erupted between the United States and Europe. The United States argued that the extension of the EEC's Common Agricultural Policy (CAP) to Spain and Portugal would result in the loss of $1 billion of agricultural exports. The U.S. Administration announced its intention to retaliate, though negotiations are under way in the Organization for Economic Cooperation and Development (OECD) to defuse the crisis [*The New York Times*, 4/25/86].

Due to politically entrenched price support systems in the EEC, the United States, and Japan, agriculture has traditionally been treated as an exceptional sector outside the GATT's purview. That may change as the costs of agricultural price supports and export subsidies rise and trade tensions escalate. In an attempt to increase discipline in agricultural trade, a Committee on Trade in Agricultural Products was established in the GATT in 1982 to explore both price supports and subsidies. The conflict in April between the United States and the EEC may have come at an auspicious time; the United States sought to give a political push to international discussions of agricultural trade by raising the issue at the Tokyo summit [*The New York Times*, 4/26/86].

Trade in Manufactures and Services

There are two important developments to watch in 1986 in the area of trade in manufactures and services. One is the continuing move toward various **discriminatory arrangements**. These include sector-specific measures aimed at **restricting trade**, such as "orderly marketing agreements" (OMAs) and "voluntary export restraints" (VERs), in products such as steel and textiles [see TD/B/1081, Part 1]. Driven to action by the strong dollar, protectionist forces introduced a flood of trade bills in the United States in the fall of 1985. In December, President Reagan vetoed the highly restrictive Jenkins bill, aimed at LDC textile exporters, but with the promise that the restrictive Multi-Fibre Agreement would be "aggressively" renegotiated [*Far Eastern Economic Review*, 1/16/86]. Those negotiations begin this summer.

There are also sectoral deals aimed at **liberalizing trade,** like the "market-opening, sector-specific" (MOSS) negotiations between the United States and Japan over a number of high-technology products. Regional and bilateral arrangements, such as the Caribbean Basin Initiative, the Lomé Convention, and the U.S.-Israel free trade zone, have also increased in number or expanded in scope. In April, President Reagan won congressional approval to launch negotiations with Canada for a free trade agreement [The New York Times, 4/24/86]. Like all customs union agreements, however, these integrationist schemes divert external trade even as they create sectoral trade.

The second development is the launching of a **new GATT round of trade talks.** A number of developing countries, led by India and Brazil, blocked preparations in July 1985 because of their objection to the inclusion of services on the agenda. In October, the United States won unanimous approval for its proposal to start the preparatory process. As Arthur Dunkel, the GATT's General Director, remarked, "There are bloody battles ahead, but the debate is no longer over procedure—it is over the substance of the negotiations" [The New York Times, 3/10/85].

There are several major issues on the trade policy agenda; each presents unique political difficulties [Michael Aho and Jonathan David Aronson, Trade Talks (New York: Council on Foreign Relations, 1985), pp. 36-58]. Increased market access has been a constant goal of all trade talks. Tariffs among the advanced industrial states have already been reduced to very low levels as the result of previous rounds. Trade liberalization now means rolling back nontariff barriers, which have proliferated in recent years, reaching agreement on the use of "selective safeguards" to protect ailing industries, and getting new players into the trade policy process. The most important new actors are the **newly industrializing countries (NICs)** of East Asia and Latin America. The NICs have been the victims of quota arrangements but are now under pressure to "graduate" from their developing-country status by opening their markets and relinquishing various preferences. The United States for example, has tightened the access of the NICs to the benefits of the Generalized System of Preferences [The Wall Street Journal, 4/2/86]. The political difficulty is that the NICs have been most competitive in those sectors experiencing difficulties in Europe and the United States, such as footwear and steel. It is unclear what concessions the advanced industrial states will make in order to convince the NICs to participate in the new round.

The United States has taken the lead in putting services—banking, insurance, telecommunications, data processing, and transport—on the GATT agenda. Services account for a growing share of employment and GNP in the advanced industrial world yet are covered by no multilateral accords. The LDCs have resisted introducing services into the GATT for a number of reasons [The New York Times, 11/10/85]. "Trade" in services frequently takes the form of direct investment, which developing countries feel they have a right to monitor and control. The financial sector, sometimes state-owned, has typically been an instrument of development policy; the introduction of foreign banks might lessen government control over the allocation of resources. The LDCs also fear that those services in which they have an advantage, such as construction, are unlikely to be discussed. There are also practical problems in negotiating services, including the fact that the regulation of these industries does not generally fall under the authority of trade ministers.

"**Industrial targeting,**" particularly in high-technology industries, has generated substantial trade conflict among the United States, Europe, Japan, and the NICs. Some economists argue that special government support, including subsidies for research and development and targeted financial and fiscal incentives, may create longer-term competitive advantages. Where several governments are backing "national champions" in the same sector, trade and industrial policies are likely to conflict. U.S.-Japanese trade in semiconductors has been one battleground in this debate, with the United States charging that government policies and open markets in the United States have contributed to Japanese dominance in the industry [*The Economist*, 1/11/86]. Defining which domestic policies are appropriate will be a difficult task, since national preferences for government intervention vary widely.

A number of other issues have also been raised. These include counterfeiting, the defense of intellectual property, and trade-distorting investment regulations, such as local-content and export requirements. Discussion of these issues has been opposed by some developing countries that feel they fall outside the appropriate scope for GATT activity. Institutional reform of the GATT itself will be on the agenda of the upcoming round [*The Wall Street Journal*, 1/2/86]. Dispute-settlement procedures are weak, and the role of the GATT in surveillance of changes in the trade policy environment could be enhanced. The creation of a more independent executive or an ongoing consultative process are reforms likely to be tabled, raising the issue of the relationship between a reformed GATT and UNCTAD.

The difficulties in bringing the new round to a successful conclusion are numerous [Aho and Aronson, *Trade Talks*, ch. 2]. Given the large number of issues suggested for inclusion, defining an agenda could take several years. Important political tradeoffs, both among and within countries, are required to make the talks go forward. In addition, the international environment has changed. The world has become more interdependent economically, there are more actors in the trade policy game than ever before, and the global economy has entered a period of slower economic growth, higher unemployment, and surplus capacity in a number of sectors. A number of issues have not been resolved from the last round of trade talks, including a code on safeguards. Completion of the new round could take a full decade.

4. Transnational Corporations, Science, and Technology

After many years of relative inhospitality to transnational corporations (TNCs), governments of both industrialized and developing countries have grown more receptive to **direct foreign investment (DFI)** in the 1980s. In this decade, transnational capital flows have amounted to $10 billion per year. Today, the equity value of foreign companies and their subsidiaries abroad totals approximately $630 billion [*The CTC Reporter*, Centre on Transnational Corporations, Spring 1986].

Most DFI originates in developed economies and these same economies absorb more than three-quarters of all investment inflows. In recent years, the United States has emerged as the world's most important net absorber of DFI, and today the U.S. share of world inflows is between 45 and 50 percent, compared to 9 percent in the early 1970s. Such rapid increases in investment flows to the United States could not have occurred without some decline, or at least stagnation, in investment flows to other areas of the world. Indeed, investment inflows to Western Europe and many developing countries have declined substantially. Since 1981, DFI in developing countries has fallen by almost 25 percent and prospects for an early recovery are dim. For many of these countries, DFI is the primary source of export earnings and foreign exchange reserves. In some developing countries, the share of foreign capital relative to the national capital stock ranges from 10 to 50 percent [*Ibid.*].

DFI and the presence of TNCs can work both for and against the host country. Under appropriate conditions, TNCs can contribute to development by providing capital, technology, managerial skills, export revenues, and external markets. Sometimes, however, important decisions affecting the economic, political, and social structure of the host country are taken at corporate headquarters thousands of miles away. Problems may arise when TNCs transfer technologies that have been developed under conditions very different from those in the host country, as was the case in Bhopal, India. A vertically integrated TNC may practice transfer pricing and thus avoid payment of high local taxes, and some TNCs may try to evade local jurisdiction or even interfere in host politics by relying on the political strength of their home governments.

A number of the United Nations' most ambitious and controversial involvements in the international transfer of technology have been efforts to formulate codes of conduct to regulate transactions between TNCs and host governments. Thus, the United Nations established the United Nations Centre on Transnational Corporations (CTC) in New York in 1974, and shortly thereafter work began on a Code of Conduct for TNCs. The next year, two other sets of negotiations on TNCs began at the United Nations Conference on Trade and Development (UNCTAD) in Geneva, one on restrictive business practices and the other on the transfer of technology. In 1978, the United Nations held the United Nations Conference on Science and Technology for Development in Geneva. These efforts were an attempt to alter the bargaining position of TNCs—perceived as very powerful by LDC and socialist governments—to promote the economic and technological development of the third world. Since then the climate for international investment has changed. Saddled with enormous debt, many LDCs and socialist countries have come to see DFI as an attractive source of capital and TNCs as less intrusive than commercial banks and the International Monetary Fund. Although they continue to criticize commercial and political practices undertaken by some TNCs, they are no longer as interested in policies that may discourage foreign investors, such as stringent national or international regulations.

In the midst of economic crisis, LDCs have been forced to accept the tenets of a liberal economic order, tenets which they may believe are not well suited to their own economic systems. The only code agreed to thus far is the UNCTAD code on restrictive business practices, which extends to developing countries the protection of Western-style competition and antitrust principles. Negotiations on the other codes continue into their second decade with few signs of progress.

Code of Conduct for Transnational Corporations

The Commission on Transnational Corporations convened in June 1985, January 1986, and April 1986 to discuss a text put forth by a committee of experts on an **International Code of Conduct for Transnational Corporations** [E/C.10/1986/18]. This text takes into account the legitimate interests of both host countries and TNCs, with a view to encouraging DFI, public and private, and also to strengthening the position of LDCs in negotiations with TNCs. By April, differences over language had narrowed considerably. The code focuses on political and technical issues. Its provisions are limited to the economic sectors traditionally given highest priority in DFI decision making: mining, agriculture, and manufacturing. The negotiators have agreed on approximately 80 percent of the code, including sections on transfer pricing, taxation, ownership and control, and environmental protection. Points of contention include applicability of international law, fair and equitable treatment, observance of domestic laws, noninterference in political affairs, and nationalization and compensation procedures. LDCs argue that TNCs should be subject to the laws of the host government, whereas industrialized countries contend that TNCs should be regulated by international law. The host governments believe that TNCs should be treated in the same manner as national enterprises are treated and demand the right to protect their own infant industries as a necessary step toward self-sufficiency. There is no agreement on who should decide what is adequate, just, or appropriate compensation in cases of nationalization or expropriation. While many host countries will settle on the book value of an enterprise, most TNCs argue that the book value does not accurately represent the firm's actual worth.

The political will necessary to reach a final agreement on the code seems lacking. Other regulatory schemes on a regional basis, such as the Andean Pact, have almost fallen apart, and even the U.N. Centre has begun to look more favorably on DFI, noting that both LDCs and TNCs can benefit.

Transnational Corporations and Apartheid

The U.N. Centre is also engaged in a program of research entitled "The activities of TNCs in Southern Africa and the extent of their collaboration with illegal regimes in that area." This issue now has center stage at many sessions of the Commission on Transnational Corporations [TNC/370]. Many countries condemn the more than 1,000 TNCs that still operate and invest in critical and strategic sectors of the South African economy, namely, mining, electronics, computers, chemicals, arms, and nuclear energy. They argue that such investment sustains the pro-apartheid regime and perpetuates the illegal occupation and plunder of Namibia. Since 90 percent—or $17 billion, according to 1983 figures—of foreign investment in South Africa, however, is undertaken by the United Kingdom, the United States, West Germany, France, and Switzerland, industrialized countries have resisted international resolutions that would control or limit such investment [*The Washington Post*, 8/7/85]. These countries have sought to preserve their national prerogatives in this area, but public pressure has forced some of them, including France, Canada, and the United States, to pass domestic legislation condemning apartheid and the illegal occupation of Namibia and restricting new investment in South Africa.

Increasing social ferment in Southern Africa has compelled the Commission to take prompt action. It appointed a nongovernmental group of experts, the Panel of Eminent Persons, to study ways in which TNCs can challenge apartheid laws and so encourage the South African Government to eliminate apartheid. The Panel recommended that South Africa rescind its Influx Control Laws and Group Areas Act by January 1, 1987. If no action is taken by this date, TNCs should withdraw from South Africa. In April 1986, the Commission's governmental delegates gave strong, albeit not total, support to the spirit of the Eminent Persons' recommendations. Some industrialized states have already enacted their own legislation on this issue, including Canada, Australia, and the United States. But none of this legislation is as far-reaching as the Panel's recommendations.

United Nations Conference on Science and Technology for Development

The worldwide slowdown in economic growth and international trade, and the deterioration in the terms of trade for third world countries, have made it impossible for newly industrializing nations to maintain export levels and collect the foreign exchange to import essential commodities and to service their debt burden. Meanwhile, the industrialized states of the North have made remarkable scientific and technological progress. The impact of these innovations portends profound economic and social change in industry, education, and health care, among other areas. The future of North and South are linked. There can be no lasting growth for the developed countries if the developing countries remain excluded from the benefits of research and development, 95 percent of which takes place in the developed world. Today there is potential for scientific and technological advances in the less-developed world.

The United Nations Centre for Science and Technology for Development was established in recognition of the necessity of scientific and technological progress to sustain development in industrializing nations. The **Vienna Programme of Action,** produced by the 1979 United Nations Conference on Science and Technology for Development (UNCSTD), provides policy guidance for the Centre. Concerned that scientific and technological progress had not benefited LDCs, the Vienna Programme's resolutions are designed to restructure, increase the effectiveness of, and restore the importance of multilateral channels for international scientific and technological cooperation.

In 1985, the Intergovernmental Committee on Science and Technology reviewed United Nations and regional efforts to implement the Vienna Programme [A/CN.11/61; A/CN.11/62; A/CN.11/63]. The Committee examined the direction the program has taken in order to modify strategies for the second half of the decade in light of recent developments. Its review concluded that there is a shortage of research and development facilities and that existing facilities are not linked to industrial and agricultural production. The Committee urged national governments, international organizations, and industrialized donor governments to provide incentives and support for a redirection of research and development. It recommended that the U.N. system build a technical infrastructure for public knowledge. (One such effort is the attempt by the United Nations Industrial Development Organization (UNIDO) to launch a new International Centre for Genetic Engineering and Biotechnology in Trieste and New Delhi that will establish a global network of affiliated centers.) The Committee also observed that the Vienna Programme is still underfunded.

The Committee was more positive in its assessment of regional science and technology programs, finding evidence of regional research networks, although there has been relatively less improvement in infrastructural development financing, science and technology information-sharing, and the choice, acquisition, and transfer of technology.

These issues were also discussed at the sixth session of UNCSTD's Advisory Committee for the Coordination of Information Services (ACCIS). This session dealt with **global information networks** on science and technology. According to ACCIS, a number of obstacles stand in the way of cooperation among developing nations and with developed nations: the prohibitively high travel costs involved in the exchange of scientists and technicians; a lack of knowledge about ongoing efforts in less-open societies; the reluctance of advanced industrialized nations to share technology with potential competitors in the world market; and bargaining difficulties inherent in negotiations between developed and developing nations concerning technology transfer. ACCIS is attempting to overcome these obstacles by creating an international data bank that will link the separate data banks of regions, sectors, and states.

Despite efforts at the regional, subregional, sectoral, and global level, nothing can substitute for national endeavors to mobilize human and financial resources for scientific and technological development. Locally funded and administered programs for technical education, as well as the stimulation of local corporate research and development, are just as critical for LDC technological development as a reliance on external sources of technology. Societies could derive significant benefits if governments were to link their science and technology policies to foreign investment policies. For example, the Mexican Government has sought to develop indigenous computer capabilities through the creation of several national research and development centers on computer technology, which receive part of their funds from foreign investors in the computer sector.

The International Transfer of Technology

UNCSTD projects attempt to transfer technology that will increase LDCs' access to the achievements of science, allowing them to accelerate their development and increase their participation in the world economic system, [*Update*, UNCSTD, 12/85]. Most UNCSTD projects, however, are limited to the transfer of technology already in the public domain. Proprietary knowledge that is owned by persons or firms is often more sought after by advanced LDCs and is usually more commercially valuable. TNCs are the primary conduits and suppliers of proprietary technology. TNCs transfer technology through such means as investment and licensing, management contracts and turnkey plans. In the 1970s, LDCs took steps to regulate nationally the transfer of technology in order to shift bargaining power from the foreign supplier to the host recipients. Many countries retain this technology transfer legislation, although in the present economic climate it is not enforced as strictly.

At the initiative of LDCs, countries in 1973 began to negotiate an **International Code of Conduct on the Transfer of Technology** at the United Nations Conference on Trade and Development (UNCTAD). From 1975 through 1979, much progress was made, but since then there has been little movement. The last international conference, which was held in May 1985, was characterized by one Western observer as "a complete failure in terms of any progress toward consensus and agreement between various groups of nations." Two major areas of disagreement preclude conclusion of the code. The first concerns restrictive business practices—the heart of the code. Industrialized countries argue that practices which may have a deleterious effect on competition should be banned, using a rule of reason standard. LDCs counter that practices which have any adverse effect on development should be prohibited per se—a much tougher standard. Restrictive business practices include export restrictions, tie-in clauses, and grant backs. The second major area of disagreement concerns party autonomy on choice of law and international law. Developing countries argue that local authorities should be allowed choice of law; industrialized countries advocate an international law standard.

Owing to the impasse on negotiations, the 40th General Assembly called on the President of the United Nations Conference on an International Code of Conduct on the Transfer of Technology and the Secretary-General of UNCTAD to hold informal consultations with states regarding measures to speed the conclusion of a code. In April 1986, the President of the Conference suggested to the states that a series of five or six informal consultations on areas of substantive disagreement take place in Geneva in the summer of 1986. Exact textual language will not be discussed at these consultations, should they take place; rather, governmental representatives will try to resolve disputed principles and goals. The disputed principles and goals, of course, are the basis of the disputes over textual language. At present, no other negotiating conferences on the code are scheduled, yet no state has taken the initiative to abandon the code exercise. The 41st General Assembly will take up the question of what is to be done regarding the future of the code, but little progress is expected.

IV
Global Resource Management

1. Food and Agriculture

The past year has been one of rebuilding and regrouping on food and agriculture issues in the international community. Global food production and stocks have rebounded. The immediate African food emergency has eased. Food policy work, particularly in the areas of food security and small-scale agriculture, has gone forward. There have been significant changes in international institutions and their leadership. Meanwhile, the underlying disarray in the world's food system, which resurfaces periodically in times of global or regional food shortages, shows few signs of durable improvement.

Just before completing its work in December 1985, the 40th General Assembly adopted its annual resolution on food and agricultural problems. Reflecting discussions of the Economic and Social Council (ECOSOC) earlier in the year in Geneva, the resolution noted the "imperative need to keep food and agricultural issues at the centre of global attention, particularly the situation in African countries." The General Assembly encouraged prompt action to press forward with national food strategies, conclude lagging negotiations to replenish the International Fund for Agricultural Development (IFAD), provide additional resources to the International Development Association, strengthen the Food Aid Convention and the Global Information and Early Warning System on Food and Agriculture, and address the crippling problem of third world indebtedness [A/Res/40/181].

The years 1985 and 1986 are expected to prove generally favorable from the standpoint of **global food production** and stocks. The Food and Agriculture Organization of the United Nations (FAO) estimated 1985 world cereal production at 1,831 million tons, "an increase of 30 million tons on last year's harvest and well above trend. Better than average harvests were achieved in all major producing regions of the world, with record outputs in a number of countries. With both production and beginning season stocks at high levels, world cereal supplies in 1985/86 are estimated to have increased by 4 percent." The 1986 world cereal crop outlook as of March was "mostly favourable," although, as in 1985 and as with food stocks, the global data masked generally weaker performance in developing than in developed countries [FAO, *Global Information and Early Warning System on Food and Agriculture Food Outlook,* Mar. 1986].

As 1986 progressed, it became apparent that the immediate food shortages in **Africa** had eased considerably. The FAO's **Early Warning System report** for March indicated abnormal food shortages in six African countries as contrasted with 21 countries in the same month the previous year. African food production, which had been 40 million tons in 1984, reached a record 54.5 million tons in 1985, with still higher levels projected (as of April) for 1986 [FAO, *Food Supply Situation and Crop Prospects in Sub-Saharan Africa,* 4/21/86]. Whereas in February 1985 some 30 to 35 million people in 20 countries were in need of external assistance, with many of them not being reached, the number by April 1986 was placed at 19 million, mostly in five countries, with most of them already receiving assistance.

The year's major international event in the food field was the General Assembly's **Special Session on the Critical Economic Situation in Africa.** The first-ever Special Session devoted to the needs of a single continent, the meeting was held May 27-31 in New York after a crash planning process of only five months. It reflected the generally acknowledged need to harness the widespread international concern about the African food emergency expressed in 1983-85 for the formidable medium- and longer-term challenges of the sub-Saharan region. Convened in response to a request from African governments, the Special Session built on a five-year **African Priority Programme for Economic Recovery (APPER)**, prepared with the assistance of the Economic Commission for Africa and approved by the Organization of African Unity. The Session, which had before it many other resolutions and reports as well, sought, in the words of Secretary-General Pérez de Cuéllar, "to translate the broad areas of agreement into comprehensive and integrated action." The Chairman of the four preparatory committee meetings, Edgard Pisani, viewed it not as a pledging conference but as a forum for seeking agreement on "the basic questions of attitudes, of priorities, of economic and social policy" [OEOA, *African Emergency,* Feb.-Mar. 1986].

The Special Session adopted unanimously a Programme of Action for African Economic Recovery and Development, 1986-1990. It acknowledged the steps taken by African governments to restructure their economies and called upon the international community to increase substantially its support for African efforts. Although no specific financial commitments were made, the final document placed priority needs for the period at $128.1 billion.

The Action Programme endorsed in large measure the APPER strategies, emphasizing recovery and development in the food and agriculture sector. It called for upgrading emergency preparedness, augmenting investment in agriculture, adopting more remunerative food-pricing policies, recognizing and supporting women's roles in food production, and giving greater attention to drought and desertification control and to sectors that support agriculture. It called upon the international community to adopt policies that promote sustained, noninflationary growth in the international economy, eliminate protectionism, and address African commodity concerns. Donors pledged to place greater emphasis on non-project aid and to work to increase multilateral concessional assistance.

In the area of **food and agriculture policy**, work during the year by a number of agencies continued to refine understanding of hunger and food insecurity. In March, the World Bank published a policy study, *Poverty and Hunger: Issues and Options for Food Security in Developing Countries*, which delineates the basic connection of hunger with lack of purchasing power rather than with food shortages per se. In addition to illustrating policy options for various developing countries, the study also stakes out more clearly the World Bank's interest in food security at the household as well as the national and international levels.

The 23rd Conference of the FAO in November 1985, at the time of the FAO's 40th anniversary, approved a **World Food Security Compact.** The Compact, which is not legally binding, articulates "the moral values and lines of action which should guide governments and non-governmental organizations and individuals in attaining the commonly shared objective of improved world food security and the elimination of hunger and malnutrition." It called on governments to discharge their "primary responsibility for ensuring the food security of their peoples," on NGOs to help create broader public support for world food security, and on individuals to carry out their "sacred obligation" to advance that cause [*Report of the Conference of FAO Twenty-Third Session,* III 1, V 1].

The connection between food security and national security also became more widely understood during the past year. In four of the six sub-Saharan African countries remaining on the FAO's critical list, mentioned earlier— Ethiopia, the Sudan, Mozambique, and Angola—civil strife was found to be a major factor in denying access to adequate food. While tradeoffs between military expenditures and investments in the agricultural and other social sectors are no secret, the close correlation between war and hunger in Africa brought home the point in the aforementioned General Assembly resolution that "the maintenance of peace and security . . . are important for improved economic conditions and enhanced food security" [A/Res/40/141].

Another policy area that received more attention in 1985 and 1986 was that of **women in development.** With the conclusion of the United Nations Decade for Women in 1985, the Voluntary Fund for the United Nations Decade for Women, established in 1976, became an autonomous entity—the United Nations Development Fund for Women (UNIFEM)—within the United Nations Development Programme [cf. *Issues Before the 40th General Assembly of* *the United Nations*, p. 122ff]. In addition to continuing to fund pilot projects in support of women's productive roles, the Fund is now giving greater emphasis to incorporating its insights into the policies and programs of other international agencies. Food and agriculture agencies are encouraged to approach the women-in-development issue as a development issue rather than as a woman's issue.

Also attracting major attention were policies dealing with the relation between **refugees and development.** The needs of the world's 10 million refugees had been highlighted at the second International Conference for Assistance to Refugees in Africa (ICARA II) in mid-1984 [cf. *Ibid.*, p. 119ff]. Reflecting the ICARA II view of "the complementarity of refugee aid and development assistance," U.N. agencies have given increased attention to incorporating development components into refugee projects as well as to addressing refugee needs in development activities. A workshop in December 1985 sponsored jointly by the Office of the United Nations High Commissioner for Refugees (UNHCR) and nongovernmental groups explored concrete ways for making the desirable operational and administrative connections.

A final area of special policy interest during the year was that of **food trade.** There was continuing concern about how the major food-exporting nations' attempts at expanding their international food markets affect the efforts of the developing countries to become self-reliant in food [cf. *Ibid.*, p. 89]. The Wheat Trade Convention was extended for another five years from July 1, 1986, but with its activities restricted to information-sharing rather than the trade-management provisions some developing countries had sought. Renewed attention was also given to South-South food trade. In April, the FAO reported that, side by side with unmet African food aid and commercial requirements, "unutilized exportable surpluses of 2.0 million tons" existed in seven sub-Saharan African countries [FAO, *Food Supply Situation*, 4/21/86].

The last year has also been a time of transition for a number of key international organizations. Perhaps the most encouraging development was the replenishment of **IFAD,** the agency that embodies what many consider the preferred approach to the alleviation of hunger: facilitation of the efforts of small farmers and the rural poor in the world's poorest countries. The impasse that imperiled IFAD's future had been a major concern of the international community [cf. *Issues Before the 40th General Assembly*, pp. 88-89].

After almost three years of negotiations, IFAD's 141-nation Governing Council in January 1986 finalized agreement on funds of $500 million for the period 1986-88, $300 million of which were to come from the industrialized (Organization for Economic Cooperation and Development [OECD]) countries and $200 million from OPEC. Non-oil-exporting developing countries promised to provide an additional $24 million. When the $40 million not then in hand failed to materialize ($24 million from the OECD group, $16 million from the OPEC nations), IFAD's second replenishment resources eventually settled out at $460 million. Although the new funds were less than half the $1.1 billion of IFAD's first replenishment (1981-83), they will sustain IFAD for a period in which attention will be directed to ways of better providing for IFAD's mission.

At the same meeting, IFAD's Governing Council gave unanimous approval to the creation of a Special Programme for Sub-Saharan African Countries affected by drought and desertification. An additional $300 million was approved for this purpose over a four-year period. IFAD's President, Idriss Jazairy, described the Council's action as providing "a ray of new hope for the millions of people of this region who have been devastated by drought and desertification over a period of many years" [IFAD Press Release 86/15]. In May, the first project using funds from the Special Programme was approved: an agricultural rehabilitation program in Mauritania.

Other institutional developments that helped advance the cause of international food security included the extension in May 1985 of the Food Financing Facility for another four years and the conclusion of a new **Food Aid Convention**. The Facility, created in 1981 within the International Monetary Fund to assist countries experiencing serious food production shortfalls and severe balance of payments problems, had been used 11 times for a total of almost $1 billion in borrowings [World Bank, *Poverty and Hunger*, p. 51]. The Food Aid Convention, which commits signatory nations to provide 7.6 million metric tons of food aid annually, was extended for another three years from July 1, 1986, though not at the level—upwards of 10 million tons—for which many had hoped. Reflecting recent experience, the text of the Convention allows its Chairman to convene a Special Session in response to severe production shortfalls in one region rather than requiring that such shortages be worldwide before this might occur.

A more controversial development was the decision, announced on May 1, to phase down the **United Nations Office for Emergency Operations in Africa (OEOA)** beginning July 1, closing it altogether on October 31. Since its inception in January 1984, OEOA has succeeded in facilitating a more coordinated response by the U.N. system to the African food crisis. Using a team of 24 substantive staff, most of them seconded from UNDP, the United Nations Children's Fund (UNICEF), the World Food Programme, UNHCR, and the U.N. Secretariat, OEOA is widely credited with spearheading an international effort that saved many lives. OEOA worked with officials of African governments to enhance their capacity to manage the relief operation, at the same time assisting outside agencies in their planning and delivery of relief matériel. During the 14 months beginning November 1, 1984, governmental and private resources valued at $2.9 billion were committed to Africa [DPI Press Release ND/259, 5/1/86].

The decision to reduce OEOA staff to seven professionals through October and then to disband OEOA as a separate office entirely seemed premature to some. Real overall improvements notwithstanding, some countries and regions within countries will probably continue to have food and non-food needs that fail to be met. The fact that a number of developing country governments, with OEOA help, have set up emergency interagency groups to respond to future food shortages is a positive step, though it does not supplant the need for continued coordination at the international level. That the OEOA decision was pressed by donor governments, some of them reluctant to provide additional resources for medium- and longer-term development activities, also caused concern.

It is a time of transition for the **World Food Council** as well. The Council's ministers at its 1985 Session requested a review of its effectiveness and recommendations for strengthening it. A small Advisory Group concluded in a report released in February that "the Council has taken a number of commendable initiatives and has achieved some success in many areas of critical importance to the improvement of the world food situation." The report also noted that the "wide mandate" entrusted to the Council in the wake of the 1974 World Food Conference "was not supported by commensurate authority and resources" [The World Food Council, *Report of the Advisory Group*, February 14, 1986, para. 56].

The Advisory Group concluded that since the "disarray" in the world's food system and the lack of coordination among food institutions continue, the Council's life and mission should be extended. It recommended strengthening the Council "through improvements in its organization, *modus operandi* and programmes and methods of work, but very modest additions to its resources and the staff" [*Ibid.*, para. 75]. Although the Advisory Group rejected two more drastic options—a major upgrading of the Council's work and a redesigning of its role—the proposed strengthening of the Council is likely to prove a constructive step. The Advisory Group's report and recommendations were discussed at the Council's June 1986 meeting in Rome, and the consensus was that the Council's work should be continued and strengthened within its existing terms of reference and budget.

The World Food Council is also undergoing a transition in leadership. Its presidency has shifted from Eugene Whelan of Canada, who has held the post since 1983, to French Agriculture Minister Henri Nallet. Maurice J. Williams, who, as Executive Director since 1979, has upgraded the quality of the Council's work, stepped down in May and was replaced by Gerald Ion Trant, formerly Senior Assistant Deputy Minister of Canada's Department of Agriculture. The Council's activities in the past year have included a series of regional workshops on food issues. The Asia Session, held in May in New Delhi and Guangzhou (Canton), featured an exchange of experience between Asian and African food policy-makers.

Leadership changes are taking place elsewhere as well. Barber Conable, a former member of the U.S. House of Representatives, replaces A. W. Clausen as President of the World Bank, effective July 1. Another American, William H. Draper III, formerly President and Chairman of the Board of the Export-Import Bank of the United States, replaces F. Bradford Morse, who has served as Administrator of the United Nations Development Programme since 1979 (and since January 1985 as OEOA Coordinator). On January 1, 1986, Jean-Pierre Hocké, a Swiss, replaced Poul Hartling, a Dane, as High Commissioner for Refugees.

A final institutional issue that bears on the ability of the international community to deal with still unresolved problems in the world's food system is the financial crisis of the United Nations itself. As of mid-1986, the impact of the crisis on the work of international agencies in the food and agriculture sector appears limited. However, it may be only a matter of time before the system's policy work and its operational and information activities are affected.

2. Population

The United States, in the past a leading proponent of family planning as well as the largest donor to international population assistance programs, has withheld $10 million of its 1985 pledge to the United Nations Fund for Population Activities (UNFPA) and there is uncertainty about its contribution to the Fund in 1986. The withholding of UNFPA funds by the United States, donor of over $2.5 billion in population assistance during the past two decades, has led to a crisis that threatens the activities of multilateral and nongovernmental family planning organizations. **The United States has denied funding for UNFPA** on the basis of charges that the organization is involved "in the management of China's population program, which allegedly includes coercive abortion and involuntary sterilization" [Popline, 9/85].

In March 1985, following intensive media attention to the Chinese population program and its supposed coercive and involuntary nature, and under pressure from conservative groups, M. Peter McPherson, Administrator of the Agency for International Development (AID), requested congressional approval to withhold $10 million of the $46 million grant mandated by Congress to the UNFPA for 1985. Despite the fact that all U.S. donations to UNFPA are held in segregated accounts which cannot be used for programs in China [Popline, 9/85], McPherson argued that withholding the pledge was necessary to disassociate the United States from human rights violations in China [AID News Release, 3/30/85].

In the summer of 1985, as a result of McPherson's request, Congress passed the Kemp-Inouye-Helms Amendment to the Fiscal Year 1985 Supplemental Appropriations Bill "banning all federal aid for groups that 'support or participate in the management of' Government population programs that coerce abortion or sterilization" [The New York Times, 2/5/86]. On September 25, the funds to UNFPA were withheld when McPherson, exercising the authority delegated to the Secretary of State by the President and redelegated to McPherson, certified that UNFPA was participating in the management of a coercive population program in China.

Although Congress did not specifically earmark a portion of U.S. population fund monies for UNFPA for the current fiscal year, $38 million were available for UNFPA. It is not yet clear, however, that a U.S. contribution to UNFPA, reduced to $30 million by Gramm-Rudman-Hollings, will ever be sent to the Fund. The language of the Kemp-Inouye-Helms Amendment has been included in the population assistance appropriation for fiscal year 1986, and McPherson has stated that "the UNFPA program in China is fundamentally unchanged." Discussions between AID and UNFPA on the U.S. donation will be held before September 30, when McPherson must decide if UNFPA is eligible to receive U.S. funds.

In order for UNFPA to receive U.S. funding, the Administration has stated that China, in its family planning program, must act to prevent coercive abortion and involuntary sterilization, or UNFPA must "radically change its assistance to the China program . . . such as by supplying only contraceptives" [AID News Release, 9/25/85]. China has not been receptive to U.S. criticism and has repeatedly denied charges that its family planning program is involuntary. Chinese Ambassador Li Luye, speaking before the 40th General Assembly on operational activities for development in the Second Committee, accused the United States of "interfering with China's internal affairs" [*Population,* UNFPA Newsletter, 12/85].

U.N. Secretary-General Javier Pérez de Cuéllar wrote to U.S. Secretary of State George P. Shultz to "stress the importance of your government's contribution to this vitally needed United Nations program." The Secretary-General urged the United States to release the remaining $10 million of its 1985 pledge and noted that charges of coercive abortion and involuntary sterilization in China's family planning program "have been refuted by the Agency for International Development, which conducted reviews of UNFPA assistance to China in April 1984 and March 1985, by the Government of the People's Republic of China and by UNFPA itself which has conducted its own investigation into this matter" [*Popline,* 9/85].

UNFPA responded to the partial withholding of the U.S. pledge in a policy statement released on September 26, stating that "UNFPA does not support abortion or coercion in any country." The Fund noted that "it does provide support for a wide range of population programmes including data collection, research and training, information, education and communication, migration and urbanization, role and status of women, and voluntary family planning" [*Population,* UNFPA Newsletter, 10/85].

The cutoff of U.S. donations to UNFPA could drastically limit the operations of nongovernmental organizations (NGOs) that depend on the U.N. program for funding. The Population Council and the Population Institute, organizations which receive funding from both AID and UNFPA, have challenged in Federal court AID's decision to withhold U.S. contributions for the Fund. These NGOs contend that UNFPA, which provides approximately 1 percent of China's $1 billion family planning program, is not involved in the management of that country's family planning program. A decision on the case, which will determine the fate of both the remaining $10 million from 1985 and the 1986 contribution, is expected shortly.

In December 1984 the United States cut off funding for the largest NGO promoting family planning, the **International Planned Parenthood Federation (IPPF)** [*Issues Before the 40th General Assembly of the United Nations, p. 94*]. Funding was stopped because of the new Reagan Administration policy announced at the 1984 International Conference on Population in Mexico City prohibiting "private organizations operating abroad that 'perform or actively promote' abortion" from receiving federal funds. IPPF, which does not fund abortions, spends about $300,000 of its $50 million budget on abortion-related activities. Awarded the 1985 United Nations Population Award, IPPF received no U.S. funding last year, losing approximately $11.5 million in revenue.

Even with complete funding of UNFPA, the agency, which assists population-related activities in over 140 countries, receives many more requests for assistance than its limited budget allows. Joseph Speidel of the Population Crisis Committee estimates that savings of $175 billion in food, shelter, and other social necessities have been realized by family planning programs that have reduced world population by 130 million over the last 15 years. Family planning, for all who desire it, at a yearly cost of $10 per couple in developing countries, would require $4 billion in funding annually. Currently, contributions to population assistance programs, of which the United States provided $290 million in 1985, total around $500 million annually [Lester R. Brown *et al.*, *State of the World 1986* (New York, London: W.W. Norton & Co., 1986), p. 179]. For 1986 the United States has reduced its population assistance by $40 million to $250 million, and for 1987 the Administration again requested that $250 million be appropriated for population assistance, with $32 million for UNFPA.

World population, however, has continued to grow. It is estimated that 85 million people were added to the world's population in 1985, bringing the total at the beginning of 1986 to 4.9 billion. With continued growth, the world's population should reach 5 billion by mid-1987 and 6.1 billion by the year 2000. During the 1980s, annual additions to the world's population have been around 80 million and should increase to 90 million a year by the end of the century.

The annual growth rate of the world's population had declined from a high of 2.04 percent during the 1960s to 1.7 percent in 1985. The change in the annual growth rate, which is expected to decrease to 1.5 percent by the year 2000, has caused future estimates for world population to be revised downward. The decline in growth rates, however, has been more than offset by the rise in global population. World population, which continues to grow at a rate of 156 persons per minute, is projected to reach 10.5 billion around the year 2100 [Report by Rafael Salas, Executive Director of UNFPA, on *UNFPA and International Population Assistance*, 3/86].

Population statistics, such as the global growth rate and the increase of the world's population in absolute numbers, are misleading. There are significant differences between the growth rates of developing and developed nations. Ninety-two percent of the projected 1.3 billion increase in population during the remainder of the 20th century will occur in developing nations [*Popline*, 3/86]. Populations in developed countries are rising by less than 1 percent each year, while developing nations' annual population growth rates range between 2 and 4 percent. India's population, currently at 750 million, is increasing at a rate of 2.15 percent per year and will double within 37 years [*The Christian Science Monitor*, 3/24/86]. In the Soviet Union low birthrates in the Russian north have led Soviet authorities to offer incentives, such as money for each baby and lengthy maternity leaves, to increase the growth rate [*The New York Times*, 7/28/85].

⟶   **Sub-Saharan Africa** is the fastest growing region in the world, with a population growth rate of more than 3 percent, increasing from 2.3 percent a year in 1960. Africa's population, currently estimated at 553 million, is projected to increase to 877 million by the year 2000 and should triple by the year 2025. Women in Africa, where the birth, death, and infant mortality rates are the highest in the world, bear an average of six children. Among developed countries the mean is around 2. Africa's population, even if its rate of growth is drastically reduced, will continue to increase through the next century due to the continent's extremely young population, with a median age of 17.2 compared to 32.5 for the developed world.

Daniel T. Arap Moi, President of Kenya, which has the world's highest population growth rate at 4.1 percent, recently announced a four-child per family policy for his country [*Population*, UNFPA Newsletter, 10/85]. Even if his program succeeds in reducing by half Kenya's current fertility rate of eight children per couple, the country's population will grow from 20 million to 38 million by the year 2010. However, this total is 19 million less than at the current rate of fertility and in 2010 would save the country 3.2 million tons of corn, the country's staple food, an amount equal to double the corn Kenya produced in 1980 [*The New York Times*, 8/11/85]. If Kenyan women reduce their fertility rate to a replacement level of two children, the nation's population would still continue to grow for another 50 to 60 years. About 45 percent of Kenya's population is under the age of 15 and will be potential parents for the next several decades [*Population*, UNFPA Newsletter, 10/85].

In Africa, where family structures and high infant and child mortality contribute greatly to high fertility and the desire for many offspring, countries have been slower than other developing regions to adopt family planning measures. Fifteen years ago, population programs in Africa consisted of a few demographic surveys and little else. Now, however, faced with lower economic growth and living standards and land nearing the limits of its carrying capacity, African leaders have demonstrated a new desire for family planning. According to the *State of the World 1986,* "Concern about population growth is growing. Over the past 18 to 24 months, the United Nations Fund for Population Activities and the World Bank have received numerous requests from African governments for family planning assistance." Evidence from fertility surveys, however, indicates that African women show little desire to limit family size.

Most of the world's population growth through the remainder of the 20th century and into the next will take place in urban areas. **The world's urban population,** growing at a rate of 3 percent per annum, will double in around 28 years. Urban populations in the third world, expanding at 3.5 percent annually, three times the rate of developed nations, will double in only 20 years [Report by Rafael Salas, Executive Director of UNFPA, on *State of the World Population 1986,* 5/86]. The number of **"mega-cities,"** with at least 10 million inhabitants, will grow from three in 1950 (New York, London, and Shanghai) to 22 by the year 2000. Eighteen of these cities will be in developing countries, and Mexico City, the largest, will have a population of over 26 million.

There is increasing awareness that rapid urban population growth poses a serious threat to the quality of city life. The 1984 Mexico City Declaration on Population and Development noted, "Rapid urbanization will continue to be a salient feature of the future. Integrated urban and rural growth development strategies should therefore be an essential part of population policies." In this decade, UNFPA has convened the International Conference on Population and the Urban Future, held in Rome in 1980 and in May 1986 in Barcelona, Spain, and the Conference on Population and Small and Medium-Sized Cities, held in Mexico in November 1985, to address the problems posed by rapid urbanization. These conferences have examined strategies for stabilizing the growth in numbers of urban dwellers, providing services for burgeoning populations, as well as coordinating urban and rural development.

Recent emphasis has been placed on the development of small- and medium-sized cities as a means to divert rural migrants from mega-cities. Werner Fornos, President of the Population Institute, has called for the creation of a $250 million UNFPA-administered Urban Incentive Fund to provide grants for the development of "magnet cities" to ease the growth of major urban centers [*Popline,* 3/86].

The Nairobi Conference marking the end of the United Nations Decade for Women focused attention on the relationship between **women and population issues.** The delegates, concerned with improving the status of women, urged governments to make available "information, education and the means to assist women and men to make decisions about their desired number of children." The right of women to control their own fertility, previously a controversial topic, was recognized at the July conference as "an important basis for the enjoyment of other rights." The Nairobi Conference, in declaring that "family planning is women's right," called on governments to facilitate access to family planning services [*Population*, UNFPA Newsletter, 9/85]. UNFPA has recently modified its program to support the participation of women in population and development programs. For 1985, UNFPA budgeted nearly $2 million for 30 projects specifically aimed at improving the status of women [UNFPA Report of the Executive Director for 1985].

At the 40th General Assembly of the United Nations, there was little discussion of population issues. Population appears on the agenda of the Economic and Social Council (ECOSOC) every other year and will be discussed at the 41st General Assembly, where Javier Pérez de Cuéllar will report on the implementation of the section on international cooperation of the 1984 Mexico City Declaration on Population and Development.

34-Year Population Forecast

	Estimated 1986 Pop.	Projected 2020 Pop.
China	1,050.0 mil.	1,418.0 mil.
India	785.0 mil.	1,212.4 mil.
Soviet Union	280.0 mil.	359.0 mil.
Nigeria	105.4 mil.	312.0 mil.
United States	241.0 mil.	307.3 mil.
Indonesia	168.4 mil.	264.0 mil.
Brazil	143.3 mil.	241.6 mil.
Bangladesh	104.1 mil.	209.0 mil.
Pakistan	101.9 mil.	199.6 mil.
Mexico	81.7 mil.	148.7 mil.
Japan	121.5 mil.	133.4 mil.
Ethiopia	43.9 mil.	111.6 mil.
Vietnam	62.0 mil.	105.7 mil.
Philippines	58.1 mil.	101.3 mil.
Iran	46.6 mil.	93.4 mil.
Turkey	52.3 mil.	89.8 mil.

	Estimated 1986 Pop.	Projected 2020 Pop.
Egypt	50.5 mil.	89.4 mil.
Thailand	52.8 mil.	83.9 mil.
Zaire	31.3 mil.	83.0 mil.
Kenya	21.0 mil.	74.5 mil.
Tanzania	22.4 mil.	74.4 mil.
South Africa	33.2 mil.	71.5 mil.
Burma	37.7 mil.	63.3 mil.
South Korea	43.3 mil.	61.9 mil.
France	55.4 mil.	59.1 mil.
Italy	57.2 mil.	57.4 mil.
United Kingdom	56.6 mil.	56.6 mil.
West Germany	60.7 mil.	54.5 mil.
Sudan	22.9 mil.	52.3 mil.
Colombia	30.0 mil.	50.5 mil.
Uganda	15.2 mil.	48.9 mil.
Algeria	22.8 mil.	48.3 mil.
Argentina	31.2 mil.	46.2 mil.
Spain	38.8 mil.	45.6 mil.
Poland	37.5 mil.	44.9 mil.
Iraq	16.0 mil.	40.2 mil.
Morocco	23.7 mil.	39.8 mil.
Peru	20.2 mil.	39.1 mil.
North Korea	20.5 mil.	37.7 mil.
Venezuela	17.8 mil.	35.9 mil.
Afghanistan	15.4 mil.	34.8 mil.
Nepal	17.4 mil.	32.9 mil.
Canada	25.6 mil.	32.7 mil.
Taiwan	19.6 mil.	28.4 mil.
Romania	22.8 mil.	28.3 mil.
Yugoslavia	23.2 mil.	26.6 mil.
Malaysia	15.8 mil.	26.1 mil.
Sri Lanka	16.6 mil.	24.1 mil.
Australia	15.8 mil.	22.0 mil.
Czechoslovakia	15.5 mil.	17.8 mil.

Source: Population Reference Bureau (1986)

3. Energy

Throughout 1985, the Organization of Petroleum Exporting Countries (OPEC) unsuccessfully attempted to reconcile the desire of many of its 13 member states and other major petroleum exporters to maintain high production with the decrease in worldwide demand for oil. Two emergency meetings of OPEC in July 1985 failed to result in an agreement to reduce OPEC production from over 17 million barrels to about 14 million barrels per day [*The New York Times*, 3/24/86]. Prices for oil continued on their downward course to about $30 a barrel until January 1986, when a price freefall brought prices down as low as $10 a barrel. Prices stabilized weeks later at $13 to $14 a barrel. The sharp decline resulted from an effort on the part of Saudi Arabia and its Gulf allies to force OPEC members to abide by production quotas by flooding the market and thereby depressing prices [*The New York Times*, 3/23/86].

In April 1986, labor strife forced Norway, a major non–OPEC oil producer, to reduce its North Sea oil production. Nevertheless, OPEC members, meeting the same month, were unable to agree on a reduction formula that might have raised prices. Also in April, members of the International Energy Agency (IEA), including most Western industrial democracies, overwhelmingly rejected a proposal to increase prices through discussions between oil consumers and oil producers.

As some economies go boom while others go bust, the sudden turnabout in oil power is straining the international banking system and altering political relations. Oil-producing countries that rely heavily on oil revenues for their economic well-being have suffered serious financial consequences as a result of the dramatic price fall. On the other hand, oil-importing countries have reaped the benefits of cheaper oil, including substantial decreases in the cost of living.

The 29th General Conference of the **International Atomic Energy Agency** (**IAEA**), held in Vienna in September 1985, reaffirmed the commitment of the IAEA to worldwide cooperation in the peaceful development of nuclear energy. The IAEA is concerned with international safeguard systems, nuclear waste disposal, technical cooperation, and nuclear power and trade. At this meeting, Hans Blix was reappointed as Director General of the Agency for another four-year term. In his statement to the 40th General Assembly in October 1985, Blix noted the IAEA's strengthening of safeguard activities despite a zero growth budget; its first inspection of the Soviet Union's nuclear installations in August 1985; and Beijing's announcement that China would open some of its nuclear reactors to IAEA inspectors.

In addition to the IAEA's regular budget for 1986 ($98.68 million), the Agency earmarked $31 million from member states' voluntary contributions for its Technical Assistance and Cooperation Fund—a 25 percent increase over last year's level. The IAEA 29th Conference also adopted seven resolutions that addressed such issues as South Africa's nuclear capabilities, protection of peaceful nuclear installations against armed attacks, amendments to the Agency statute, physical protection of nuclear material, and Agency staffing [*IAEA Bull.*, no. 4, Winter 1985]. The 41st General Assembly will once again review the annual report of the Agency [A/Res/40/8] and the Agency's records of the 40th Session.

A **United Nations Conference for the Promotion of International Cooperation in the Peaceful Uses of Nuclear Energy** was first proposed at the 32nd General Assembly in 1977 [A/Res/32/50]. After years of disagreement over nuclear fuel safeguards and nuclear weapon proliferation, the 40th General Assembly has finally approved the 66-nation Preparatory Committee recommendation that the Conference be held from March 23 to April 10, 1987, in Geneva [A/40/47, para. 25]. The Preparatory Committee will meet prior to the Conference in Vienna in November 1986 [A/40/47, para. 41].

The United Nations' involvement in energy matters has led to the reaffirmation of the importance of the further **development of energy resources of developing countries** [A/Res/40/208]. Studies will continue to monitor and analyze trends in energy exploration and development, taking into account the results of a joint United Nations Development Programme (UNDP)/World Bank Energy Sector Assessment Programme, which will report its findings to the 41st Session through the United Nations Economic and Social Council. Many developing countries are accelerating efforts to find, assess, and exploit domestic energy resources [DTCD: *Energy Activities* (New York: DTCD, 1985), p. 1]. In an August report [A/40/511] the Secretary-General called for even greater attention to efforts to develop energy resources of developing countries. The Department of Technical Co-operation for Development (UN/DTCD), the energy branch of the United Nations responsible for exploration, development, and use of nonnuclear energy, is now conducting projects costing $84.7 million. The DTCD receives most of its funding from UNDP and developing-country recipient governments. There are 15 technical cooperation projects in energy planning currently under way in such areas as Angola, Ethiopia, Peru, and Central America. In addition to energy planning, projects are being undertaken in areas of electricity supply, petroleum development, coal development, geothermal energy, solar energy, wind energy, and biomass, as well as multisource projects (involving at least two of the areas mentioned).

With the drop in oil prices, new questions have arisen about **new and renewable sources of energy.** The issues involved relate to long-term research and development for renewable resources, notwithstanding short-term variations in the price of oil. A **United Nations Conference on New and Renewable Sources of Energy** took place in Nairobi, Kenya, in 1981 [A/AC.218/9], but the 40th General Assembly failed to give much attention to the implementation of the Nairobi Programme of Action for the utilization of new and renewable sources of energy [A/40/100, item 84(n)], and the Programme does not rate high on the agenda items for the 41st Assembly. During the third session of the 40th General Assembly, a report was submitted that reviewed and assessed the trends, policy measures, and activities of the United Nations system in the field of new and renewable sources of energy [A/AC.218/9]. The report found a "substantial reduction of energy consumption per unit of gross domestic product (GDP) in developed market economies (19 percent reduction of energy consumption between 1973 and 1984; and a 36 percent reduction of oil consumption per unit of GDP)" [Ibid.]. The report also noted that the economic incentive for conservation was preserved until recently because of the increase in the value of the U.S. dollar against other currencies in 1981. Energy prices have actually fallen to levels comparable in real terms to those prevailing in the early 1970s [Ibid.].

The problem of how to **finance the development of energy resources of third world countries** is also under consideration. The 39th General Assembly called for the creation of an **"energy affiliate"** of the World Bank and also called upon member states "to take appropriate measures to this end in relevant forums" [A/Res/39/176]. A report on the 40th General Assembly by the Secretary-General reiterated the need for an "energy affiliate" of the World Bank [A/40/637]. However, the report notes little progress in this area, except for the establishment of a new energy financing program by the International Finance Corporation (IFC).

The 41st General Assembly will tackle the recent effects of the dramatic drop in oil prices as well more long-term problems: the establishment of an agency and method of implementation to finance energy resources in the developing countries; the need to emphasize and direct interest in the development and utilization of new and renewable sources of energy; and the problems attendant to the development of nuclear energy, such as waste disposal and possible terrorist attacks on nuclear energy reactors [*Bulletin of the Atomic Scientist*, Mar. 1986, pp. 17–25].

4. Environment

The General Assembly will *not* consider environmental issues at its 41st Session, although it will debate some major issues that combine environment, politics, and economics.

The **United Nations Environment Programme (UNEP)** is experimenting with **biennialization,** a two-year schedule for its Governing Council sessions. For the first time since UNEP was established, its Council of 58 governments did not meet this year. As a result, there will be no environmental report to this session of the General Assembly. Next year, the Governing Council will meet and report to the 42nd Session [UNEP/GC 11/2].

The experiment is motivated in part by the need for savings at a time when contributions to UNEP are stagnating, as well as by a general agreement that UNEP should devote more time to program implementation and less to preparing for Council sessions. The General Assembly itself has decided [A/38/429] to make the work of its Second (Economic and Financial) Committee biannual by allocating the oversight of programs to odd or even years.

UNEP's experiment in biennialization has potentially negative aspects. According to one UNEP official, they are:

1. "While the cat's away, the mice will play": Some governments are concerned about loosened control over UNEP's policies and programs.

2. A few governments are not represented in Nairobi where UNEP is headquartered and, therefore, cannot participate in "off-year" briefings [UNEP/ GC 13/2].

3. UNEP programs may lose some visibility and momentum without annual, top-level governmental scrutiny.

In May 1987, the UNEP Governing Council will debate and decide whether to continue to meet every two years. But insofar as the General Assembly is concerned, the decision has little effect, for from now on it will review UNEP on odd years, along with such other programs as human settlements, science and technology, women, U.N. volunteers, and special economic assistance plans [A/39/217].

This does not mean that in even years environmental issues will be overlooked. Many are so vast and of such basic importance that they supersede administrative boundaries: famine in Africa, nuclear fallout and disarmament, the exploitation of Antarctica. As environmental problems are interrelated so are the solutions, requiring cooperation at international, national, and local levels among government officials, scientists, engineers, business leaders, and grass-roots groups.

Nowhere was this more amply illustrated than in Africa, where, in the mid-1980s, drought and famine afflicted half the continent. It was Africa's second major famine in a decade, and officials feared wide-scale hunger would continually recur if nothing were done to restore the continent's natural resources through development that was environmentally sound.

To confront the problem at its most basic level, Africa's environment ministers met in Cairo on December 16–18, 1985. From this meeting, organized by UNEP, the United Nations Economic Commission for Africa (ECA), and the Organization of Africa Unity (OAU), the **Cairo Programme for African Co-operation** was launched [UNEP/AEC.1/2, Annex I]. The African ministers' objective was to feed people and fuel development. To restore their continent's degraded environment, the ministers agreed on a comprehensive list of economic, technical, and scientific activities.

Two massive pilot projects were approved. Three villages in each African country—150 in all—and 30 pastures in semi-arid areas will test the concept "small is beautiful"—economically, socially, and environmentally. The goal is self-sufficiency in food and energy using local skills and experience so as to improve village conditions and put a check on urban migration.

In the second pilot project, eight scientific networks will be developed or strengthened to provide technical support for the "greening" of Africa. And, although their list of problems and projects is daunting, the environment ministers focused on four priority areas, setting up committees on: deserts and arid lands; rivers and lake basins; seas; and forests and woodlands.

Eight Western governments, including the United States, welcomed African solutions for African problems and pledged practical assistance for environmental projects [UNEP/AEC.1/2, Dec. 18, 1985].

Successful scientific cooperation during the 1957–58 International Geophysical Year led to the **1959 Antarctic Treaty.** Treaty membership is small and dominated by industrialized countries. The 12 original signatories (Argentina, Australia, Belgium, Chile, France, Japan, New Zealand, Norway, South Africa, the United Kingdom, the United States, and the Soviet Union) have since been joined by six others (Poland in 1977, West Germany in 1979, India and Brazil in 1983, and China and Uruguay in 1985), and only these 18 can make policy on Antarctica. Fourteen other nations (Czechoslovakia, Denmark, Netherlands, Romania, East Germany, Bulgaria, Peru, Italy, Papua New Guinea, Spain, Hungary, Sweden, Finland, and Cuba) have acceded to the treaty, but they are observers only and may not participate in decision making [Interview with Vladimir Golitsyn, U.N. lawyer].

For 27 years, such antagonists as the United States and the Soviet Union and Argentina and the United Kingdom have safeguarded one-tenth of Earth's land surface through the Treaty, keeping it much as it has always been—ecologically pristine, demilitarized, and nuclear-free—so that Antarctica can be a subject for scientific research. This research has discovered extraordinarily rich natural resources. Estimates of oil reserves run in the billions of barrels. The biological harvest is bigger. Every year a million tons of Antarctic krill are caught—tiny shrimplike creatures that support the entire Southern Ocean ecosystem.

The Treaty nations have been cautious in exploiting Antarctic fisheries. Their **Convention on the Conservation of Antarctic Marine Living Resources** came into force in 1982, the same year Antarctica came before the United Nations. The agreement states that decisions to harvest should calculate the effect on dependent species—referred to as "the ecosystem as a whole principle" [Robert Repetto, *World Enough and Time: Successful Strategies for Resource Management* (New

Haven: Yale University Press, 1986), p. 117].

Many third world countries have been pressing for a **global regime to govern Antarctica** so all can share its wealth. The developing-nation argument is that Antarctica is the **common heritage of mankind**, a concept similar to that used in Law of the Sea negotiations. By 1982–83, Malaysia had enough support to bring the issue to the United Nations. Although Antarctica since then has appeared regularly on General Assembly agendas, Antarctic Treaty nations so far have successfully opposed the Malaysian drive for a **U.N. committee on Antarctica** [*Issues Before the 40th General Assembly of the United Nations*, 103–106].

Meanwhile, the Antarctic Treaty Consultative Parties are conducting negotiations in secret. Their long-awaited **minerals regime** is of particular interest to the developing nations, because of the potential profits from oil exploitation in Antarctica. Treaty nations were invited to tell the Secretary-General about their progress toward a minerals agreement so that he could report to the 41st Session [A/40/156B]. But observers expect no such report will be forthcoming at this session [Interviews with Jean-Claude Faby, UNEP; Pat Scharlin, formerly International Earthcare Center of Sierra Club; Vladimir Golitsyn]. The General Assembly also urged that Antarctic Treaty nations "**exclude the racist *apartheid* regime of South Africa from participation**" [A/40/156C], a request which the Treaty states so far have refused.

Another version of politics and the environment also became an issue during the 40th Session of the General Assembly. The Second Committee spent days debating the wording of one preambular paragraph before it adopted the **resolution on international cooperation in the field of the environment** [A/40/200]. The argument came about when the Soviet Union proposed an amending paragraph dealing with the "arms race and the environment." Some Western countries took strong exception to it—even though they had accepted much stronger language on the same subject at a previous session. The squabble reached such proportions that, for the first time, a General Assembly resolution on environmental cooperation required a vote. Six Western nations—France, Israel, Portugal, the United Kingdom, the United States, and West Germany—abstained.

During the same week of the 40th Session, the General Assembly decided, peaceably and without a vote, to convene an **International Conference on the Relationship Between Disarmament and Development** from July 15 to August 2 in Paris; but in June of 1986 it was decided to postpone that conference. A likely topic for discussion is the negative impact of war and the arms race upon environmental security [A/40/155]. UNEP's other arms race-related activities include publications in conjunction with the Swedish International Peace Research Institute (SIPRI) and a seminar on security and the environment.

5. Law of the Sea

By May 1986, the 1982 **United Nations Convention on the Law of the Sea**—
a comprehensive treaty covering all ocean uses and developments—had been
ratified by 29 out of the 60 required for its entry into force. This is the third
year that the Preparatory Commission established to prepare for the Convention's entry into forces has met to draft implementing rules for the deep-
seabed mining regime and the International Tribunal for the Law of the Sea
that were created by the Convention. A report on the Commission's progress,
as well as on other aspects of the Convention, will be presented by the Secretary-General to the 41st General Assembly.

The United States, the United Kingdom, and West Germany have not
signed the Convention, finding unsatisfactory its provisions on deep-seabed
mining in areas beyond national jurisdiction, and the United States has also
chosen not to participate in the work of the Preparatory Commission. These
countries' concern about the provisions of this section are shared to varying
degrees by most of the other industrialized nations whose companies have
been involved in pioneering seabed minerals development. Their reluctance
to ratify the Convention has acted as a deterrent to still other states, which
fear that without the assessed contributions of the largest industrialized nations, they will have to provide a larger portion of the funding to launch the
institutions established by the Convention.

From its beginning, the work of the **Preparatory Commission** has been
considered crucial to the entry into force of a widely accepted Convention.
States from all regional and interest groups emphasize the importance of
drafting implementing rules for the Seabed Mining Code that clarify and
make more precise the Convention's provisions. Some think this process itself
will remove some of the objections to the Convention that have prevented
more widespread ratification; still others believe a handful of changes in the
Convention will probably be required as well.

Despite universal support for the Convention's provisions other than
those on mining the seabed, a number of states have enacted national marine
laws that are inconsistent with the Convention's rules of national sovereignty
and jurisdiction. These actions could have the effect of unraveling the agreed
regime of law for ocean use and provoke conflicts among states. Some countries have already approved such laws based on **assertions of unique circumstances**; West Germany, for example, has extended the limit of its territorial
sea to as much as 16 miles in certain areas to ensure tanker safety. This led
one pundit to coin the term "creeping uniqueness" for the next wave of national marine claims that may undermine agreed ocean law, the wave of the
1960s having been termed "creeping jurisdiction" [*Oceans Policy News*, Newsletter of
Citizens for Ocean Law, 2/86].

More recently, the United States Government formally protested claims by Ecuador and Chile to the continental shelf [*Oceans Policy News*, 3/86] as inconsistent with the Convention. The Soviet Union and other countries of Eastern Europe have similarly objected to assertions made by the Philippines with regard to archipelagic waters. Nevertheless, ocean law experts still credit the adoption of the Convention with reducing the excessiveness of national claims.

The Office of the United Nations' Special Representative on the Law of the Sea, Satya Nandan of Fiji, offers U.N. member states information and advisory services to assist in implementing the new comprehensive regime of ocean law and in monitoring state practices. For this purpose it collects and indexes national laws in the marine field and issues a bulletin of documents and reports on a wide range of actions relevant to the development of international ocean law. The Secretary-General's report to the 40th General Assembly [A/40/943] contains an excellent overview of these developments and of the work of Nandan's office [*Oceans Policy News*, 1/86]. Among the documents issued in 1985 were *Multilateral Treaties Relevant to the United Nations Convention on the LOS* [U.N. sales publication No. E.85.V.11] and *Pollution by Dumping: Legislative History of Articles 1, Paragraph 1(5), 210 and 216 of the UN Convention on the LOS* [U.N. sales publication No. E.85.V.12].

A current priority of the Preparatory Commission's work concerns implementation of Resolution II of the Law of the Sea Conference, which established an interim regime to protect the already significant investment of pioneer seabed mining enterprises and to provide a bridge to the Convention's regime. Registration of these **Pioneer Investors** by the Preparatory Commission gives them preferential rights over any other applicant except the **International Seabed Authority's** (ISA) operational mining arm, the **Enterprise**, in the award of mining contracts by the ISA, and at the same time imposes obligations regarding development of the Enterprise.

Problems have arisen in implementing Resolution II that were not envisaged at the time it was adopted by the Law of the Sea Conference in 1982. As a consequence of differences about the provisions of the Convention, four of the entities specifically identified in Resolution II as eligible for registration as Pioneer Investors did not apply. These were the four multinational consortia that have been issued licenses to explore for manganese nodules under the domestic legislation of the United States, the United Kingdom, and West Germany. Of the four that have made application—France, India, Japan, and the Soviet Union—three did so without first resolving problems of overlapping mine sites, a prerequisite under Resolution II. In addition, so extensive is the overlap between the Soviet Union and France and Japan that they are seriously limited in their ability to adhere strictly to another requirement for registration by the Preparatory Commission as contemplated in Resolution II and the Convention: that of parallelism—the division of all application areas into equal parts, one mining site for the Pioneer Investor and one for the Enterprise.

At the request of the Commission, Chairman Joseph S. Warioba has been attempting to promote a solution to these problems. The result to date is an understanding reached by the applicants in Arusha, Tanzania, in February 1986. It deals collectively with the overlap among the three state applicants, the matter of reserved areas for the Enterprise, the relinquishment of allocated areas once the actual mine site is defined, and the future accommodation of the four multinational consortia. Informal consultations on the **Arusha Understanding** among the members of the Commission will be pursued as a matter of priority at the summer session, scheduled to be held from August 12 to September 5. Also yet to be formalized are the Commission's rules for registration—work that was set aside awaiting resolution of these other problems. The impending departure of Chairman Warioba, recently appointed Prime Minister of Tanzania, is generally regarded as an unfortunate development for the Commission, in view of his effectiveness in promoting solutions to problems for which Resolution II was unable to provide all the answers.

Registration of applicants continues to be viewed as the single most important decision before the Preparatory Commission, since it gives life and status to the regime established by Resolution II and to basic tenets of the Convention itself. The importance attached to registration can also be attributed to the continuing actions conducted under the domestic laws of the United States, the United Kingdom, and West Germany that are criticized by the Commission as efforts to circumvent the Convention's regime. The issuance of U.S. national mining licenses in August and October 1984 was first condemned by the Commission in 1985. At its spring 1986 meeting, the Commission similarly deplored licenses issued by the United Kingdom and West Germany in late 1984 and late 1985, respectively, adopting a strongly worded declaration [LOS/PCN/28] when called to a vote by East Germany, despite efforts by the developing nations to promote a more conciliatory consensus version. The seven countries voting against the declaration were Belgium, Canada, France, Italy, Japan, Luxembourg, and the Netherlands; ten countries abstained.

Recent projections of the economics and feasibility of commercial seabed mining have produced varied reactions as to the speed at which the Preparatory Commission should work. Experts maintain that the drop in world metals prices will delay prospects for commercial development of **manganese nodules** until well into the second decade of the 21st century [Marne A. Dubs, "Minerals of the Deep Sea: Myth and Reality," *The New Order of the Oceans: The Advent of a Managed Environment*, ed., Giulio Pontecorvo (New York: Columbia University Press, 1986)]. A computer study produced for the Commission by the Government of Australia [LOS/PCN/

SCN.2/WP10/Add.1] concludes that the aggregate price of the four primary metals found in manganese nodules—copper, cobalt, nickel, and manganese—would have to double before deep-seabed mining could approach the minimum 18 percent discounted cash flow rate of return on investment required by private operators.

Some observers of the law-of-the sea process maintain that this leaves ample time to seek consensus on a revised seabed mining package. Others express concern that the Convention may enter into force without adherence by most of the seabed mining countries and that it may then be far more difficult to work out an acceptable mining regime.

The training of personnel for the Enterprise—an obligation assumed by registered Pioneer Investors—is also affected by the predicted long delays in commercially viable mining. Though the Pioneers do not wish to shirk their training obligations, neither do they wish to activate these duties prematurely, entering into long-term, open-ended obligations that might be pushed well beyond those contemplated in 1982.

The regular work of the Commission is organized into five separate working groups: the informal plenary is considering matters related to implementation of Resolution II and draft rules for administrative, procedural, and budgetary aspects of the ISA; special commission one (SCN.1) is attempting to address the problems of land-based developing-nation producers likely to be affected by competition from deep-seabed mineral production; SCN.2 is considering training programs and alternate operational modes to launch the Enterprise, with some discussion of how its launch should relate to the delay in prospects for commercial seabed mining operations; SCN.3 is reviewing draft regulations for the mining code governing prospecting, exploration, and exploitation of manganese modules; and SCN.4 is drafting rules of procedure for the International Tribunal for the Law of the Sea.

Although the Preparatory Commission has been making good progress in all these forums, its sense of purpose has been affected by the combined uncertainties of future support by the industrialized nations, complications in the registration process, and doubts about the commercial viability of seabed mining. The success of its continuing efforts to implement these and other portions of the Convention requires that governments take a firm hand in organizing and directing the work of the Commission.

6. Antarctica

This is the fourth year that Antarctica will be debated in the First Committee of the General Assembly. In 1986, it will have before it an updated and expanded study of the Secretary-General's report on Antarctica produced in 1984 [A/39/583, Parts I and II]. The update will address three issues: (1) availability of information from the Antarctic Treaty Consultative Parties to the United Nations on their respective activities in, and their deliberations regarding Antarctica, (2) the involvement of the relevant specialized agencies and intergovernmental organizations in the Antarctic Treaty System, and (3) the significance of the 1982 United Nations Convention on the Law of the Sea in the Southern Ocean [A/40/156A]. The General Assembly has also invited the Antarctic Treaty Consultative Parties (ATCPs) to inform the Secretary-General of their negotiations to establish a regime regarding Antarctic minerals, so that he can submit to the Assembly for the 41st Session a report containing the replies [A/40/156B]. A third resolution adopted by the General Assembly in December 1985 urges the ATCPs to exclude the "racist *apartheid* régime" of **South Africa** from participation in meetings of the ATCPs at the earliest possible date and invited the states parties to the Antarctic Treaty to inform the Secretary-General of actions taken in this regard [A/40/156C].

Participants in the 1985 debate were in the end unable to reach agreement on a consensus resolution as had occurred the previous two years, primarily due to disagreeements on the third resolution. While there were no negative votes on the three resolutions, the 18 ATCPs and the vast majority of the Non-consultative Parties (NCPs), the now 14 nations that have acceded to the Antarctic Treaty but do not hold decision-making status, sought as a group not to participate in the vote. Nevertheless, China, India, Peru, and Romania voted in favor of the South African resolution; China abstained on the other two; and Peru abstained on the minerals-related resolution, while Romania supported it. The ATCPs noted that "it is a matter of great regret to members of the Antarctic Treaty that the tradition of consensus decisionmaking . . . has this year been broken."

The ATCPs have therefore decided as a group not to respond to the information requests in the first two resolutions, although they remain willing to provide information on Antarctica to the international community and adopted various policies to do so at the most recent biennial consultative meetings in 1983 and 1985. It appears that most of the NCPs will go along with this decision, but not all of them. Malaysian efforts to establish a United Nations committee on Antarctica have been unsuccessful to date. This question will probably come up again at the 1986 General Assembly session.

During the 1985 General Assembly debate, there was a slight shift in emphasis from previous years, when the Antarctic Treaty System (ATS) as a whole seemed to be under attack. Although many countries still support application of the **common heritage of mankind principle** to Antarctica, which was applied to the seabed beyond national jurisdiction in the 1982 Law of the Sea Convention, they are less adamant about reconstituting the whole of the ATS with universal, one-nation, one-vote membership; instead, they are concentrating calls for a universal regime on the minerals regime that the ATCPs began negotiating in 1982. On the other hand, the call for expulsion of South Africa would undermine the ATS, since Antarctic decision making takes place by consensus, and it is difficult to conceive of a situation where South Africa would go along with such a consensus.

Meetings under the ATS continue apace. The fifth annual meeting of the Commission and Scientific Committee, established by the 1980 Convention on the Conservation of Antarctic Marine Living Resources (CCAMLR), takes place at their headquarters in Hobart, Tasmania, Australia, in September. Additional conservation measures for Southern Ocean finfish were adopted at the 1985 meeting, but the Commission's task is hampered by a lack of data and information necessary to assess the need for conservation measures. Every effort is being made to encourage states that are party to CCAMLR to submit the information required so that the 1986 meeting can act. Another priority area for action in 1986 is agreement on how to implement the system of observation and inspection called for under the CCAMLR.

With respect to minerals, the eighth meting in the negotiation to produce a legal regime governing the possibility of **mineral resources development** in Antarctica took place in Hobart, Australia, in April 1986, and it appears that Japan will host another meeting in Tokyo in the fall. The ATCPs are seeking to conclude an agreement in 1987. Two sets of discussions are taking place in this forum: frequent informal consultations among heads of delegation on the key issues, and working group sessions on (1) legal issues such as compliance and enforcement, liability, dispute settlement, amendment, and withdrawal; (2) guidelines for operators planning to submit applications to explore and develop minerals; and (3) environmental issues. The key issues are the composition and decision-making procedures of the institutions of the regime and how they relate to each other, and participation in the institutions of the regime, in activities approved pursuant to it, and in potential benefits from such activities. One important accommodation required if the negotiations are to succeed is that between claimant and non-claimant states in Antarctica, the other between parties to ATS regimes and the wider international community, given the unresolved issue of ownership of the area and its resources.

Another recent development in the ATS was the decision at the VI Special Consultative Meeting in Brussels, Belgium, on October 7, 1985, that the People's Republic of China and Uruguay qualified for Consultative (decision-making) status under the Antarctic Treaty by virtue of their scientific research activities in Antarctica.

At the XIII Consultative Meeting in Brussels immediately following, two working groups were established to consider (1) the operation of the ATS, including questions of document availability and appointment of observers; and (2) environmental issues, including environmental impact assessment (eia), procedures for science and logistic activities, establishment of additional protected areas, data and monitoring requirements for effective long-term conservation in Antarctica, revising the procedures and standards for waste disposal in Antarctica, and potential environmental consequences of tourism and the increasing concentration of activities in Antarctica in general.

Most of the environmental issues were referred to the nongovernmental **Scientific Committee on Antarctic Research (SCAR)** for further information and advice, and several additional protected areas were adopted. With respect to the operation of the ATS, the ATCPs agreed to establish national contact point(s) to improve dissemination of information on the system, such as reports of Consultative Meetings, the Handbook, and the annual exchange of information on scientific plans and results, as well as information on the location of scientific data and samples and on bibliographies and other sources of published works related to all Antarctic matters. In addition, they declassified documents from the first three Consultative Meetings and will take up those from the next four at their 1987 meeting.

The next meeting will also reconsider the establishment of a secretariat in 1987, as the need for information grows and coordination within the ATS and with SCAR becomes more important. On the latter topic, the ATCPs finally agreed to invite observers from two international organizations to the 1987 meeting, although these will come from "within the system": CCAMLR and SCAR. Moreover, the NCPs now have a permanent invitation to attend regular consultative meetings.

Finally, SCAR held a biennial meeting in San Diego in June, where it took up the various requests for advice from the Brussels meeting as well as its normal agenda of Antarctic scientific issues. SCAR is involved in a joint working group with the International Union for the Conservation of Nature and Natural Resources (IUCN) to draft a long-term conservation plan for Antarctica, bearing in mind the projected increase in scale, type, and intensity of Antarctic activities.

As the General Assembly continues its involvement in questions of Antarctic governance, "all states" are urged to "resume cooperation with a view to arriving at a consensus on all aspects concerning Antarctica," in the words of a declaration adopted by the foreign ministers of the Non-Aligned Movement on April 18, 1986. It is clear that consensus will gel only around efforts that build on the ATS, acknowledging the existence of claimant and non-claimant positions alike and the concept of decision-making rights based on some level of experience in Antarctica. Parties to the ATS must indicate in concrete terms that this need not preclude greater involvement on the part of interested states and international organizations in all forms of Antarctic activity.

V
Human Rights and Social Issues

1. Human Rights

The Preamble to the United Nations Charter affirms a "faith in fundamental human rights, in the dignity and worth of the human person, in the equal rights of men and women and of nations large and small" [U.N. Department of Public Information, *The United Nations at Forty: A Foundation to Build On* (New York: United Nations, 1985), p. 132]. One of the purposes of the organization outlined in Article 1 is to promote and encourage "respect for human rights and for fundamental freedoms for all without distinction as to race, sex, language or religion." The Charter gives the General Assembly the responsibility for studying and recommending ways in which fundamental rights and freedoms can be realized.

These Charter provisions have fostered the creation of permanent and ad hoc bodies for the study of particular human rights issues and for the drafting of human rights instruments. The General Assembly is the highest policy-making body in the U.N. with regard to human rights. By calling on other U.N. human rights bodies to conduct studies or to draft conventions on particular rights topics, the General Assembly initiates U.N. activity in various human rights fields and gives final approval to proposals drafted by these other bodies. On adoption by the General Assembly, these reports and instruments can spur the creation of additional committees or offices to monitor their implementation.

The Commission on Human Rights was set up in 1946. Its first order of business was to draft an international bill of rights. Eleanor Roosevelt, who headed the Commission, divided this work into three stages: first, to define basic rights and freedoms; second, to enact binding legal obligations, or covenants, to protect those rights; and third, to institute mechanisms to aid their implementation.

The first stage was completed in 1948 with the adoption of the **Universal Declaration of Human Rights.** In 30 articles, the Declaration sets forth the fundamental rights and freedoms to which all men and women are entitled, including freedom from torture, slavery, arbitrary arrest and detention; the right to work and to form trade unions; the right to own property and to vote; freedom of movement and residence; the right to seek asylum in other countries; the right to equality before the law and to a fair trial; and the right to be presumed innocent until proven guilty. The General Assembly called the Universal Declaration "a common standard of achievement for all peoples and all nations" [*The United Nations at Forty*, p. 133].

It was not until 1966, however, that the United Nations' work in the field of creating binding legal obligations was largely fulfilled. International legal obligations were set by the two Covenants negotiated by the Human Rights Commission and adopted by the General Assembly—the International Covenant on Civil and Political Rights (with the Optional Protocol on Civil and Political Rights) and the International Covenant on Economic, Social and Cultural Rights. Together, the Universal Declaration and the two Covenants form the Bill of International Human Rights.

Because international issues are inherently political and involve fundamental questions of national sovereignty, the United Nations' ability to enforce human rights mechanisms remains distinctly limited and observance of fundamental human rights is still far from universal. In fact, as the United Nations attempts to define human rights in more specific terms or to monitor rights violations more rigorously, the international consensus wanes. Measures that address the relationship between the individual and the state are often seen as intrusions on national sovereignty. For example, by June 1986, ratification of the Universal Declaration was nearly universal, but the Covenant on Civil and Political Rights had been ratified by only 83 of the 159 member states and the Covenant on Economic, Social and Cultural Rights by 87. Only 37 states had ratified the Optional Protocol on Civil and Political Rights, which permits the United Nations to accept complaints concerning rights violations from individuals in ratifying states. (Notable among the nations that have failed to ratify the two Covenants is the United States.)

Although the three stages enunciated by Mrs. Roosevelt continue to guide the work of the United Nations in human rights matters, they have been somewhat redefined. The Bill of International Human Rights, which remains the primary standard-setting mechanism, has been augmented over the years by conventions on a number of specific human rights issues. Current efforts at standard setting increasingly focus on "the right to development." The Proclamation of Teheran of 1968 and General Assembly resolutions thereafter have affirmed the notion that the enjoyment of social and economic rights is a requisite for the realization of civil and political rights. Several Western governments, defining human rights in terms of the rights of individuals and rejecting the notion of collective rights for states or peoples, see in such declarations the possibility that civil or political liberties could be put aside to accommodate the social or economic development of the state. The United States has registered its objection to recent General Assembly resolutions that make note of the interdependence of economic and social rights and civil and political rights [A/40/983]. The subject will be discussed at the 41st General Assembly [A/C.3/40/L.60] and at Assembly sessions for years to come.

The United Nations' human rights activities tend to emphasize standard setting more than attempts to bring the conduct of national governments into compliance with those standards. Integral to U.N. compliance efforts is the work of the Human Rights Committee, which reviews nations' reports on human rights progress and receives complaints from individuals concerning abuses. The primary tools used by the Human Rights Committee in implementing human rights standards are fact-finding and intervention in particular cases of rights abuse.

The United Nations' importance lies in its ability to expose human rights violations and to bring the pressure of international opinion to bear on the oppressors on the basis of the standards set by the U.N. bodies. Through reports, studies, fact-finding missions, and general debate, the human rights bodies within the United Nations system have broadly disseminated the standards set by the Universal Declaration, and its provisions have been incorporated into the legal systems of many nations, especially newly independent countries. The General Assembly has also adopted several resolutions encouraging the establishment of national institutions for promoting and protecting human rights and will consider a report from the Secretary-General on this subject at the 41st Session [A/Res/40/123].

Standard Setting

The main achievements of the General Assembly have been in defining human rights standards that are not only acceptable to the international community but are, in fact, more stringent than those applied by any single country. The human rights activities of the General Assembly, then, are greater than the sum of its parts: The U.N. continually strives to bring the conduct of all member nations into compliance with the Declaration, Covenants, and various conventions.

The Third Committee of the General Assembly receives reports on human rights questions from the Secretary-General, the Economic and Social Council (ECOSOC), the Committee on Human Rights, the Commission on Human Rights and its Sub-Commission on the Prevention of Discrimination and Protection of Minorities. Debate in the Third Committee on the issues, draft declarations, and recommendations of these bodies has been characterized as "acrimonious" by Jay H. Long, the Principal Officer of the Office of the Under-Secretary-General for Political and General Assembly Affairs [DPI/NGO/SB/85/32].

Yet despite this acrimony, significant majorities and a surprising international consensus have permitted the adoption of key human rights instruments and fact-finding and intervention activities along a number of thematic lines. Some of the major themes emerging in the U.N.'s work include those relating to the status of refugees and stateless persons; protection of the rights of workers; the abolition of slavery; political rights of women and discrimination against women; the rights of children, including the exploitation of child labor; independence for colonial countries and peoples; racial discrimination, especially apartheid; torture; and intolerance, discrimination, or persecution based on religious identity. For example, the Sub-Commission on Prevention of Discrimination and Protection of Minorities of the Commission of Human Rights is at work on a draft Body of Principles and Guidelines on the Rights and Responsibilities to Promote and Protect Human Rights and Fundamental Freedoms. At the request of the General Assembly, the Sub-Commission has also examined human rights in relation to scientific and technological developments, with the goal of drafting a body of guidelines, principles, and guarantees on such matters as the use of computerized personal files. The Sub-Commission adopted a resolution on the **administration of justice and the human rights of detainees** and recommended that its study on the subject be published and disseminated as widely as possible.

Many of the U.N. human rights instruments have been negotiated by the **Commission on Human Rights**, which remains the principal U.N. body for the protection of human rights and provides policy guidance for U.N. activities in human rights. The Commission, which has been expanded to 43 member nations since its founding in 1946, is an intergovernmental body that meets annually to examine human rights violations and general human rights situations in particular countries or regions and to review the United Nations' implementation activities. Member countries are elected by ECOSOC; the specific representatives of these countries are appointed by their governments.

During its February-March 1986 session, the Commission reviewed a report by the Secretary-General on U.N. advisory services to countries that request such assistance to implement international human rights conventions and on the Secretary-General's role in facilitating bilateral assistance in this area [HR/2890]. The Commission also continued its work on standard-setting—the development of declarations, conventions and other human rights instruments—with particular regard to the rights of the child: of indigenous peoples; of religious, ethnic, and other minorities; and of people suffering from mental disorders or detained because of such disorders [HR/2890]. The possibility of a **Convention on the Rights of the Child** has been considered at each session of the General Assembly since 1959, when the Assembly unanimously adopted the Declaration of the Rights of the Child [HR/2889]. During the 40th Session, the Assembly asked the Commission on Human Rights to give priority to work on the draft convention.

The 40th General Assembly also requested the Commission to give special attention to violations of the **right to self-determination,** especially under conditions of foreign military intervention, aggression, or occupation [A/Res/ 40/24]. The 41st General Assembly will consider violations of the right to self-determination in all countries, but particularly in Kampuchea and Afghanistan, in light of the Commission's work and a report from the Secretary-General. It is unlikely, however, that the Assembly will reach a consensus on compliance measures because of the reluctance of many member states to set a precedent by singling out particular instances of military or other intervention or aggression. The exception has been the situation in Southern Africa; the General Assembly has voted to impose sanctions on the Government of South Africa for its interference in Angola and Namibia and for its apartheid policies.

Another U.N. body that brings issues before the General Assembly is the **Human Rights Committee,** which was established to monitor compliance with the Covenant on Civil and Political Rights when it went into force in 1976. The Committee consists of 18 human rights experts who act in a personal capacity [HR/2822]. Within a year of ratifying the Covenant (and every five years thereafter, or when the Committee so requests), states that are parties to the Covenant are required to submit reports to the Committee on their progress in implementing the Covenant. The Human Rights Committee studies and reviews these reports and also monitors national legislation in these areas. Under the Optional Protocol to the Covenant, the Human Rights Committee will consider (in closed meetings) communications from individuals concerning rights violations.

The Human Rights Committee will continue to address some of the issues taken up in the 1985 session, including the increasing problem of late reports from states parties and the lack of response by some governments to the Committee's requests for additional information [HR/2821]. The General Assembly has taken note of the effects of this problem on the various human rights bodies and has asked the Secretary-General to address the matter [A/40/ 983].

The Committee regularly prepares "general comments" in the form of recommendations to governments of additional measures to be taken in implementing specific articles of the Covenant [HR/2882]. During 1985 and 1986, the Committee prepared such comments on the position of aliens under the Covenant and considered drafts of general comments on the rights of people belonging to minority groups. The **Declaration on the Human Rights of Individuals Who are not Nationals of the Country in which They Live,** adopted by the 40th General Assembly, defines the term "alien" very broadly; to add to the Declaration's effectiveness, further qualification of the legality of the alien's presence in the territory of the states is required [A/C.3/40/12; A/Res/40/144].

Another item on the Committee's agenda was the relationship between human rights activities and the 1986 **International Year of Peace.** Assistant

Secretary-General for Human Rights Kurt Herndl has noted the "close link between the maintenance of peace and respect for human rights: The more that governments through their actions demonstrated respect for human rights and fundamental freedoms, the more one would be able to avoid conflicts between men and states and would have a better opportunity for preserving peace in the world" [UNIS/1040]. In this connection, the Committee has requested the Secretary-General to distribute its general comments on the prevention of war in relation to the right to life, especially with regard to nuclear weapons and the possibility of thermonuclear war [HR/2698].

In addition to its Charter responsibilities in the field of human rights, the Economic and Social Council (ECOSOC) was given special monitoring and implementation responsibilities by the Covenant on Economic, Social and Cultural Rights. In 1985, ECOSOC resolved to establish a **Committee on Social and Cultural Rights** to monitor implementation of the Covenant, a move welcomed by the Third Committee of the General Assembly [A/40/983]. The members of the committee, scheduled to commence operations in 1987, will be experts from countries selected by ECOSOC, who will act in their personal capacity.

During its first session of 1986, ECOSOC continued to carry out its mandate to act as the Special Rapporteur in matters relating to **summary or arbitrary executions**, the subject of General Assembly resolutions in Sessions 36 through 39 [see A/Res/36/22, A/Res/37/182, A/Res/38/96, and A/Res/39/110]. The Assembly, which urged all U.N. bodies to cooperate in the preparation of the Special Rapporteur's final report, will consider the report and recommendations of the Commission on Human Rights during the 41st Session [A/Res/40/143].

Article 68 of the Charter instructs the Economic and Social Council to "set up commissions in economic and social fields for the promotion of human rights." The Commission on the Status of Women, set up in 1946 as one of the six original functional commissions of ECOSOC, met during February and March 1986 to discuss ways in which it could strengthen its role in coordinating all U.N. programs for women and to examine the status of the **Convention on the Elimination of All Forms of Discrimination against Women**, adopted in 1979. As of May 1986, 87 states had become parties to the Convention [UNIS/WOM/114]. During the 40th General Assembly, the Third Committee adopted recommendations for implementing the "forward-looking strategies" contained in the final report of the World Conference to Review and Appraise the Achievements of the United Nations Decade for Women, held in Nairobi in the summer of 1985. The Secretary-General will present a report to the 41st Session on measures to strengthen the Commission [DPI/NGO/SB/85/32].

The 41st General Assembly will review the report of the Secretary-General on a **new international humanitarian order** [A/40/348] and will debate comments received on this report. Assistant Secretary-General for Human Rights

Kurt Herndl has stressed the importance of this order because it encompasses not only human rights but humanitarian law [DPI/NGO/SB/85/31].

The Assembly will also consider the progress of the Working Group on the Drafting of an **International Convention on the Protection of the Rights of All Migrant Workers and Their Families.** The Working Group will meet during the 41st Session to continue the reading of the second draft convention [A/C.3/40/L.70].

The **Convention against Torture, Other Cruel, Inhuman or Degrading Treatment or Punishment,** adopted at the 39th Session, obligates states to make torture a "punishable" offense in their laws. At the close of the 40th Session, it had been signed by 44 states and ratified by 4, although it had not yet entered into force [DPI/NGO/SB/85/31]. A Committee Against Torture will be set up under the Convention to monitor compliance. It will examine reports from states, undertake confidential investigations, and make visits to member states (although the signatories can choose to disallow such visits), and it can receive complaints from individuals [*Issues Before the 40th General Assembly of the United Nations,* p. 109].

In March 1985, the Commission on Human Rights appointed a Special Rapporteur to examine questions relevant to torture. Also during 1985, the Third Committee adopted resolutions calling on all governments to ratify the Convention against Torture and calling on all governments, organizations, and individuals to contribute to the United Nations Voluntary Fund for Victims of Torture, which was established by the General Assembly in 1981 [A/40/982].

Country-Specific Issues

During the 40th Session, the General Assembly adopted resolutions that expressed "deep concern" over continuing rights violations in four countries: Afghanistan, Chile, El Salvador, and Iran [DPI/NGO/SB/85/32]. Since that time, the Assembly has adopted a more conciliatory approach to both Chile and El Salvador. Continuing rights violations in **Guatemala**—including involuntary disappearances, secret detentions, repression, killings, and forced participation of rural and indigenous populations in "civilian patrols" organized by the military—were also a concern, but here the General Assembly saw reason to express "the hope that the [November] elections [would] be the first step in a process leading to complete and effective enjoyment of human rights by the people of Guatemala." It also noted "with satisfaction the set of provisions to safeguard human rights and fundamental freedoms contained in the new Constitution" and urged the newly elected government to continue to cooperate with the Special Rapporteur in bringing human rights violations to an end [A/Res/40/140]. The Assembly has dropped Guatemala from its list of countries to monitor; instead, Guatemala will report only to the Human

Rights Commission. The Guatemalan constitution that went into effect in January 1986 provides for the establishment of both a national commission and a commissioner for human rights.

The 40th General Assembly was the first to consider human rights reports on countries other than those of Latin America. At the request of the Assembly, the Commission on Human Rights appointed individuals to examine and prepare reports on the human rights situations in Iran and Afghanistan; reports on these two countries, as well as on Chile and El Salvador, will be considered by the 41st Session.

The Commission's report on **Iran** cited such violations of human rights as persecution of minorities, notably among members of the Baha'i faith; torture; cruel and degrading treatment and punishment; arbitrary arrests and detentions; and a lack of recognition of the right ot a fair trial [A/Res/40/141]. The General Assembly has asked the Commission to study ways to secure protection of these rights in Iran.

The 41st General Assembly will consider a report of the Special Rapporteur on human rights conditions in **Afghanistan**, particularly the effect on women and children of the continued Soviet occupation and the ongoing conflict. The Assembly has expressed concern that widespread disregard for human rights now threatens "not only the lives of individuals but of whole groups of persons and tribes" [A/C.3/40/L.48/Rev.1]. The Assembly has also expressed alarm at the common practice of torture and summary execution of political opponents of the regime and at the consequences for civilians of indiscriminate bombardments and military operations. Authorities in Afghanistan continue to refuse to cooperate with the Special Rapporteur and with the Commission on Human Rights.

Rights violations in **El Salvador** on the part of government and insurgent forces in that country's civil war again led the 40th General Assembly to request that both sides respect the rules of war outlined in the Geneva Convention of 1949 [A/Res/40/139]. The General Assembly also expressed its regret that talks between the government and insurgents have been interrupted. The Special Representative appointed to monitor the situation will continue to observe the extent to which both sides respect the rights of civilians, prisoners of war, the wounded, and health personnel, both civilian and military. The General Assembly has again urged that "all States refrain from intervening in the internal situation in El Salvador" in any way that prolongs and intensifies the war.

The General Assembly has expressed its concern about human rights in **Chile** at each session since the 29th in 1974. To the surprise of many, the United States—which in recent years has generally refrained from public criticism of the Chilean Government—in early 1986 was sponsor of the resolution condemning human rights abuses in Chile that was placed before, and passed by, the Commission on Human Rights. It remains to be seen whether the United States will undertake such initiatives in the future.

The urgency of the political crisis in South Africa has given new impetus to the Assembly's discussion of South African human rights violations. During the 40th Session, the General Assembly resolved to organize a world conference on sanctions against South Africa in response not only to South Africa's policy of apartheid but to its intervention and aggression against neighboring Southern African states [DPI/NGO/SB/85/32]. The **World Conference on Sanctions against Racist South Africa** was held June 16 to 21, 1986, in Paris. It was organized by the U.N. Special Committee against Apartheid in cooperation with the Organization for African Unity and the Movement of Non-Aligned Countries [*U.N. Chronicle,* April 1986]. Representatives of 130 nations participated, although the United States, West Germany, and Great Britain—South Africa's principal trading partners—boycotted the conference [*New York Times,* 6/21/86]. The conference issued a 17-page statement calling for sweeping economic sanctions against South Africa and urging the United States and Great Britain to reconsider their opposition to such sanctions. The conference also urged an end to all cooperation with the Pretoria Government on military and nuclear matters and a global boycott of companies that do business in South Africa.

The General Assembly has continued to appeal to members and U.N. bodies to intensify efforts to implement the **International Convention on the Suppression and Punishment of the Crime of Apartheid,** adopted in 1973. The Special Committee against Apartheid compiles lists of individuals, organizations, and institutions that it believes are responsible for committing crimes under the Convention [A/Res/40/27], while ECOSOC is charged with implementation of the program of action for the Second Decade to Combat Racism and Racial Discrimination. A recent ECOSOC report examines the economic consequences for South Africa of a divestment of capital and business by foreign investors in that country.

In February 1986, the Security Council echoed the General Assembly's repeated condemnations of South Africa, warning South Africa against "committing any acts of aggression, terrorism and destabilization against independent African states and its use of mercenaries" [UNIS/1046]. The Council also demanded the immediate dismantling of apartheid.

Discussion of apartheid continues in the Committee on the Elimination of Racial Discrimination, formed in 1969 when the **International Convention on the Elimination of All Forms of Racial Discrimination** was adopted. The Convention's 124 signatories have agreed to condemn apartheid and to take measures to eradicate such policies in their own countries [HR/506]. In November 1985, the First International Conference in Solidarity with Peoples under Racial Discrimination, held in Libya, issued "The Tripoli Declaration," which denied the authority of the Pretoria regime, condemned apartheid, and expressed solidarity with the people of Southern Africa.

The 41st Assembly will also debate the report of the **Special Committee to Investigate Israeli Practices Affecting the Human Rights of the Population**

of the Occupied Territories. During the 40th Session, the Assembly passed a resolution calling upon the Israeli Government to release all Arabs detained or imprisoned "as a result of their struggle for self-determination" [A/Res/40/161]. In the past, Israel has denied all allegations of rights abuses, characterizing such charges as politically motivated [*Issues Before the 38th General Assembly of the United Nations*, p. 120].

The Commission on Human Rights and the Sub-Commission also examined the situations in Paraguay, Pakistan, Albania, Ethiopia, Haiti, and Zaire. The human rights situation in scores of other countries was considered in public discussion and in reports on such specific issues as torture, executions, and disappearances. The Human Rights Committee examined 29 reports from individuals in various countries who were alleging rights violations.

Over the next year, the human rights work of the United Nations will once again be hindered by the lack of international consensus on the proper role of international and intergovernmental organizations in protecting human rights. The work of United Nations special committees and special rapporteurs—often criticized by independent human rights groups for failing to report evenhandedly on the situations in given countries—can only become less effective if states fail to cooperate with their efforts. Nations that view U.N. efforts to enforce human rights obligations as an abridgement of national sovereignty will continue to balk at any initiative taken in the 41st Session to implement the declarations, conventions, and resolutions adopted by the General Assembly in previous years.

2. Refugees

In a speech in New York at the 40th anniversary of the United Nations in 1985, President Reagan singled out the **United Nations High Commissioner for Refugees (UNHCR)** for special praise within the family of U.N. operational agencies. The President's attention to the UNHCR acknowledged the humane treatment of refugees from civil and political strife as a central concern of the United Nations since the post–World War II effort to solve Europe's problem of displaced persons. Gradually, the work of the United Nations with refugees has expanded around the globe, illuminating (in the words of the newly elected High Commissioner, Jean-Pierre Hocké) the "universality of the problem of forced exile" [speech to representatives of states members to the Executive Committee of the High Commissioner's Program, 1/31/86]. Despite the inherent contentiousness of refugee problems, the U.N. system has shown a continuing ability to meet human needs in the midst of political limitations.

With the December 1985 election of Mr. Hocké, a Swiss official with the International Committee of the Red Cross, many observers expressed the hope that a new era of candor over refugee problems had begun. In particular, the new High Commissioner began his term by acknowledging that long-standing juridical instruments for addressing refugee problems, namely, the 1951 Convention on the Status of Refugees and the 1967 Protocol, "no longer fully take account of the complexities inherent in the phenomena of exile which are evident today" [*Ibid.*]. His predecessor, Poul Hartling, had also sought to strengthen the legal basis of the UNHCR's mandate.

While it is unlikely that full-scale revisions of these standards will be presented during the 41st General Assembly, numerous refugee issues will arise. The scope of refugee problems has hardly diminished in the last year. Reliable estimates place the number of refugees today at approximately 10 million [U.S. Committee for Refugees, *World Refugee Survey 1985* (New York, Washington, D.C.: American Council for Nationalities Service, 1985)]. Measured numerically, the worst refugee problems are the concentrations of Afghan refugees in Pakistan, Palestinians around Israel and its occupied territories, and Ethiopians in the Horn of Africa. Reports on actual figures vary, but in each of these cases the refugee populations in question are in the millions.

The General Assembly has in recent years passed resolutions calling for reports from the High Commissioner on refugee problems in specific countries. The 41st Session will receive reports on the current situation in Somalia, Ethiopia, Djibouti, Sudan, and Chad [A/40/1007]. In addition, a report on the general situation of refugees from Namibia and South Africa currently living in several countries in Southern Africa will be submitted [*Ibid.*; see also A/Res/40/ 133, 134, 135, 136, 137, 138].

Most pressing from an institutional perspective are the **expanding financial needs for meeting refugee crises**. The UNHCR has traditionally ended the year with a modest financial surplus that allowed it to meet costs that arose before donor states completed payments on pledged assistance. The unprecedented level of emergency needs in 1985 left the agency facing the early months of 1986 with very restricted room for financial maneuver as the new program cycle began. By the end of 1985, expenditures in Somalia, Ethiopia, and Sudan alone exceeded $100 million within a total budget of almost $500 million. In addition to its annual pledging conference for donor nations, the UNHCR solicited supplementary funds in 1986 for **Special Programs of Emergency Relief Assistance in Africa** [EA/COM 7/85-86, February 1986]. By February 1986, less than 10 percent of an estimated $80 million in requested additional funding had been pledged or paid for meeting current emergency needs [*Ibid.*]. Concern over the use of U.N. funds prompted a General Assembly resolution in late 1985 calling for a full financial report and audit of several U.N. agencies, including the UNHCR, to be presented at the 41st General Assembly [A/41/50, p. 17].

The long-term needs of African refugees had been addressed in 1984 by the second **International Conference for Assistance to Refugees in Africa (ICARA II)**. The intentions of ICARA II, which for the most part were directed at combining relief assistance to refugees with long-term development aid, were largely overshadowed by the magnitude of the relief crisis of 1984–85. A resolution at the 40th General Assembly therefore reemphasized "the complementarity of refugee aid and development assistance." The resolution also called on the United Nations Development Programme (UNDP) to expand its involvement in refugee situations in Africa, and asked the Secretary-General and the officials of interested bodies such as the Organization of African Unity, the UNDP, and the UNHCR to monitor follow-up to ICARA II. The Secretary-General will report on this process to the 41st Session as part of a comprehensive report on the current refugee situation in Africa [A/Res/40/117].

The longest-standing refugee problem before the General Assembly is that of the Palestinians. Since 1949 a special agency, the **United Nations Relief and Works Agency for Palestine Refugees in the Near East (UNRWA)**, has been charged with providing assistance to Palestinians displaced at the time of the formation of Israel in 1948 and in the course of subsequent hostilities. Notably weaker than the UNHCR (UNRWA, for instance, is not charged with reponsibility for the legal protection of refugees it serves), the agency has led a precarious existence for more than 35 years. Its existence and funding are extended on a yearly basis by resolution of the General Assembly; UNRWA was included in the list of U.N. agencies required to undergo an audit prior to the 1986 General Assembly [A/41/50, p. 17]. A resolution passed at the 40th Session noted with regret that "no substantial progress has been made in the programme endorsed by the General Assembly . . . of 26 January 1952 for the reintegration of refugees either by repatriation or resettlement." At the 41st Session, the Secretary-General will report on progress made on a number of matters related to the feeding, education, repatriation, and protection of Palestinians [A/Res/40/165].

The nature of the contemporary refugee problem has in recent years been analyzed from the perspective of **human rights and mass exoduses** [E/CN.4/1503]. The 40th Session of the General Assembly adopted a resolution stressing the need to "improve international cooperation aimed at prevention of new massive flows of refugees," and decided to review the matter again during the current session [A/Res/40/149]. At the 40th Session, a specially formed Group of Governmental Experts submitted their findings on averting new refugee flows [A/40/385, Annex.]. In December 1985 the Secretary-General was charged with presenting a report to the 41st Session on the progress that has been made on this issue over the past year [A/40/166]. To that end, the Group of Governmental Experts has been preparing further recommendations for the General Assembly on international cooperation in averting new refugee flows.

Averting refugee flows depends on the ability of interested parties to address root causes; many of those most interested in averting new flows are developed nations that must shoulder the responsibilities of resettlement and care. To a large extent, successful handling of such complex matters will depend upon the ability of leaders in the UNHCR and elsewhere to marshal the political will to bring refugee issues the attention they require. Shortly after his election, Mr. Hocké stated that "I have good reason to believe that [the refugee] problem can be defused, and that in the long run it can be fought even at its roots" [*World Refugee Survey 1985*, p. 4].

Three recognized solutions to refugee problems remain at the heart of organized international response. The preferred solution of the three is **voluntary repatriation**: willingly returning to one's own home and family. This is also the most difficult, often requiring elaborate agreements between refugees and the political and economic powers that forced them to flee their homes in the first place. The difficulty of repatriation can be seen in the numbers: the most successful repatriation of recent years was the 1983–84 return of 32,000 Ethiopians from Djibouti. Other successes through March 1985 were the return of 23,000 Ugandans from Zaire, 5,800 Ugandans from Sudan, 2,200 Laotians from Thailand, and 2,300 Salvadorans from Honduras. Elsewhere, levels of success in repatriation programs are even smaller [*Ibid.*, p. 38].

More complex than repatriation is the second most favored solution, **local settlement and integration**. This solution is dependent on the willingness of host governments to provide land and facilities to allow refugees to be integrated into the local culture and economy. This is often difficult for poor nations, though it is often the poorest (such as the Sudan, where one out of every 20 residents is a refugee) that have shown the most willingness to accommodate refugees. Some nations that have had difficult experiences integrating refugees into local cultures are resistant to any notion of long-term local settlement. To some degree, the willingness of Thailand to serve as a short-term country of asylum for Southeast Asian refugees is dependent on the continued willingness of Western nations to offer resettlement abroad. Some 230,000 Cambodians along the Thai-Cambodian border who have fled civil strife at home are not recognized as bona fide refugees, in part in order to assure that their stay in Thailand is a temporary one. Salvadoran refugees in Honduras have faced similar pressures from the Honduran Government, which has been hesitant about the possibility of settling Salvadorans on a long-term basis.

The least desirable solution of refugee problems is ironically also the best known, namely **third country resettlement**. This solution takes refugees farthest from their own homes and families; it is frequently also the most expensive solution. In the decade since 1975, slightly over 2 million refugees have been resettled in third countries. Recent trends in developed Western nations have been away from expanded levels of refugee resettlement. One matter frequently discussed within the United Nations is the proper treatment of refugees rescued by boats at sea, an area in which the UNHCR has been active in recent months [A/40/12 Add. 1, p. 27]. Numerous governments have offered resettlement opportunities to refugees rescued under such circumstances.

The plight of refugees at sea draws attention to a key aspect of the mandate of the High Commissioner, namely, the **legal protection of refugees**. Frequently left outside their homeland and without clear protection under the law, refugee populations around the world have come to rely on U.N. officials to secure their rights. One of the most common protections extended to refugees under U.N. mandates is freedom from *refoulement*, or forced repatriation against their wishes.

A matter of physical as well as legal protection that has drawn increasing attention in recent years is the growing frequency of **armed attacks on refugee camps** and the **attempts to militarize camps**. These phenomena have become common in refugee camps in Central America, Africa, and Asia. Such attacks had been condemned by a resolution at the 39th General Assembly [A/Res/39/140]. However, during 1985 "the basic rights of refugees in different areas of the world . . . continued to be disregarded, and in particular refugees were . . . exposed to pirate attacks, other acts of violence, military and armed attacks, arbitrary detention and refoulement" [A/40/12 Add. 1, p. 33]. Such problems indicate the UNHCR's need, in the words of the new High Commissioner, for "the decisive support of Governments. Their political will to see UNHCR effectively carry out its mandate constitutes the real guarantee for the success of the Office's activities" [Hocké speech, 1/31/86].

3. The Status of Women

The **"forward-looking strategies for the advancement of women to the year 2000,"** adopted unanimously by the summer 1985 conference in Nairobi that marked the end of the United Nations Decade for Women 1975-85 [A/Conf.116/28/rev.1], has had an impact on a variety of the social and political issues dealt with by the United Nations—especially, but not exclusively, on the improvement of the status of women. The strategies outline the obstacles to achieving equality, development, and peace (the themes of the decade), and propose steps that must be taken to overcome these obstacles at the national, regional, and international levels.

The wide-ranging strategies call for everything from pure drinking water to government-sponsored child-care to reducing global expenditures on armaments. Enormous effort went into achieving consensus on these strategies at the women's conference [*The InterDependent*, July/August 1985]; and the 40th General Assembly heartily endorsed the strategies and called on governments, agencies, and nongovernmental organizations to encourage the promotion of women as "equal partners with men in public and political life" [A/Res/40/101]. The General Assembly stressed that the "primary responsibility" for translating the forward-looking strategies into "concrete action" lay with the individual states [A/Res/40/108]. The Secretary-General will report on the implementation of the strategies at the 41st General Assembly [A/41/50/95d].

The General Assembly also called for special attention to the role of women in promoting peace and cooperation and the further implementation of the 1982 Declaration on the Participation of Women in Promoting International Peace and Cooperation. The Secretary-General will report on the implementation of this declaration during the 41st General Assembly [A/41/50/95a].

The **Committee on the Elimination of Discrimination Against Women (CEDAW)** held its fifth session in 1986. The committee—made up of 23 experts nominated by national governments but serving in a personal capacity—is charged with monitoring compliance with the Convention on the Elimination of All Forms of Discrimination Against Women. At the time of the meeting, 20 additional states had become parties to the Convention—a legally binding document outlining measures to eliminate gender discrimination. As of May 22, a total of 93 states had signed the Convention, and 87 states have ratified or acceded to it since it was adopted in 1979 [CEDAW/c/12/L.1]. (The United States signed the Convention in Copenhagen in 1980 but has yet to ratify it and is therefore ineligible to nominate an American to serve on CEDAW.) The General Assembly again called for ratification and accession to the treaty by all states, "taking into account the World Conference to Review and Appraise the Achievements of the United Nations Decade for Women: Equality, Development, Peace"[A/Res/40/39].

The committee of experts heard reports from Czechoslovakia, Denmark, Ecuador, El Salvador, Mongolia, Portugal, Venezuela, and Vietnam in fulfillment of their obligation as parties to the Convention. At the same time, the committee continued to wrestle with fundamental problems of interpreting its role and with improving the efficiency of its work. Of special concern is article 21 of the Convention, which provides for the making of "suggestions and recommendations" by the committee in its annual reports [CEDAW/c/12/L.1/add.19]. At its Fifth Session, CEDAW formed a working group to make recommendations on this matter [wom/352].

On the basis of the group's report, the committee recommended that after presenting their first report, states parties should report every four years and include obstacles encountered in implementing the Convention. The committee suggested that states parties should consider establishing public institutions (national machinery) to ensure the effective elimination of discrimination against women. CEDAW also passed a resolution in support of the objectives of the International Year of Peace [CEDAW/c/12/L.1/add.18] and heard the report of the Co-ordinator for the Improvement of the Status of Women in the Secretariat [pr/wom/357]. The committee supported the position that **women in the United Nations** should be fully integrated at all policy-making levels and that this process should not be inhibited by financial constraints. The 41st General Assembly will hear reports from CEDAW on its work [A/41/50/94a] and from the Secretary-General on the status of the convention [Ibid./94b].

The five **regional commissions**, which were to play a key role in promoting women's advancement at the regional level and were directed to appoint a staff member to handle this aspect of their work, received close scrutiny at the 40th General Assembly. The Assembly took them to task for their "inadequate response to the need to incorporate the interests of women in their social and economic policies and programs"—including the general failure to appoint a staff member, as directed [A/Res/40/105]. Further, they asked that the Secretary-General report on the measures that the regional commissions have taken to incorporate women's concerns in their policies and programs during the 1988–89 biennium [A/41/50/95c].

The United Nations is also strengthening the bodies it created to advocate improvements in the status of women. These bodies include the Commission on the Status of Women, the United Nations Development Fund for Women, and the International Research and Training Institute for the Advancement of Women.

The **Commission on the Status of Women (CSW)** was formed in the early years of the United Nations to support equality for women. Charged with preparing the World Conference, CSW has now taken the lead in organizing U.N. efforts to continue the momentum of the women's decade through the year 2000. A key element of this will be the implementation of the forward-looking strategies within the U.N. system and among member states. The General Assembly asked the CSW to recommend measures to implement the strategies. In order for CSW to play this pivotal role, the General Assembly requested that CSW be strengthened. The specific recommendations include adequate support services, routing all reporting through CSW to the Economic and Social Council to the General Assembly, proposals for streamlining the agenda and eliminating overlap in reports, and increasing the number of members and frequency of meetings [A/Res/40/108/13–17].

The General Assembly approved the mandate of the **United Nations Development Fund for Women (UNIFEM**—formerly the Voluntary Fund for the United Nations Decade for Women) to encourage aid agencies to address women's needs and to help women's groups with development projects. UNIFEM's own projects this year have focused on women farmers and on water supply, including relieving the burden placed on women by the task of fetching water. As UNIFEM heads toward its second year as a separate entity in "autonomous association" with the United Nations Development Programme (UNDP), the General Assembly called for increased funding [A/Res/40/104]. UNDP, through the Secretary-General, will submit a report on UNIFEM's activities to the 41st General Assembly [A/41/50/95b]. In addition to supporting UNIFEM's work, UNDP developed a strategy for increasing its capacity to incorporate women into development projects [DP/1986/L.14].

The 40th General Assembly refined the long-term agenda of the **International Research and Training Institute for the Advancement of Women (INSTRAW)** by calling for increased research, training, and information activities, and by encouraging cooperation between INSTRAW and other agencies doing similar work. The General Assembly also called for increased funding from states members and other sources to the United Nations Trust Fund for INSTRAW [A/Res/40/38]. The Secretary-General will report on INSTRAW's activities before the 42nd General Assembly. Reports will be every two years.

The Secretary-General continues to speak in favor of ensuring that the United Nations improves the status of women within its own system. "Only when women participate fully in all aspects of the Secretariat's work, and only when women's experience is sufficiently reflected in the composition of the organization's staff," he said at the United Nations celebration of International Women's Day, "will the Secretariat be able to maximize its effective contribution at every level to the improvement of the status of both men and women worldwide" [sg/sm/3837/wom/348]. The 40th General Assembly adopted a resolution encouraging initiatives by the Secretary-General [A/Res/40/258b]. The mandate of the Co-ordinator for the Improvement of the Status of Women in the Secretariat has been extended through 1987 and a steering committee to monitor progress has been formed [A/Res/40/108/19].

The special needs of **rural women**, a major focus of the conference, was addressed by the 40th General Assembly. The General Assembly called for an increased focus on the needs of these women and a comprehensive report by the Secretary-General, to be delivered at the 44th General Assembly, on the status of, and strategies for, the improvement of the condition of rural women [A/Res/40/106].

The General Assembly reiterated its concern for the prevention of prostitution [A/Res/40/103] by calling for the report prepared by the Special Rapporteur of ECOSOC in 1982 to be issued as a U.N. document. A new resolution about domestic violence called for research by the Secretary-General on the subject from a "criminological perspective" and proposed ten measures for individual states to adopt to deal with the matter [A/Res/40/36]. The latter is an example of how far the United Nations' ability to deal with these issues has evolved in the course of the decade: At the mid-decade conference in Copenhagen, the subject of domestic violence was shelved as one beyond the purview of the United Nations.

In addition, many of the specialized agencies—the United Nations Fund for Population Activities (UNFPA), UNDP, the International Labour Organisation, (ILO), the United Nations Children's Fund (UNICEF), the International Fund for Agricultural Development (IFAD), the Food and Agriculture Organization of the United Nations (FAO)—are devoting an increasing amount of their funding and planning to include measures to bring women into the social, political, and economic mainstream. "Planners have begun to realize," says Margaret Snyder, head of UNIFEM, "that women in low-income societies throughout the world are not just exhausted mothers of malnourished children—not simply the victims of crisis. They are the providers of food, fuel, water and often of the whole family income—the sustainers and developers of their families, communities and countries. Thus the fate of women is a critical determinant of the fate of whole societies" [*The Christian Science Monitor*, 12/17/85].

4. The Information Issue

"Questions relating to information" has been on the agenda of the General Assembly since its 33rd Session, and communications issues have been the center of discussion at the United Nations Educational, Scientific and Cultural Organization (UNESCO) biennial conferences since 1974, when the Soviet Union introduced the controversial "Draft Declaration on the Role of Mass Media" [UNESCO 18 C/35]. The issue that has received the most attention has been the third world's call for a **New World Information and Communication Order (NWICO)**. Based on 12 principles forged in UNESCO debates, the NWICO has as its intention the establishment of a more balanced flow of information between the developed and the developing nations [UNESCO Resolution 4/19 (1980)].

It is claimed that developed nations possess about 90 percent of the electronic communications equipment in the world and that the flow of international news is dominated by four Western agencies: Associated Press, United Press International, Agence France-Presse, and Reuters. The control of the news media by the West, the third world nations contend, has led to biased, revolution- and disaster-oriented reporting that ignores the development needs and achievements of their countries.

The issue, though, extends beyond a call for accurate and even-handed reporting. "Information is a basic resource without which full participation in today's world is impossible," states a recent report by the Senior Interagency Working Group for Communications Development Assistance on U.S. communications policy. "It is highly destabilizing," the report adds, "to allow the world to remain separated into two groups of countries: a small group that is information-rich and a larger group that is information-poor." Increasingly, communications and information are considered, along with food, shelter, clothing, and health care, as basic developmental needs for the third world. The U.N. system, through the NWICO, has worked to expand the communications and information capabilities of the third world.

Debate over the implementation and definition of the NWICO has been extensive and controversial. The United States cited the issue of the NWICO as a major reason for its withdrawal from UNESCO at the end of 1984. Communication issues were predominantly discussed at the UNESCO General Conference held in Sofia, Bulgaria last fall. UNESCO spends only about 10 percent of its budget on communication programs.

The debate on the NWICO has split the international community into ideologically separate groups. Western nations, strong supporters of a media free from government control or interference that can act as an extralegal check to governments themselves, have viewed the NWICO as an attempt by certain countries to impose international controls on the media. UNESCO debates, which have included efforts by some to institute an international licensing system in order "to protect" journalists, are viewed suspiciously as attempts to implement censorship and to control journalists' access to news sources.

In contrast to the Western model, the print media in 25 percent of the countries in the world (all are developing countries with the exception of Poland) are partly free, according to Freedom House. These developing countries practice "guided journalism" in which journalists may not dissent from government policy. Twelve Latin American countries currently license journalists. According to Freedom House criteria, 41 percent of the world's countries have print media that are not free. These include most of the countries in the Soviet bloc, where media is viewed as the servant of the state and considered as a tool for the achievement of socialist state goals.

Western nations, suspicious of a "hidden agenda"—that NWICO is in essence an effort to legitimize state control of the media—have attempted to limit the role of government in the implementation of the NWICO against the wishes of many East bloc and developing countries, which favor a more active governmental role. The West has also called for studies on the "watchdog" role of the press—a bugbear to the Soviet bloc [Leonard R. Sussman, "No Detente in International Communications," in *Freedom in the World: Political Rights & Civil Liberties 1985-86* (Westport, Conn: Greenwood Press, 1986), p. 96].

Recently, however, **UNESCO** has taken a less controversial stance on information issues. More than a year prior to the General Conference, the rhetoric began to subside with the U.S. announcement that it would withdraw from UNESCO at the end of 1984 unless the organization's budgetary and press-freedom policies were changed [*Issues Before the 39th General Assembly of the United Nations*, p. 139]. In 1985, faced with a loss of the U.S. contribution, 25 percent of UNESCO's budget, and the British threat to follow the United States out of UNESCO, the organization's 51-nation Executive Board in a June meeting decided to downgrade the more controversial aspects of the UNESCO program and emphasize more practical measures to build communications infrastructure in the third world [*The New York Times*, 6/23/85]. Also at the Executive Board Session, at the insistence of the West the normative definition of the NWICO as "an evolving and continuous process" was reaffirmed [*Issues Before the 40th General Assembly of the United Nations*, p. 127].

Changes recommended by the Executive Board were approved at the Sofia Conference in the fall of 1985. East-bloc attempts to reverse the Executive Board's consensus on NWICO as "an evolving and continuous process" were defeated, and studies on the "watchdog" role of the press were preserved [*Freedom in the World*, p. 96].

At the General Conference, UNESCO, its budget reduced from $374.4 million for 1984–85 to $307.2 million for 1986–87 due to the U.S. withdrawal, approved cuts in its more controversial programs, including communication. Low priority was assigned to "reflective" programs, such as conferences on the definition of the NWICO and on the protection and licensing of journalists. Ninety percent of the $35 million communications budget for 1986–87 was allocated for operational activities for the development of infrastructure and human resources [A/SPC/40/SR.29]. The delegates at the Sofia Conference called for the development of a "plurality of media sources" and gave "high priority" to the training of communication personnel, the establishment of media infrastructures, and the strengthening of the **International Programme for the Development of Communication (IPDC)** [UNESCO Resolution 3.1/5 (1985)].

IPDC, concerned with pragmatic steps toward the implementation of the NWICO, was created at the 1980 UNESCO Conference in Belgrade, Yugoslavia, for the purpose of separating the concrete "action" program of UNESCO's communication activities from the rhetoric of the more "reflective" programs. IPDC, primarily concerned with the technical aspects of communication—the training of personnel and the building of media infrastructure—has received over $8 million in voluntary contributions since it was officially started in 1982. At the beginning of 1986, IPDC had provided over $5 million in funding for 148 communication development projects [UNESCO/NYO/86–1B]. In January 1986, IPDC's 35-member Intergovernmental Council approved 61 more projects with a total budget of $2.3 million. The United States, which has not donated funds to IPDC's general fund, has provided "funds-in-trust" (the donor country selects the beneficiary) to finance media training courses in the United States.

Debate on the NWICO in the General Assembly and in the United Nations Committee on Information, unlike that in UNESCO, has intensified. The resolution on **"Questions relating to information"** has received decreasing Western support over the past several sessions. Approved by consensus in 1980 [A/Res/35/201], six voted against the resolution in 1984 [A/Res/39/98], and at the 40th Session, sections A and B of the final text received 19 and 16 nays, respectively [A/Res/40/164]. The resolution was passed overwhelmingly with the support of the Group of 77 (G-77), the negotiating bloc of the third world, and the Eastern bloc.

In June, the **Committee on Information**, which reports on these matters to the United Nations, was unable to agree by consensus on a report because of Western objections to the G-77 text. The draft report omitted the phrase describing the NWICO as "an evolving and continuous process," included in UNESCO resolutions since 1983. Again in August, when the 69-nation committee reconvened, an impasse was reached, and in the roll-call vote the Western delegates were defeated by 41 to 14 [*Freedom in the World*, p. 9].

The Information Committee, responsible for reviewing the operations of the United Nations' Department of Public Information (DPI), will have before it at its next session a U.S. General Accounting Office report on the DPI released in April 1986. The report, titled "United Nations: Analysis of Selected Media Products Shows Half Oppose U.S. Interests," evaluated DPI materials on four topics of interest to the United States—apartheid, new world orders, Palestine, and disarmament—in terms of content considered "contrary to U.S. policies and/or interests." The report concluded that about half of the materials studied were contrary to U.S. interests. The accuracy of the report, prepared at the request of Senator Arlen Spector (R-Pa.), has been challenged by DPI. "By selecting for a quantitative analysis only those topics on which the United States finds itself in a minority, the study's conclusions were inevitably misleading," DPI charges [DPI/Note No. 4558].

In Copenhagen, DPI joined with UNESCO to sponsor a roundtable in April on the NWICO. The meeting brought together 25 journalists, communication experts, and policy-makers to discuss the international flow of information, media freedom, access to communication, the "watchdog" role of the press, and other communication issues. The report of the roundtable, approved unanimously, will be submitted to the UNESCO General Conference and to the U.N. General Assembly. Another roundtable has been proposed for 1987.

5. Other Social Issues

According to one Western diplomat, the General Assembly's Third (Social, Humanitarian and Cultural) Committee is "very contentious" and filled with a "great deal of argument" [Interview with *Issues Before the 41st General Assembly*]. If there is one area of common concern for the committee, though, it is that of social issues such as the problems and needs of the world's youth, the disabled, and the elderly. The entire international community speaks out in support of these underprivileged groups. Resolutions concerned with these issues attract numerous sponsors and are adopted by consensus. Votes, however, do not translate into donations. U.N. programs for these groups are notoriously underfunded, and matters are likely to worsen this year as the United Nations' fiscal crisis deepens.

International Youth Year (IYY), coinciding with the 40th anniversary of the General Assembly, was not exceptional. Officially designated as International Youth Year: Participation, Development, and Peace, it was celebrated with little enthusiasm at the General Assembly. Sessions of the United Nations World Conference for International Youth Year, held November 13–15 at plenary meetings set aside by the 39th Assembly for the discussion of youth-related issues and the commemoration of IYY, were sparsely attended. Because of tight scheduling at the 40th Assembly, many of the speeches by the "youth delegates," who ranged in age from 15 to 60, were delivered late at night in the empty hall of the General Assembly.

The General Assembly, however, demonstrated its support for IYY by passing four resolutions related to youth at its 40th Session, rather than the standard three. Resolution 40/14, entitled "International Youth Year: Participation, Development, and Peace," had over 95 sponsors, more than any other resolution passed by the 40th General Assembly [A/40/855]. The problems of youth, defined by the United Nations as persons between 15 and 24 years of age, are considered annually by the United Nations' Third Committee. The lack of employment, training, and educational opportunities for young people was discussed at the 40th Session [A/40/64]. The General Assembly called for efforts to ensure the rights of youth to education and work [A/Res/40/15], and urged member states to increase opportunities for this sector of the population [A/Res/40/16].

The Trust Fund for IYY, set up to finance the preparations for and the activities of IYY, received very few contributions in 1985. Programs and events to celebrate the international year were severely limited by lack of support for the Trust Fund, which as of May 1985 had reached only $120,000. **Failure to attract financial backing** for IYY is attributable to (1) lack of international support for what many delegates considered largely a Romanian initiative to honor the son of Ceausescu, the ailing leader of that country; and (2) "institutional fatigue" at the United Nations as a result of the "proliferation of commemorative years and decades" [*Issues Before the 40th General Assembly of the United Nations*, p. 128].

IYY, envisioned as a process to review the state of youth and to develop strategies to meet their needs, has proceeded according to a three-step agenda: (1) selection of objectives; (2) implementation of the program of action; and (3) assessment of program results and follow-up planning, begun in 1979 when the General Assembly designated 1985 as a commemorative year for youth [GA/7185]. Much of the discussion on IYY centered on this final phase, and although the official year has ended, follow-up activities will continue. The Trust Fund for IYY will be maintained for the implementation of programs and policies established during the year, and the 41st General Assembly is likely to approve a request that the Trust Fund be included in the United Nations annual pledging conference. U.N. officials are hopeful that these changes will attract more donations. By the beginning of 1986, the Trust Fund had risen to $227,913. In addition, the General Assembly has recommended that the national committees established to carry out the objectives of IYY be maintained to implement the follow-up program. At the 41st General Assembly, the Secretary-General will deliver a report evaluating the results of IYY [A/40/85].

The 40th Session drew attention to **the needs and problems of the elderly,** some 227 million persons aged 65 and over. The Secretary-General emphasized the large numbers of elderly living in developing regions in his report on the first review and appraisal of the implementation of the International Plan of Action on Aging. In 1985, 55.4 percent of the world's elderly lived in developing countries, and by the year 2025 that figure will rise to more than 70 percent. The burdens caused by this drastic shift in population structure will be borne largely by those nations with the least economic and social resources [E/1985/6].

The United Nations Trust Fund for Aging, established to provide seed money for the development of third world programs for older persons, received requests for assistance far beyond the extent of its resources. The Trust Fund, totaling only $628,000 at the end of 1985, was included for the first time in the United Nations Pledging Conference for Development Activities as a result of resolution 1985/28 of the Economic and Social Council (ECOSOC).

The supporters of fiscal restraint prevented an expansion of the U.N. program for aging at the 40th General Assembly. Concerned that the elderly have largely been ignored by the U.N. system, the Ambassador of the Dominican Republic called for the creation of a UNICEF-like organization for the aged. The United States and the Soviet Union, two of the organization's more parsimonious members, opposed the plan as too costly. A preliminary version of resolution 40/30 introduced by the Group of 77 would have created a "working group" of the Third Committee to study expanding the program of the Plan of Action on Aging adopted by the World Assembly on Aging, held in Vienna in 1982. That was considered too expensive as well, and in its stead the Third Committee recommended that the Secretary-General prepare a report on expanding the U.N. program on aging. In February, the Secretary-General sent a letter to all member states requesting their views on "ways and means" for the United Nations to promote the Plan of Action. The Secretary-General's report will be taken up at the first meeting of ECOSOC in 1986, and the Council's recommendations will be considered "as a matter of high priority" at the 41st General Assembly [A/40/928].

The year 1987 marks the midpoint of the **United Nations Decade of Disabled Persons**. The Secretary-General will convene in 1987 a meeting of experts, comprised mainly of disabled persons, to review the progress of the Decade at the halfway point, as requested by the 39th General Assembly in resolution 39/26. Secretary-General Pérez de Cuéllar will submit to the 42nd General Assembly a report on the progress of the Decade, including the responses of member states to a questionnaire monitoring the implementation of the 1982 World Programme of Action Concerning Disabled Persons [A/40/880]. On the adoption of the World Programme of Action at the 37th Session, the General Assembly proclaimed 1983–92 the United Nations Decade of Disabled Persons, during which members states were encouraged to implement the Programme.

Donations to the Trust Fund for the International Year of Disabled Persons (IYDP), created originally for IYDP in 1981 and extended by the Assembly for the duration of the Decade, have proceeded slowly. Renamed the Voluntary Fund for the United Nations Decade of Disabled Persons in 1985, it totaled only $1.6 million at the beginning of 1986. A total of 25 states have donated to the Fund. To increase donations for the Decade, the Fund was included in the United Nations Pledging Conference for Development Activities for the first time in 1985, and the General Assembly authorized the Secretary-General to accept "special purpose contributions" from donor countries that choose to finance particular projects [A/Res/40/31].

Crime as an international problem was dramatically illustrated at the 7th **United Nations Congress on the Prevention of Crime and the Treatment of Offenders,** by Professor Manuel Lopez-Rey, chairman of the committee that performed the preparatory work for the 1985 Congress. He noted that, "In 1980 the world population was in rough figures four billion. That was more or less the number of offenses committed that year" [*The InterDependent*, Sept./Oct. 1985].

The Congress, established in 1950, met in Milan, Italy, and by the end of its two-week session on September 6, had adopted 25 resolutions and agreed on "six legal instruments designed to set international standards." The Milan Congress proceeded largely without controversy, focusing on both "common crime" and on criminal acts characteristic of modern society, such as computer crime [*Ibid.*]. A measure of the success of the 7th Congress was its ability to deal with sensitive political matters, such as terrorism, by consensus [DPI/NGO/85/26]. The Milan Plan of Action, approved by consensus, called for "the formation of an international terrorism information network, to be primarily concerned with preventative measures." International cooperation was also mentioned in the discussion on combating organized crime. Delegates at the Congress spoke on the importance of sharing information, easing extradition procedures, and other measures in dealing with organized criminals who operate across national borders.

The 40th General Assembly endorsed the resolutions of the Milan Congress and adopted the Milan Plan of Action by consensus, [A/Res/40/32]. In addition, the Assembly adopted the Standard Minimum Rules for the Administration of Juvenile Justice ("The Beijing Rules") as recommended by the Milan Congress, calling on member states to accept legal standards on such topics as the age of criminal responsibility and the rights of juveniles [A/Res/40/33]. The Assembly also adopted the Declaration of Basic Principles of Justice for Victims of Crime and Abuse of Power [A/Res/40/34]. Resolution 40/36 brought attention to women as victims of crime by calling for comprehensive measures dealing with domestic violence. The 40th Assembly, in resolution 40/35, also looked ahead to 1990, requesting that the "development of standards for the prevention of juvenile delinquency" be included on the agenda of the 8th U.N. Crime Congress [A/40/881].

Drug abuse and illicit drug trafficking, a topic discussed at the Milan Congress, is receiving a great deal of attention at the United Nations. In May 1985, before a meeting of ECOSOC, the Secretary-General, in accordance with resolution 39/143, proposed a ministerial-level world conference on illicit drugs be convened in 1987. The General Assembly acted on the Secretary-General's recommendation, and in resolution 40/122 decided to convene an International Conference on Drug Abuse and Illicit Trafficking in June 1987 in Vienna. In December, the Secretary-General appointed Tamar Oppenheimer (Canada) Secretary-General of the Conference; and in February, the Commission on Narcotic Drugs, acting as the preparatory body for the Conference, met to discuss the agenda [SOC/NAR/342]. Delegates to the planning body urged that "irrelevant" political questions be avoided and the Conference deal with substantive issues directly related to the problems of drug abuse and illicit trafficking. The Commission will reconvene in February 1987 to finalize the agenda for the Conference [SOC/NAR/352].

International support for such a conference has grown over the past few years as many drug supplier nations have begun to experience internal drug-related problems. According to Jon R. Thomas, former Assistant Secretary of State in the Bureau of International Narcotics Matters, "Drug abuse is on the increase around the world" [*The New York Times*, 3/26/86]. The United Nations' International Narcotics Control Board reports that the illegal traffic is so pervasive and generates such vast volumes of capital "that economies are disrupted, legal institutions are menaced, and the very security of some states is threatened." The political dangers posed by drug trafficking were dramatically illustrated in Colombia in April 1985, when drug dealers assassinated the Minister of Justice after the Government had raided a drug processing center and seized ten metric tons of cocaine in March [*The InterDependent*, May/June 1985]. The Central American nation of Belize, considered by the United States as the most important narcotics trafficking center in the region, has experienced a growing use of cocaine by its citizens. The Government of Belize has implemented a massive education program on the dangers of drug trafficking, and Belize Prime Minister Manuel Esquivel, while in New York for the 40th General Assembly, remarked, "If we allow this to continue, we could lose our Government—our Independence" [*The New York Times*, 10/27/85].

At the 39th General Assembly, Latin American nations reversed themselves, displaying an openness in dealing with drug-related problems and taking the lead in the international fight against drug abuse and trafficking. A resolution introduced by Venezuela at the 39th General Assembly and sponsored by several Latin American countries called for the creation of a new international convention against traffic in narcotic drugs and psychotropic substances [A/Res/39/14]. The need for a new international convention has been stressed because of the multinational character of drug trafficking. Drug traffickers "have no respect for national boundaries" and quickly relocate when they feel pressure in one country, according to U.S. Deputy Attorney-General

D. Conell Jensen at a conference on drug trafficking held by the Organization of American States in April [*The New York Times*, 4/27/86]. The international convention, being prepared by the Commission on Narcotic Drugs, is to be a new legal instrument that will seal loopholes in existing treaties, such as the 1961 Single Convention in Narcotic Drugs and the 1971 Convention on Psychotropic Substances, to strengthen international action against illicit drug traffic [*The InterDependent*, May/June 1985]. The new convention will be discussed at the International Conference in 1987.

In response to another long-standing problem, the 1982 General Assembly declared 1987 the **International Year of Shelter for the Homeless (IYSH)**, recognizing the need to deal with the deteriorating and inadequate conditions of shelter and basic services for the more than one billion disadvantaged in both developing and developed countries. Currently, one quarter of the world's population is inadequately housed and approximately 100 million have no shelter at all; and the current international housing crisis will worsen as the world's population increases by another 1.5 billion by the year 2000.

The Commission for Human Settlements, the intergovernmental body responsible for organizing the year, and the United Nations Centre for Human Settlements (HABITAT), the agency responsible for coordinating programs and activities for the year, have highlighted the plight of the homeless and those without any "real" home, such as squatters, and are also attempting to secure from neighborhoods a renewed commitment to rebuild. A multifaceted global IYSH plan has been fashioned to urge nations to improve shelter for the homeless, to assess their shelter needs for the year 2000, and to identify national IYSH projects by 1987. One hundred and thirty countries have voiced interest in participating in the activities of the year, and over 300 IYSH projects have been identified. During 1987, nations are to design housing policies and programs for the poor and the disadvantaged. The IYSH agenda calls for the implementation of these national shelter strategies as well as for the demonstration of new methods for the improvement of shelter and housing. The required budget for the IYSH program was estimated in 1983 to be $4.3 million. As of April 1986, only $2.7 million, 60 percent by developing nations, had been pledged for the international year.

VI
Legal Issues

The Sixth Committee of the United Nations handles legal issues that confront the organization. Some of its projects are almost as old as the most important of all legal documents, the U.N. Charter. A troubling phenomenon is increasingly evident in the Sixth Committee's work. Document peddlers combat procedural hounds in an annual ritual of predictable debates. Efforts to produce additional treaties or declarations on topics already extensively codified (such as the non-use of force) mask the real problem—how to make existing rules of law and the U.N. agencies responsible for them work. Even those members trying to revitalize the organization sometimes obstruct efforts; for example, by retreating from such U.N. institutions as the International Court of Justice. Nonetheless, the Sixth Committee's work is vital and arguably has the most lasting impact on world affairs.

1. The International Court of Justice

On April 7, 1986, the United States' 40 years of accepting the compulsory jurisdiction of the International Court of Justice (ICJ), known as the World Court, ended [24 Int'l Legal Mats. 1742 (1985)]. The U.S. termination followed two years of American efforts to throw out the controversial action brought to the ICJ by Nicaragua, alleging U.S. involvement in military and paramilitary actions against the Sandinista Government in Nicaragua [see Issues Before the 40th General Assembly of the United Nations, p. 134]. The U.S. State Department justified the termination on the grounds that most other states (notably the Soviet Union and its allies) had never accepted the compulsory jurisdiction of the ICJ, that the ICJ had been abused for political reasons, and that continued acceptance "would be contrary to our commitment to the principle of the equal application of the law and would endanger our vital national interests." However, Washington pledged to continue to use the ICJ on a voluntary basis. With the consent of Italy, the United States submitted to a special chamber of the ICJ a long-standing dispute concerning the Italian subsidiary of two American corporations [24 Int'l Legal Mats. 1745 (1985)].

Meanwhile, with the United States absent from the proceedings, oral arguments in **Nicaragua versus the United States** were heard in September 1985. On June 27, 1986, the ICJ rendered its long-awaited judgment. By a vote of 12 to 3 (with the American, British, and Japanese judges dissenting) the Court rejected the justification of collective self-defense maintained by the United States in connection with the military conflict and held that the United States, by supporting the contra forces and engaging in certain attacks against Nicaragua and the laying of mines in its internal or territorial waters, had broken customary international law. The ICJ also held that the U.S. trade embargo against Nicaragua had contravened the Treaty of Friendship, Commerce and Navigation between the two states, that the United States should immediately cease and refrain from committing illegal acts against Nicaragua, and that the United States is obligated to make reparations to Nicaragua [ICJ Communiqué No. 86/8; *ICJ Reports 1986*]. The United States is not expected to honor the judgment, but Nicaragua will pursue its claim for damages before the ICJ and probably in U.S. federal courts [*The New York Times*, 6/28/86].

In contrast to the U.S. retreat from the ICJ, Canada announced on September 10, 1985, that it was broadening its acceptance of the compulsory jurisdiction of the ICJ to include disputes regarding "the conservation, management or exploitation of the living resources of the sea, or in respect of the prevention or control of pollution or contamination of the marine environment in marine areas adjacent to the coast of Canada." Canada had previously exempted such disputes from ICJ jurisdiction [24 Int'l Legal Mats. 1729 (1985)].

The ICJ reached three decisions on African boundary disputes in 1985 and early 1986. It established the principles and rules for **Libya and Malta** to follow in order to delimit their respective continental shelf areas by special agreement [*ICJ Reports 1985*, p. 13]. On December 10, 1985, the ICJ ruled primarily in favor of Libya in Tunisia's application for revision and interpretation of the ICJ's 1982 judgment concerning delimitation of the continental shelf between **Tunisia and Libya.** The Court called upon both countries to implement the 1982 judgment [*Ibid.*, p. 192]. The frontier dispute between **Burkina Faso and Mali,** which has been before the ICJ since 1983, degenerated into armed conflict in late December 1985. Both countries sought assistance from the ICJ for "provisional measures" to stop the fighting. Following a ceasefire agreement on December 31, the Court indicated that Burkina Faso and Mali should withdraw their forces behind lines to be determined by agreement between the two parties, failing which the ICJ would order the terms of the troop withdrawal. The ICJ also reaffirmed the administration of the disputed areas as it prevailed prior to the armed actions [*ICJ Reports 1986*, p. 3].

By June 1986, the ICJ had not yet delivered an advisory opinion on Judgment No. 333 of the U.N. Administrative Tribunal, which upheld the Secretary-General's refusal to extend the contract of a Soviet citizen, **Vladimir V. Yakimetz,** who worked on the staff of the Secretariat. Yakimetz defected to the United States in 1983, alleging that Soviet citizens working for the Secretariat functioned under the orders of the Soviet Mission to the United Nations, a practice which would violate Article 100 of the U.N. Charter. The Soviet mission reportedly pressured the Secretary-General not to rehire Yakimetz [*The New York Times*, 7/17/84].

2. The Effectiveness of the Organization

Since its establishment in 1975, the Special Committee on the Charter of the United Nations and on the Strengthening of the Role of the Organization has labored under an intractable paradox. Although it has been asked to make proposals for strengthening the role of the United Nations because of perceived inadequacies in its present structure, the Special Committee also has been effectively forbidden from making proposals to change that structure (for example, by amendment to the U.N. Charter). Therefore, every proposal is the target of crippling criticism by those delegations which, in the words of an Egyptian delegate, continue "to see the Charter as a holy book which could not be improved or interpreted" [A/C.6/40/SR.40].

Of the Special Committee's three projects, its primary one of strengthening the role of the United Nations in **maintaining international peace and security** remains tied to a revised working paper prepared by Belgium, West Germany, Italy, Japan, New Zealand, and Spain [A/AC.182/L.38/Rev.2; *Issues Before the 39th General Assembly*, p. 146; *Issues Before the 40th General Assembly*, p. 135] and a new paper submitted by Czechoslovakia, East Germany, and Poland [A/AC.182/L.48]. The Western paper, a weaker version of previous drafts, encourages states to approach the Security Council at an early stage and, if appropriate, on a confidential basis. It proposes that the Security Council should consider holding periodic meetings and consultations. The Western paper also urges the Security Council, the General Assembly, and the Secretary-General to consider greater use of their fact-finding capabilities. In the past, the Soviet bloc has labeled the working Western paper "totally unacceptable," arguing that it runs contrary to the Charter by placing the functions of the Secretary-General and the General Assembly regarding peace and security on the same level as, and in some cases above those of, the Security Council where the Soviet Union can exercise its veto power [A/C.6/40/SR.37, 38, 40]. Also concerned about tampering with the Charter, many Western and third world members have expressed interest in, but have not fully backed, the working paper's proposals. After a dispute over procedure, the Sixth Committee avoided a controversial vote on a draft resolution by Libya which called for the Special Committee to accord priority to examination of "the abuse of the unanimity rule of the permanent members of the Security Council" [A/C.6/40/L.13/Rev.1; A/C.6/40/SR.50].

The working paper of the three socialist states deals with the "lasting validity of the purposes and principles" of the Charter, and lists general steps that could be taken by states to "implement more effectively" the objectives and principles of the Charter [A/AC.182/L.48]. At the 1986 working session of the Special Committee, procedural squabbles arising from submission of the two working papers broke out. Another deadlock appears on the horizon for this issue.

The Special Committee also considered working papers on the establishment of a commission for good offices, mediation, and conciliation for the **peaceful settlement of disputes** [A/38/343, Annex; A/C.6/39/L.2]. Drafted by Nigeria, the Philippines, and Romania, the working papers recommend the establishment of a commission, fully integrated in and subordinate to existing organs of the United Nations, for the purpose of facilitating early and equitable solutions to international disputes, to defuse crises and to prevent conflicts between states. For example, before a dispute was brought before the Security Council, the Council or the General Assembly could recommend to the parties the use of such a commission made up of states not parties to the dispute. At a minimum, the commission could clarify the issues and offer suggestions for negotiations before the dispute is brought to the Council or the Assembly. The prospects for a commission are dim. Although nonaligned countries in large part have backed the proposal, the Soviet bloc has rejected it as an encroachment on the competence of the Security Council [A/C.6/40/SR.38, 40, 42], while the United States and many of its allies have found the proposal too ambiguous and unnecessary in light of the underutilization of existing U.N. mechanisms [A/C.6/40/40, 41, 42; L/2560].

The time may finally have arrived when the study of the **rationalization of procedures** at the United Nations "should be considered over and done with," as one Brazilian delegate put it [A/C.6/40/SR.40]. Although a revised working paper submitted by France and the United Kingdom is still under consideration [A/AC.182/L.43/Rev. 1], some delegations have argued that there is little more to add to the results already achieved [A/40/33] and that the Anglo-French working paper focused on the General Assembly to the exclusion of other principal U.N. organs, such as the Security Council [L/2560]. But the recent recommendations to improve the efficiency of the organization made by former presidents of the General Assembly [A/40/37] and by the Asian-African Legal Consultative Committee [A/40/726] may add new grist to the mill.

3. Peace and Security

Recognizing the futility of soliciting any support from Western nations for its proposed world treaty on the **non-use of force,** the Soviet Union has called for a U.N. declaration on the subject as an intermediate step. The Soviet initiative of October 7, 1985, was embodied in the General Assembly's resolution on non-use of force which, like previous years' resolutions, was supported by the Soviet bloc and nonaligned group but opposed by the West

[A/C.6/40/SR.50; A/Res/40/70]. Despite the initiative, the decade-old deadlock between East and West in the Special Committee on Enhancing the Effectiveness of the Principle of Non-use of Force in International Relations saw no improvement, although slight progress in shaping a declaration was reported at the 1986 working session. The Soviets and some nonaligned supporters ultimately want a treaty that essentially would "restate" the U.N. Charter in more detail, outlawing the use of force or threat of force against the territorial integrity or political independence of any state, prohibiting the use of armed force involving any type of weapon (including nuclear or other weapons of mass destruction) on land, sea, in the air, or in outer space, and outlawing any kind of assistance to any state to use force. Further, no state could justify resort to force in violation of the obligations assumed under the world treaty [A/AC.193/L.3].

Ten nonaligned countries still seek (although with diminished enthusiasm) even broader coverage for the treaty, so that economic or political coercion or hostile propaganda, as well as subversion, pressure, intimidation, support of terrorism, covert attempts to destabilize governments, and the use of mercenaries would be illegal. Their working paper, however, advocates the use of force by certain peoples to achieve self-determination and independence as well as to liberate occupied territories and to eliminate racism, colonialism, and apartheid [A/34/41/Corr.1; A/36/41].

Many Western nations, led by the United States, see in the Soviet proposal a strategy to prohibit the West from using nuclear weapons in self-defense. More generally, when states use force they always have "legal" explanations, such as the U.N. Charter's right of self-defense. What is needed, the West argues, is not further declaratory instruments, but implementation and improvement of the effectiveness of existing international norms [A/40/41]. The United States has been joined by France and Australia in calling for the Special Committee on the U.N. Charter to add non-use of force to its project on the maintenance of peace and security, rather than pursue it further as a separate agenda item by another Special Committee narrowly focused on the conclusion of a world treaty [A/C.6/40/SR.10,12].

One of the more amorphous and seemingly impossible tasks confronting the Sixth Committee is defining and then doing something about the **principle of good-neighborliness between states.** Launched by Romania in 1979, this agenda item is now being handled by a new subcommittee which met in November 1985 to clarify and identify the elements of good-neighborliness [A/C.6/40/L.28]. Although the General Assembly has instructed the subcommittee to complete its task by the 41st Session [A/C.6/40/L.29], there is wide disagreement among members. On a conceptual level, the principle is practically universal in scope, one that arguably could encompass vast tracts of international law and countless areas of potential cooperation between neighboring states. The United States describes the concept as an attitude, not a set of legal principles that can be stated (or restated) in a new instrument [A/C.6/40/

SR.49]. A further problem continues to be the views of certain African and Arab states, which warn against any codified principle that would inhibit their efforts to eliminate apartheid or colonialism or to promote self-determination [A/C.6/40/SR.49, 51].

Over the objection of most Western delegates [A/C.6/40/SR.50], the Sixth Committee continued to consider a draft code of **offenses against the peace and security of mankind** apart from the other work of the International Law Commission (ILC) (see page 148). This is the oldest project before the ILC, dating its roots back to the Nuremberg Charter and Judgment and to a 1954 draft code adopted by the Commission [see A/40/10, par. 18]. Not until 1981, following the approval of a definition for aggression, did the General Assembly authorize the ILC to draft a revised code [A/Res/36/106]. A Special Rapporteur, Mr. Doudou Thiam of Thailand, presented his third report to the 1985 session of the ILC [A/CN.4/387 and Corr. 1 and 2], where it was decided that the ILC's earlier decision to limit the draft code for the time being to offenses committed by individuals is meant to include both "authorities of a State" and private individuals [A/40/10]. Many nonaligned states continue to press for eventual inclusion of states as subjects of the code, while both Western- and Soviet-bloc delegates adamantly reject any criminal responsibility for states.

An ILC drafting committee was requested to iron out what is meant (conceptually) by an "offence against the peace and security of mankind." One alternative is to define it as a violation of the most fundamental interests of mankind, namely, the maintenance of peace, the protection of fundamental human rights, the safeguarding of the right of self-determination of peoples, and the safeguarding and preservation of the human environment. Another alternative was simply to establish that a wrongful act has to be recognized as an offense against the peace and security of mankind by the international community as a whole. The drafting committee also was instructed to grapple with the 1974 definition of aggression (an essentially political, not legal, formulation), while the ILC would continue discussion of such situations as the threat of aggression, preparation for aggression, intervention in another state's affairs, terrorism, violation of treaty obligations, colonialism, mercenarism, and economic aggression [A/40/10]. The Special Rapporteur's fourth report will discuss war crimes and crimes against humanity. As the ILC probes deeper into the technical drafting of a code, objections to particular provisions are certain to increase.

4. Economic Relations

The **New International Economic Order** (NIEO), a proposal that dates back almost 12 years, remained on the Sixth Committee's backburner as members studied the analytical report prepared by the United Nations Institute for Training and Research [A/39/504/Add.1, Annex III]. The General Assembly has recommended that the 41st Session consider the best forum to be entrusted with the task of making some progress on the issue [A/Res/40/67]. The International Law Commission has been proposed, but many members will fight to avoid submission of the NIEO to the Commission. Another proposal has been for a group of government experts to formulate some principles. The most likely outcome at the 41st Session will be a postponement of concrete action on the NIEO for a few years.

The one tangible NIEO project under way is the preparation of a legal guide for drawing up international contracts for construction of industrial works which seeks to provide some guidance to officials of less developed countries (LDCs) and to representatives of construction companies who deal with them so that balanced and equitable contracts may be drafted [A/40/17]. Several Western delegates have expressed their disappointment that few LDCs had taken part in the preparation of the guide, even though it was specifically directed at their needs [A/C.6/40/SR.4, 5].

The core legal body within the United Nations responsible for formulating the rules of international trade is the United Nations Commission on International Trade Law (UNCITRAL). For years its major project was the drafting of a model law on **international commercial arbitration**, which it completed in June 1985 [A/40/17]. The Sixth Committee spent much of its time at the 40th Session heralding the achievement, but defeated a draft resolution from a cross-section of Western and nonaligned states which would have required that the General Assembly recommend the model law to all member states [A/C.6/40/L.7].

Most attention is now directed toward the draft **Convention on International Bills of Exchange and International Promissory Notes,** which is near final form. At the 1986 session of UNCITRAL, a revised draft of the Convention was reviewed following the previous year's settlement of several major controversial issues [A/40/17]. West Germany pointed toward continuing difficulties, however, when it reminded the Sixth Committee that the draft Convention's dual system distinguishing between rules for national negotiable instruments and those for international ones was bound to create problems and that commercial circles were unlikely to make use of the Convention [A/C.6/40/SR.4].

At the 40th Session, the General Assembly called upon governments and international organizations to provide legal security for the widest possible use of **automated data processing** in international trade in conformity with UNCITRAL's recent recommendations [A/40/17; A/Res/40/71]. UNCITRAL circulated for comment the final chapters of a draft legal guide on **electronic funds transfers.** The Working Group on International Contract Practices continues its preparation of uniform legal rules relating to the **liability of operators of transport terminals** [A/40/17].

Consideration of the draft articles on **most-favored-nation** clauses adopted by the International Law Commission in 1978 [A/33/10] was extended by the Sixth Committee until the General Assembly's 43rd Session. The reason for the delay stems from the limited number of comments received from members. Some states have proposed creating a working group to handle the issue [A/40/977].

5. International Organizations and Host Country Relations

Sixteen years after the International Law Commission started drafting it, the **Vienna Convention on the Law of Treaties between States and International Organizations or between International Organizations** was adopted by 67 of the 97 states attending a special U.N. conference in Vienna in March 1986 [25 Int'l Legal Mats. 543 (1986)]. The Convention will enter into force when 35 states have ratified or acceded to it. Modeled after the 1969 Vienna Convention on the Law of Treaties between States, the Convention is the first codification of rules pertaining to treaties entered into by international organizations. Given the high number of abstentions (23) by predominately Eastern-bloc states, the new Convention may share the fate of its 1969 counterpart, which less than 50 states have joined.

On March 7, 1986, the U.S. Mission to the United Nations informed the Soviet, Ukrainian, and Byelorussian Missions that their staffs "must be reduced in four stages over a two-year period from the current (total) level of 275 to a staffing level of 170 permanently assigned personnel by April 1, 1988." The United States accused the Soviet missions of engaging in espionage activities that threatened the national security. American officials also argued that there was no reason why the Soviet missions should be larger than the two next largest missions (United States and China) combined [*The New York Times*, 3/8/86;HQ/469].

The American move was unprecedented and a debate quickly ensued in the **Committee on Relations with the Host Country**. In the history of the United Nations, no host state had called for ceilings on or reductions in the size of missions. The U.N. Legal Counsel pointed to the 1975 Vienna Convention on the Representation of States in Their Relations with International Organizations of a Universal Character and to the Headquarters Agreement of 1947 between the United Nations and the United States to argue that while the size of missions must not "exceed what is reasonable and normal," disputes on mission staffing should be handled through consultations [HQ/469]. Failing agreement, the 1947 treaty entitles the United Nations to challenge the American decision and refer the question to a three-member tribunal, whose decision would be binding. The likelihood of any such tribunal being established, however, is nil.

The United States also imposed **travel restrictions** on all employees of the United Nations located in New York who are nationals of the Soviet Union, Afghanistan, Cuba, Iran, Libya, Vietnam, Bulgaria, Czechoslovakia, East

Germany, and Poland [ST/IC/85/48; ST/IC/85/74]. Alleged espionage and other clan-
destine activities by certain members of the U.N. Secretariat prompted this
action. The initial order in August 1985 stipulated that all official and personal travel by such nationals within the United States had to be arranged
through the U.S. Department of State's Foreign Missions Service Bureau. Personal travel would require prior approval from the U.S. Mission to the United
Nations. The Secretary-General claimed that the United States had never
brought to his attention any evidence or charges of espionage against any
member of the Secretariat. He stated that the new measures violated the
United States' treaty obligations and constituted discrimination among members of the Secretariat solely on the basis of their nationality [ST/IC/85/48]. Following months of discussions, the Secretariat and the United States agreed in
January 1986 that the Transportation Section of the Office of General Services would notify the U.S. Mission to the United Nations of official travel
of all U.N. staff members in the territory of the United States, regardless of
nationality. Staff members would continue to be permitted to arrange official
travel through agencies of their own choice. The Secretariat based its undertaking to notify the United States of all official travel on the obligations of
the host country and the United Nations to protect U.N. officials both at the
New York Headquarters and while on official travel in the United States
[ST/IC/86/4].

6. Violence by Individuals and Groups

Perhaps the most historic achievement of the 40th Session was its strong
stand against **terrorism**. The General Assembly unequivocally condemned
"all acts, methods and practices of terrorism wherever and by whomever
committed" as criminal [A/Res/40/61]. On October 8, 1985, the Secretary-General condemned all acts of terrorism, which the members of the Security
Council endorsed in a statement made by the President of the Council on
their behalf one day later [S/17554]. The Security Council also adopted a resolution which "condemns unequivocally all acts of hostage-taking and abduction" [S/Res/579(1985)].

These condemnations arrived 14 years after the General Assembly, on
the recommendation of the Sixth Committee, established an *Ad Hoc* Committee on International Terrorism. Its work effectively had been at a standstill
since 1979. The Sixth Committee has been criticized for not fulfilling its mandate in this area. The major reason for this is that the issue has become more
political than legal. While Western members pressed for general condemnation of terrorism "in all its forms and manifestations," Eastern-bloc, Arab,
and nonaligned members distinguished between terrorism and the right of
national liberation movements to pursue the principle of self-determination.
Many of these members also have sought to condemn "state terrorism," an
epithet used to refer to the United States and Israel. Ironically, in 1985 the

Reagan Administration invoked the same epithet to characterize acts of violence allegedly supported by various states, particularly Libya.

Numerous violent incidents in 1985, including the hijacking of TWA Flight 847 in June [The New York Times, 6/15/85], the Israeli raid on the headquarters of the Palestine Liberation Organization in Tunisia in October [Ibid., 8/2/85], the hijacking of the cruise liner *Achille Lauro* in October [Ibid., 10/8/85], and the murder of a Soviet diplomat in Lebanon [Ibid., 10/3/85], culminated in the multiple condemnations during the 40th Session, following intensive consultations spearheaded by the Chairman of the Sixth Committee. But the debates of the Sixth Committee continued to evidence recrimination between West and East and between Arab members and Israel [A/C.6/40/SR.18, 20, 21, 22]. Despite the existence of numerous international conventions that address primarily skyjackings and the taking of hostages, many states are not party to those conventions and there appears to be no desire to prepare a comprehensive convention on the prevention of terrorism in the near future. What more the Sixth Committee can do about terrorism when it next considers the item at the 42nd Session is under consideration.

The *Ad Hoc* Committee on the Drafting of an International Convention against the **Recruitment, Use, Financing, and Training of Mercenaries** trudged through another year of debating draft articles for convention. No real progress was recorded, because there remains a divergence of opinion as to the exact scope of the definition of mercenaries and as to whether states should be held liable for illegal mercenary activities under the convention. Western members sought greater specificity in the definition of punishable crimes and offenses, and opposed broad application of the convention to armed conflicts. Soviet-bloc and nonaligned members pushed for expansive definitions that would make anyone who, either during war or during times of peace, engaged in any of a host of hostile activities subject to the convention [A/40/43; A/C.6/40/SR. 13, 14, 15]. One of the more biting criticisms leveled by Western delegates during the Sixth Committee debates concerned the low level of participation by nonaligned members in the *Ad Hoc* Committee's sessions [A/C.6/40/SR. 14]. The Sixth Committee will once again consider the issue at the 41st Session (agenda item 132).

The Sixth Committee annually surveys measures undertaken to enhance the protection, security, and safety of **diplomatic and consular missions and representatives**. The U.N. Legal Counsel reported at the 40th Session that incidents against diplomats were increasing in number and that for the first time since reporting of incidents had been requested of member states [A/Res/35/168], a U.N. official had been fatally attacked. But he also noted that governments were taking measures to find and punish those responsible [A/C.6/40/SR.6]. Numerous conventions exist on the subject of diplomatic protection and immunity, and the General Assembly continues to encourage members to join each of those conventions [A/40/453; A/Res/40/73]. A general consensus appears to have formed that adequate legal provisions exist in the conventions but that the political will to implement them and make the law effective was still lacking [A/C.6/40/SR.6, 7]. The United States has joined with other delegations, however, to favor the establishment of a consultative mechanism among member states to consider measures against states that fail to carry out their obligations under the Convention on the Prevention and Punishment of Crimes Against Internationally Protected Persons, including Diplomatic Agents [A/C.6/40/SR.7].

7. Outer Space

The Committee on the Peaceful Uses of Outer Space (COPUOS) achieved a significant breakthrough in June with the adoption of a set of draft principles on remote sensing by satellites. Since the first U.S. Landsat remote-sensing satellite was launched in the early 1970s, a number of Soviet-bloc and developing countries have argued that operators of remote-sensing satellites should not be allowed to gather and distribute data about a country without first obtaining that country's permission, given the economic and national security value of such information. The United States and other developed nations have responded that the free flow of information will benefit all countries. The 15 principles adopted in June make no mention of prior consent rights, and in general reflect the U.S. position. One principle declares that remote-sensing activities shall be carried out for the benefit and in the interests of all countries, taking into particular consideration the needs of developing countries. Another principle states that states carrying out remote-sensing activities should make available to other states opportunities for participation on mutually agreed terms [OS/1245]. The draft principles now go on the agenda of the 41st General Assembly, where they are expected to be adopted.

The Legal Sub-Committee on COPUOS will continue to consider three other thorny issues. A working group reached consensus on a set of principles to regulate the use of **nuclear-power sources** in outer space. In particular, consensus was reached on requiring states that launch space objects with nuclear-power sources on board and those possessing space monitoring and tracking facilities to provide timely information to potential target states and the Secretary-General in the event of a malfunction that could bring the object hurtling back to earth. But codification remains a distant goal.

A second working group looked at two issues. Since 1983 the Legal Sub-Committee has been discussing a Soviet proposal to establish the **boundary of outer space** at an altitude not exceeding 110 kilometers above sea level and to allow for innocent passage at lower altitudes through the airspace of one state of another state's space object for the purpose of reaching orbit or returning to earth. Western states are opposed to defining or delimiting outer space on the grounds that it is unnecessary and would not help to secure any state's sovereignty or security. Further, they argue that no practical definition or delimitation of outer space has yet been demonstrated. This issue will have little chance of advancing in the 41st Session.

The Legal Sub-Committee is also unlikely to make progress on the issue of regulating the geostationary orbit—an orbital band about 22,000 miles above Earth's equator. A satellite in geostationary orbit stays in the same position relative to a fixed point on Earth, which is a useful characteristic for communications satellites in particular. With current technology, however, only a limited number of satellites can be placed in that orbit without interfering with each other, and the orbit is becoming crowded. Developing nations in particular fear that by the time they develop their own communications satellite systems, there will be no room left in the geostationary orbit. Consequently, they have argued for the right to reserve slots. The industrialized nations contend that advancing technology will enable countries to place communications satellites closer together before crowding becomes a serious problem; and they want the International Telecommunication Union to continue to assign slots on a first-come first-served basis.

8. The International Law Commission

The International Law Commission (ILC) continues its unpublicized but essential task of codifying the law of nations. The 41st Session, however, will pay particular attention to the ILC because the terms of some of the ILC's 34 legal experts are expiring and new experts must be elected (agenda item 17[b]). There is much prestige and influence at stake for member states. Having its nominated legal expert elected to the ILC means that a member state can have a greater impact on the development of international law.

Codification work on four draft conventions dominates the ILC's work, along with consideration of a draft Code of Offences against the Peace and Security of Mankind (see page 141). At the end of its 1985 session, the ILC had provisionally adopted 27 draft articles on the **status of the diplomatic courier and the diplomatic bag not accompanied by diplomatic courier**. Two new draft articles regarding ships employed in commercial service and arbitration were added to the 15 draft articles already provisionally adopted for codification of **jurisdictional immunities of states and their properties** [A/40/10].

A new Special Rapporteur, Stephen McCaffrey of the United States, was appointed by the ILC to shepherd the Commission's work on the **law of the non-navigational uses of international watercourses**. He submitted a preliminary report with his recommendations on the future course of the ILC's work

[A/CN.4/393]. The ILC endorsed the report, but no draft articles have yet been adopted on this complex topic. The ILC has provisionally adopted five draft articles on **state responsibility**. At its 1985 session, the definition of an "injured state," no mean feat, was agreed upon [A/40/10; A/40/447].

9. Other Legal Issues

In a surprise development, informal consultations were held during the early days of the 40th Session to deal with both the substance of a draft **Declaration on Social and Legal Principles Relating to the Protection and Welfare of Children** and the procedure required for its adoption by the Sixth Committee. The Declaration, which focuses on adoption, would not impose legal obligations on member states but would serve only as a guide for national legislation. A draft Declaration strongly pushed by the Netherlands was reviewed and most participants agreed that it needed only minor amendments [A/C.6/40/L.8]. But an immediate decision was opposed by some Islamic states and by the Soviet Union, so the Sixth Committee agreed to hold informal consultations early in the 41st Session with the aim of adopting a declaration by consensus [decision 40/422; agenda item 139].

The 41st Session also will consider the report of the Secretary-General on **draft standard rules of procedure for U.N. conferences** [A/40/611 and Add.1; agenda item 138]. Most of the proposed rules follow closely the rules of procedure of numerous U.N. conferences covered during the past decade. Those procedures, which have to a considerable extent become standardized, were generally based on ones used by the General Assembly and to some extent those of the Economic and Social Council. In particular, the proposed rules follow closely the rules of procedure of the United Nations Conference on New and Renewable Sources of Energy [A/Conf. 100/2].

Finally, an open-ended working group of the Sixth Committee will continue its consideration at the 41st Session of a draft **Body of Principles for the Protection of All Persons under Any Form of Detention or Imprisonment**. The report of the working group has been circulated for comment [A/C.6/40/L.18], but chances of U.N. adoption of the principles soon is remote, not to mention implementation of the principles through changes in national criminal laws.

VII
Administration and
Budget

1. U.N. Budget and Finance

It is widely recognized that the United Nations' growing financial crisis is in reality a political crisis arising from lack of agreement among the various member states on how to finance and utilize the organization and for what purposes. The restoration of the United Nations' financial stability requires a readiness on the part of member states to address, in a spirit of give and take, the fundamental and controversial issues related to the organization's budgetary and programming procedures.

Although the issue of finances has been on the General Assembly's agenda for many sessions, it has never had such urgency as today, when the United Nations faces the possibility of being unable to meet its payroll and its bills. And it is the first time that the General Assembly, meeting in **special resumed session** in Spring 1986, has had to take emergency steps to avert such a situation.

The financial crisis, although precipitated by the large-scale withholdings of assessed payments by the United States, is not wholly of America's making. Four interrelated factors, all of long standing, have made their contribution as well. Among these are the slowness with which many members pay their assessed dues; the refusal of some members—although this is impermissible under the Charter—to pay their share of the costs of activities they oppose, something that tends to be cumulative rather than seasonal; the low level of the United Nations' working capital ($100 million of an annual budget of about $800 million); and the United Nations' lack of borrowing power. These four factors have been responsible for the organization's **endemic cash flow problems**, and the strain on the United Nations' ability to cover its expenses has grown greater with each passing year. By the end of 1985, 18 member states, including four of the five permanent members of the Security Council, had combined withholdings of about $120 million; unpaid dues for 1985 and earlier years had reached a grand total of $225 million.

In spite of problems such as these, the United Nations has managed, if barely, to keep itself financially afloat year after year. But it is now wrestling with a new emergency that would test its viability even if it were in a much more robust financial state. The United States, which provides a quarter of the organization's revenues, has embarked on a series of withholdings that may total 10 percent—or more—of the U.N. regular budget, although the actual sum remains unclear at present.

As of June the following congressional and administrative measures to cut a total of $80 million had already been enacted or seemed likely to be acted upon: (1) **the Kassebaum amendment,** which requires a 20 percent cut in the U.S. contribution unless a system of weighted voting is introduced for financial decision making (something considered highly improbable); (2) legislation sponsored by Representative Don Sundquist (R-Tenn.) intended to deny the U.S. contribution to the salaries of Soviet-bloc U.N. staff members in protest against their having to relinquish part of their paychecks to their own governments; (3) a downward recalculation of the formula by which the United States repays the United Nations for its tax reimbursements to U.S. nationals working in the Secretariat; and (4) nonpayment of the U.S. share of the difference between the budget proposed by the Secretary-General last September and the U.N. budget adopted last December (the difference reflects inflation, exchange rate fluctuation, and additional program costs). It is possible that, if the Gramm-Rudman-Hollings budget-cutting mechanism is triggered by the failure of the Reagan Administration and the Congress to agree on a budget package within the deficit target level established by the legislation, still further cuts in U.S. payments to the United Nations might become mandatory.

This array of withholdings is to a large degree a result of general calls for fiscal restraint and budget cutting in the United States. The United Nations, without a strong constituency in the U.S. Congress to intercede in its behalf, is more likely to suffer sharp cuts than other Federal programs.

The preceding cuts will affect the United Nations' "regular budget"—the cost of its Secretariat and its global activities. For such programs as the United Nations' peacekeeping forces, member states are assessed separately, and some member states withhold payments here too—in particular the Soviet bloc and some Arab countries. The shortfall here is greater than that for the general budget, amounting to some $240 million at the end of 1985. As a result, countries that supply contingents to these forces have not been fully reimbursed for their out-of-pocket expenses, which has been a hardship for third world suppliers. This emergency, however, affects the future of particular peacekeeping efforts alone.

The creation by the General Assembly in December 1985 of an 18-member **Group of High-Level Inter-Governmental Experts**—an initiative of the delegation of Japan—is seen by many U.N. delegations as a first step in the search for a lasting solution to the political crisis that has generated the

United Nations' growing financial one. Underlying the crisis is a tension between the principle of sovereign equality of member states, permitting the more numerous developing countries to wield considerable influence over the kinds of issues on which U.N. attention and resources are focused, and the need to set priorities and manage more effectively the United Nations' limited monies and manpower, an increasing concern of the developing countries.

The Group was given rather broad but vague terms of reference: It is "to conduct a thorough review of the administrative and financial matters of the U.N." in order to find the means of improving its efficiency of operation and thus its effectiveness in dealing with the global political, economic, and social needs for which it was created [A/Res/40/237].

The Group has had a series of organizational meetings and has narrowed down the matters on which it will concentrate in the very limited time—approximately nine months—available to it. The matters with which it will deal include setting relative priorities, managerial improvements, content and level of program budget, procedures for reaching broad agreement on central budgetary questions, and governmental sharing of U.N. costs. Complementing this effort is the work of a **two-year blue-ribbon panel** established by the United Nations Association of the United States of America (UNA-USA) to delve even more deeply into these questions, focusing not only on U.N. management but on narrowing the gap between the organization's goals and capabilities.

For the short term, the Secretary-General has formulated a number of measures to stave off the bankruptcy that threatens to overtake the United Nations in the last quarter of 1986. In a report to the resumed 40th Session of the General Assembly, he stated that a number of economy measures had already been taken by the Secretariat. These included a 20 percent reduction in travel and consultancy costs; deferral of maintenance projects; a freeze in recruitment; suspension of the promotion process; and deferment of the General Service's cost-of-living adjustment, matching that previously imposed on professional staff. In this way the United Nations will save some $30 million in 1986.

The Secretary-General also suggested that further savings of a similar amount could be made by the Assembly, among them the deferral of two major construction projects at the Headquarters of the Economic Commissions for Africa and Asia and the Pacific, which would generate cash savings of $9 million; the shortening of the 41st Session of the General Assembly by three weeks; and the curtailment or even postponement of the meetings of some other U.N. bodies. He urged that the 1986 publications program be cut back and that there be a 50 percent reduction in the acquisition plans for furniture and equipment, such as word processors. Finally, the Secretary-General submitted a 24-page list of activities that could be cut back or postponed during the current period of financial stringency.

The Assembly's watchdog financial group—the Advisory Committee on Administrative and Budgetary Questions—gave these proposals of the Secretary-General its full support and urged that the Assembly adopt them as a package. At the same time, the Committee refused to entertain the possibility that the cash flow emergency might be mitigated by borrowing or by any increase in the Working Capital fund.

On May 9, the General Assembly met to consider the Secretary-General's budget-cutting proposals. It was decided that the decision to shorten the 41st General Assembly would be made in the autumn in the light of the then prevailing financial situation. The Economic and Social Council had already acted to reduce the length of its session, convened at that time. It was also suggested that the special session on Namibia could achieve substantial savings by adjourning the General Assembly for a few days in mid-September, during which the special session could be held and thus additional travel costs avoided. Finally, it was agreed that the Secretary-General would review the other items in his report in light of the evolving financial situation and report to the 41st Session. "No project or programme would be eliminated for which adequate financial resources were available" [Press release, GA/7291].

In order to bridge the financial gap that would remain even if there were agreement to all the proposed savings, the Secretary-General urged member states to pay their past and current assessed contributions (as of June 30, 1986, $371 of $736 million of 1986 assessed contributions were still outstanding). He also suggested that the General Assembly issue an appeal to governments to make contributions to the Special Account set up some years earlier to keep the United Nations solvent and to prepay part of the 1987 assessments. But these stopgap measures presuppose that the General Assembly will, with the help of the Group of Governmental Experts, produce some long-term solutions at the coming session. Should they fail to do so, matters may become even more serious in early 1987.

2. Personnel and Administration

Personnel issues, which were scheduled to receive particularly close attention in the 41st General Assembly, have been all but overshadowed by the more pressing matter of the financial crisis. Undoubtedly, budgetary questions and the report of the 18-member Group of High-Level Inter-Governmental Experts will receive more attention in the upcoming session. Nevertheless, though it is clear that any ordinary discussion of personnel issues will be waived in this most extraordinary year, consideration of such hardy perennials as salary levels, pensions, and recruitment are certain to figure into any austerity measures taken by the 41st Session.

Continuing member-state concern about **U.N. salaries** in the face of the financial crisis is likely to give this issue special prominence in 1986 and 1987. U.N. professional salaries are determined by a comparison with the salaries of U.S. civil servants, the highest paid in the world. To this salary a post-adjustment is added, where applicable, to equalize purchasing power in all duty stations. In addition, a "margin" is added on to take account of expatriation, less favorable career development, and less security of tenure. The 40th General Assembly approved a range of 110 to 120, with a desirable midpoint of 115, for the margin between net remuneration of officials in the professional and higher categories of the United Nations in New York and officials in comparable positions in the U.S. Federal civil service [A/Res/40/244]. At that time, the General Assembly anticipated a gradual transition from 120, where the margin now rests, to the preferred level of 115, by keeping U.N. professional salaries at their current levels until the margin had itself fallen due to rising U.S. salaries. In light of the financial crisis, there is at least a possibility that the General Assembly will attempt an immediate reduction of the margin to the level set last year by cutting U.N. salaries—a guaranteed savings of several million dollars—despite the request of the Secretary-General that professional salaries not be cut. The General Assembly last year requested the International Civil Service Commission (ICSC) to return to the 41st Session with an elaboration of its methods for calculating the margin based on net remuneration and the post-adjustment, of particular interest in these troubled times.

The nettlesome area of **pensions** will also undergo renewed scrutiny before the 41st General Assembly. Three years ago, in response to an actuarial imbalance in the pension fund, which caused outflows to exceed income, the General Assembly authorized the first of several increases in the size of contributions to the pension fund by staff and participating organizations. The 40th General Assembly deferred consideration of the second stage of the increased contribution rate until the pension board releases this year's report on the actuarial situation. The Secretary-General's move to enforce the established retirement age of 60, announced in late March, may actually weaken the actuarial imbalance further. The Pension Board has lobbied for years to raise the retirement age to 62, in an effort to close the gap by reducing pension liability.

In 1985, progress was made toward regulation of two of the thorniest aspects of the pension system. The 40th General Assembly determined that the maximum retirement benefit available to any U.N. professional employee on the Under-Secretary-General or Assistant-Secretary-General level leaving the United Nations after April 1, 1986, would not exceed 60 percent of pensionable remuneration [A/Res/40/245]. The new ceiling is reduced from an earlier level of either 65 or 66.5 percent, based on starting date and length of service. This action will automatically impose a cap—at this level—on the size of the lump sum payment that employees can opt for in lieu of up to one-third of their pensions. The ceiling for lower-grade professional pensions remains at either 65 or 66.5 percent of pensionable remuneration.

Despite what are considered positive moves toward bringing U.N. pensions back into line with those of the comparator nation—the United States—the General Assembly is not yet completely satisfied with the proposed methodology for determining and monitoring pensionable remuneration. In addition, the ICSC, in cooperation with the United Nations Joint Staff Pension Board, is expected to issue a report to the 41st General Assembly suggesting possible refinements and revisions of the scale it approved in 1984.

Early in 1986, the Secretary-General put into effect a number of **cost-saving measures**, including enforcement of the 60-year-old retirement age, a freeze in recruitment, suspension of the promotion process for six months, and deferment of the cost-of-living adjustments to the salaries of General Service staff. Certain of these measures, expected to result in savings of $30 million, are likely to have some impact on two of the cornerstones of recent **personnel policy**: equitable geographical distribution of staff members, and the improvement of the status of women in the Secretariat. Article 101 of the U.N. Charter explicitly makes "efficiency, competence, and integrity" the "paramount consideration" for the selection of U.N. employees, but adds that "due regard" shall be given to establishing the widest geographical representation. Recent General Assembly resolutions concerning personnel policy have emphasized "equitable geographical distribution" and have required the Secretary-General to deliver an annual status report on his efforts to improve recruitment in this area. There was little significant progress in 1984 and 1985. According to the Recruitment Programmes Section, 11 member nations currently have no nationals on the work force at all, a slight improvement over last year. At the same time, 23 countries are underrepresented and 30 countries, all from the developing world, are overrepresented. These figures have deteriorated since last year, primarily as a result of the recent transformation of the United Nations Industrial Development Organization (UNIDO), formerly a component part of the U.N. organization, into a specialized agency. The separation of UNIDO, for example, caused five nations to fall out of range. The Secretary-General will submit to the 41st General Assembly proposals for the review of the system of desirable ranges, taking into account all relevant factors, including that of population.

There was but little change in the number of women employed by the Secretariat over the last year, although the separation of the predominantly male UNIDO did lead to an increase in the relative percentage of women employees. Nevertheless, due to the continuing efforts of the Special Co-Ordinator for the Improvement of the Status of Women, there has been significant progress in the identification of qualified candidates through increased advertising, and more extensive use of competitive examinations on the P-1 and P-2 level. The Secretary-General will report on the progress of these measures to the 41st General Assembly. Obviously, all special recruit-ment programs will be put on hold for the indefinite future as a result of the Secretary-General's recruitment freeze order. In addition, the Secretary-Gen-eral's intention to offer an experimental examination on the P-3 level have been put on hold. It is widely believed that the new examination would pro-vide a basis for objectively identifying high-quality candidates from under-represented member states.

In an odd twist, efforts to cut back on staff through a recruitment freeze and the nonrenewal of short-term contracts may prove quite a boost to the Secretary-General's two-year **Career Development Plan**, now in its second year. One of the major goals of the Plan is to improve the utilization of U.N. personnel throughout the organization. Reduction of the staff, as a result of the Secretary-General's cost-saving measures, will require the rotation of em-ployees throughout the system in order to fill vacancies in important programs.

The sole personnel item on the agenda of the resumed session, that of job classification, was deferred until the 41st General Assembly, in the wake of far more important financial considerations. Resolution of this thorny issue has been attempted since the decision was made some years ago to convert New York's five-grade General Service structure into a seven-grade system. Last year, the Fifth Committee declined to accept the proposed formula for reclassification, which would result in the upgrading of four-fifths of the Gen-eral Service positions, and consequently the salaries, held by U.N. employees. Despite pressure from the Secretary-General and the staff, a final decision on implementation of the job classification scheme was put off until this year, although it was determined that the effective date of the program would be set at January 1, 1985.

According to the U.N. Staff Union, the number of **U.N. employees im-prisoned or illegally detained** throughout the world increased over the last year. Some 30 U.N. employees are currently detained, missing, imprisoned, or believed dead. The greatest number of these incidents has taken place in Afghanistan and Syria, but there have been others in areas as politically di-verse as Poland, the Gaza Strip and the West Bank, Guatemala, and Burma. In a widely publicized development, Alec Collett, a 64-year-old British jour-nalist working for the United Nations Relief and Works Agency for Palestine Refugees in the Near East (UNRWA), was claimed to have been murdered by his captors in Lebanon in retaliation for the U.S. attack on Libya in April 1986. If reports of his death are confirmed, Collett would become the 22nd person to die in the service of UNRWA since 1982. The Secretary-General has continued his efforts on behalf of imprisoned staff members through his preferred use of energetic, behind the scenes diplomacy.

On December 5, 1985, claiming that **the United Nations Educational, Scientific and Cultural Organization (UNESCO)** was "harmfully politicized" and "inefficient and badly managed," the United Kingdom followed the United States' lead to become the second member nation to withdraw from the organization. Singapore resigned its membership just a month later. Early in 1986, striking UNESCO workers protested the job losses anticipated by the budget cuts resulting from the withdrawal of these three countries from the organization. Director-General Amadou Mahtar M'Bow has said that more than 650 posts will probably be eliminated over the next two years, and that at least 150 of the 2,100 staff members would be dismissed [*The New York Times*, 12/8/85]. At the 23rd General Conference of UNESCO, held in Sofia, Bulgaria, in November and December, an urgent appeal was made to the United States and the United Kingdom to rejoin the organization. An effort was made at the Conference to implement significant reforms, including a reduction of the emphasis on proposals for a world information order, which have been attacked by both the United States and the United Kingdom as a blow to freedom of the press. The Conference elected a Yugoslav, Ivo Margan, as President of the organization's 30-member Executive Board. Dr. Margan, a widely respected 10-year veteran of UNESCO, has been mentioned as a possible successor to the authoritarian and controversial M'Bow when his term expires in 1987.

Appendix

PRINCIPAL ORGANS OF THE UN

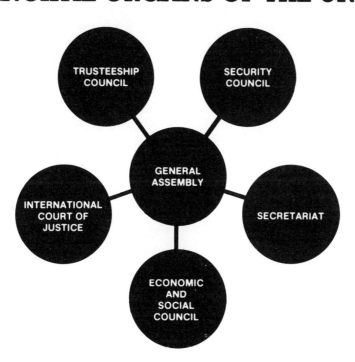

I. GENERAL ASSEMBLY

All UN members are part of the General Assembly, and each has one vote. The General Assembly controls the UN's finances, makes nonbinding recommendations on a variety of issues, and oversees and elects some members of other UN organs. The Assembly meets in plenary session from the third Tuesday in September through mid-December. As the length of the agenda has grown in recent years, there has been a tendency to resume the plenary shortly after January 1 for a few weeks in order to address all items. The Assembly can also meet in special session, as it has done for two special sessions on disarmament. Most business is delegated to the Assembly's seven main committees, which prepare recommendations for the approval of the Assembly.

President of the 40th General Assembly: Jaime de Pinies (Spain)

Main Committees

First Committee (Political and Security)
Special Political Committee (Other political issues,
  including most disarmament issues)
Second Committee (Economic and Financial)
Third Committee (Social, Humanitarian, and Cultural)
Fourth Committee (Decolonization)
Fifth Committee (Administration and Budget)
Sixth Committee (Legal)

Chairpersons

Ali Alatas (Indonesia)
Keijo Korhonen (Finland)

Omer Yousif Birido (Sudan)
Endre Zador (Hungary)
Javier Chamorro Mora (Nicaragua)
Tommo Monthe (Cameroon)
Riyadh Mehmoud Sami Al-Qaysi (Iraq)

Housekeeping Committees make recommendations on the adoption of the agenda, the allocation of items, and the organization of work.

Some Housekeeping Committees:
(1) General Committee
(2) Credentials Committee
(3) Committee on Relations with the Host Country

(4) Committee on Conferences
(5) Committee on Contributions
(6) Committee for Program and Coordination

Other Bodies Include:
(1) Board of Auditors
(2) International Civil Service Commission
(3) Joint Inspection Unit
(4) Panel of External Auditors of the United Nations, the Specialized Agencies, and the International Atomic Energy Agency
(5) Administrative Tribunal

(6) United Nations Joint Staff Pension Board
(7) United Nations Staff Pension Committee
(8) Investments Committee
(9) Advisory Committee on Administrative and Budgetary
  Questions

SPECIAL COMMITTEES THAT REPORT ON SPECIAL ISSUES:

There are some 75 such subsidiary organs. Some of these include:

(1) Special Committee on the Situation with regard to the Implementation of the Declaration on the Granting of Independence to Colonial Countries and Peoples

(2) Committee on the Exercise of the Inalienable Rights of the Palestinian People

(3) Special Committee against Apartheid

(4) Ad Hoc Committee on the Drafting of an International Convention against Apartheid in Sports

(5) United Nations Council for Namibia

(6) Committee on the Peaceful Uses of Outer Space

(7) Special Committee on Peacekeeping Operations

(8) United Nations Scientific Committee on the Effects of Atomic Radiation

(9) Ad Hoc Committee on International Terrorism

COMMISSIONS:

Three major Commissions report to the General Assembly:

(1) International Law Commission was established in 1947 to promote the development and codification of international law. It meets every year in Geneva and consists of 25 experts elected by the Assembly for 5-year terms. It prepares drafts on topics of its own choice and on topics referred to it by the Assembly and by the Economic and Social Council.

(2) United Nations Commission on International Trade Law, established in 1966, is a 36-country body that promotes the harmonization of international trade law and drafts international trade conventions. It also provides training and assistance in international trade law to developing countries.

(3) Disarmament Commission, established by the General Assembly in 1952, reports annually to the Assembly. This deliberative body makes recommendations on various problems in the field of disarmament and inter alia considers the elements of a comprehensive program for disarmament to be submitted as recommendations to the Assembly and, through it, to the negotiating body—the Conference of the Committee on Disarmament.

GENERAL ASSEMBLY (Continued)

OTHER ORGANIZATIONS CREATED BY AND REPORTING TO THE GENERAL ASSEMBLY:

Office of the United Nations Disaster Relief Coordinator (UNDRO) is a clearinghouse for information on relief needs and assistance, and mobilizes and coordinates emergency assistance.

Office of the United Nations High Commissioner for Refugees (UNHCR) extends international protection and material assistance to refugees, and negotiates with governments to resettle or repatriate refugees.

United Nations Center for Human Settlements (Habitat) deals with the housing problems of the urban and rural poor in developing countries. It provides technical assistance and training, organizes meetings, and disseminates information.

United Nations Children's Fund (UNICEF) provides technical and financial assistance to developing countries for programs benefiting children. It also provides emergency relief to mothers and children. It is financed by voluntary contributions.

United Nations Conference on Trade and Development (UNCTAD) works to establish agreements on commodity price stabilization and to codify principles of international trade that are conducive to development.

United Nations Development Program (UNDP) coordinates the development work of all UN and related agencies. It is the world's largest multilateral technical assistance program, currently supporting more than 6,500 projects around the world, and is financed by voluntary contributions.

United Nations Environment Program (UNEP) monitors environmental conditions, implements environmental projects, develops recommended standards, promotes technical assistance and training, and supports the development of alternative energy sources.

United Nations Fund for Population Activities (UNFPA) helps countries to gather demographic information and to plan population projects. Its governing body is the Governing Council of UNDP, and it is financed by voluntary governmental contributions.

United Nations Industrial Development Organization (UNIDO) is an autonomous organization within the UN that promotes the industrialization of developing countries. It is in the process of being converted into a specialized agency.

United Nations Institute for Training and Research (UNITAR) is an autonomous organization within the UN that provides training to government and UN officials and conducts research on a variety of international issues.

United Nations Relief and Works Agency for Palestine Refugees in the Near East (UNRWA) provides education, health, and relief services to Palestinian refugees.

United Nations University (UNU) is an autonomous academic institution chartered by the General Assembly. It has a world-wide network of associated institutions, research units, individual scholars, and UNU fellows, coordinated through the UNU center in Tokyo. It has no faculty or degree students.

World Food Council (WFC) is a 36-nation body that meets annually at the ministerial level to review major issues affecting the world food situation.

World Food Program (WFP) is jointly sponsored by the UN and FAO. It supplies emergency food relief and provides food aid to support development projects.

II. SECURITY COUNCIL

The Security Council has primary responsibility within the UN system for maintaining international peace and security. It may determine the existence of any threat to international peace, make recommendations or take enforcement measures to resolve the problem, and establish UN peacekeeping forces. Its resolutions are binding on all member states. It has 15 members: 5 permanent members designated by the UN Charter and 10 nonpermanent members. The latter are nominated by informal regional caucuses and elected for two-year terms; five are elected each year. Decisions on substantive matters require nine votes; a negative vote by any permanent member is sufficient to defeat the motion.

Permanent Membership
China
France
USSR
United Kingdom
United States

Term ending Dec. 31, 1986
Australia
Denmark
Madagascar
Thailand
Trinidad and Tobago

Term ending Dec. 31, 1987
Bulgaria
Congo
Ghana
United Arab Emirates
Venezuela

III. ECONOMIC AND SOCIAL COUNCIL

Under the authority of the General Assembly, ECOSOC coordinates the economic and social work of the UN and its large family of specialized and affiliated institutions. ECOSOC usually meets in plenary session twice a year for a month at a time, once in New York and once in Geneva. The 54 members of ECOSOC are elected by the General Assembly for three-year terms; 18 are elected each year.

Term expires:

Dec. 31, 1986
Argentina
Canada
China
Costa Rica
Finland
Guyana
Indonesia
Papua New Guinea
Poland
Rwanda
Somalia
Sri Lanka
Sweden
Uganda
USSR
United Kingdom
Yugoslavia
Zaire

Dec. 31, 1987
Bangladesh
Brazil
Colombia
France
Guinea
Haiti
Iceland
India
Japan
Morocco
Nigeria
Romania
Senegal
Spain
Turkey
Venezuela
West Germany
Zimbabwe

Dec. 31, 1988
Australia
Belgium
Byelorussia
Djibouti
Egypt
Gabon
East Germany
Iraq
Italy
Jamaica
Mozambique
Pakistan
Panama
Peru
Philippines
Sierra Leone
Syria
United States

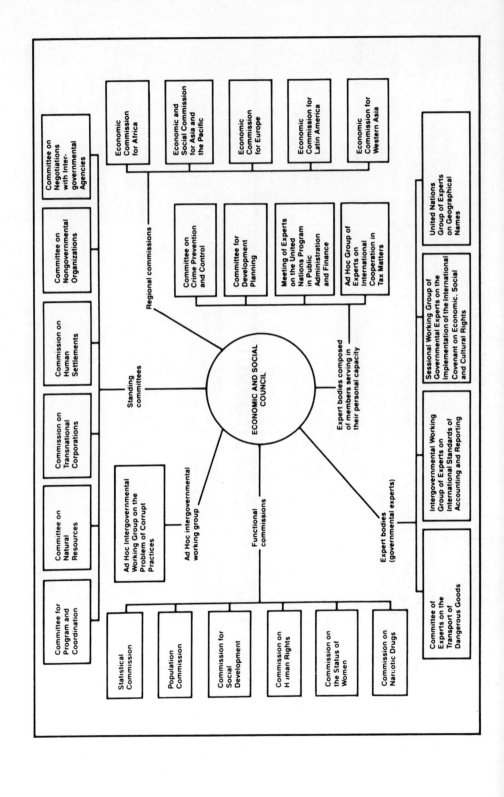

IV. TRUSTEESHIP COUNCIL

The five members of the Trusteeship Council—China, France, the USSR, the UK, and the US—are also the five permanent members of the Security Council. Only the US still administers a trust territory, the Trust Territory of the Pacific Islands. Originally, the Trusteeship Council had more members and administered 11 trust territories, but as the latter achieved independence or became parts of other states, the membership of the Council was reduced. China does not participate in the Council's work.

V. INTERNATIONAL COURT OF JUSTICE (WORLD COURT)

The International Court of Justice has 15 members, who are elected by an absolute majority of both the Security Council and the General Assembly for nine-year terms. The Court hears cases referred to it by the states involved, and provides advisory opinions to the General Assembly and the Security Council at their request. Five judges are elected every three years.

Term Expires:
Feb. 5, 1988

Jose Sette Camara (Brazil)
Platon Dmitrievich Morozov (USSR)*
Roberto Ago (Italy)
Stephen Schwebel (USA)
Mohammed Bedjaoui (Algeria)

*Resigned, 1985

Feb. 5, 1991

Nagendra Singh (India)*
Jose Maria Ruda (Argentina)
Robert Jennings (U.K.)
Guy Ladreit de Lacharriere (France)**
Keba Mbaye (Senegal)

*President of the Court
**Vice President

Feb. 5, 1994

Taslim Olawale Elias (Nigeria)
Manfred Lachs (Poland)
Shigeru Oda (Japan)
Jens Evensen (Norway)
Ni Zhrengya (PRC)

VI. SECRETARIAT

The Secretariat administers the programs and policies established by the other UN organs. It is headed by the Secretary-General (currently Javier Pérez de Cuéllar of Peru), who is elected by the General Assembly on the recommendation of the Security Council for a five-year term. The Secretary-General is authorized by the United Nations Charter to bring to the attention of the Security Council any matter that he believes may threaten international peace and security (Article 99), and may use his good offices to attempt to resolve international disputes. Under the Secretary-General are the Director-General for Development and International Economic Cooperation (currently Jean Louis Ripert of France), 26 Under-Secretaries-General, and 29 Assistant Secretaries-General. Further, the Secretariat contains a 16,000 international civil service staff (11,000 worldwide and 5,000 in New York), which carries out the day-to-day activities delegated to the Secretary-General. In the field, technical experts and economic advisers oversee economic and peacekeeping projects. Under Article 100 of the Charter, member states must recognize and respect the international character of the duties assigned to the Secretary-General and his staff.

SPECIALIZED AGENCIES

The specialized agencies are autonomous intergovernmental organizations related to the UN by special agreements. They report annually to the Economic and Social Council.

Food and Agriculture Organization of the United Nations (FAO) works to increase food production and to raise rural standards of living, and to help countries to cope with emergency food situations.

Edouard Saouma (Lebanon), Director-General
Via delle Terme di Caracalla
Rome 00100, Italy
Washington, DC Office:
1776 F Street, NW
Washington, DC 20437

International Civil Aviation Organization (ICAO) works to facilitate and to promote safe international air transportation by setting binding international standards and by recommending efficient practices. ICAO regulations are the rules that govern international flying.

Yves Maurice Lambert (France), Secretary-General
Place de L'Aviation Internationale
1000 Sherbrooke Street W.
Montreal, Quebec, Canada H3A 2R2

International Fund for Agricultural Development (IFAD) lends money on concessional terms for agricultural development proj-

ects, primarily to increase food production for the poorest rural populations.

Abdelmuhsin Al-Sudeary (Saudi Arabia), President
Via del Serafico 107, 00142
Rome, Italy

International Labor Organization (ILO) formulates international labor standards and provides technical assistance training to governments.

Francis Blanchard (France), Director-General
4 Route des Morillons, CH-1211
Geneva 22, Switzerland

International Maritime Organization (IMO) promotes international cooperation on technical matters related to shipping and provides a forum to discuss and to adopt conventions and recommendations on such matters as safety at sea and pollution control.

C.P. Srivastava (India), Secretary-General
4 Albert Embankment
London, SE1 7SR, England

SPECIALIZED AGENCIES (Continued)

International Monetary Fund (IMF) provides technical assistance and financing to countries that are experiencing balance-of-payments difficulties.

Jacques de Larosière (France), Managing Director
700 19th Street, NW
Washington, DC 20431

International Telecommunication Union (ITU) promotes international cooperation in telecommunications, allocates the radio-frequency spectrum, and collects and disseminates telecommunications information for its members.

Richard E. Butler (Australia), Secretary-General
Place des Nations
CH 1211 Geneva 10, Switzerland

United Nations Educational, Scientific and Cultural Organization (UNESCO) pursues international intellectual cooperation in education, science, culture, and communications, and also promotes development by means of social, cultural, and economic projects.

Amadou-Mahtar M'Bow (Senegal), Director-General
UNESCO House
7 Place de Fontenoy, 75700
Paris, France

usually for specific, productive projects. IFC lends to private corporations without government guarantees. IDA provides interest-free "credits" to the world's poorest countries for a period of 50 years, with a 10-year grace period.

Aldin Winship Clausen (United States), President
1818 H Street, NW
Washington, DC 20433
New York office: 737 Third Avenue, 26th fl.
New York, New York 10017

World Health Organization (WHO) conducts immunization campaigns, promotes and administers research, and provides technical assistance to countries that are improving their health systems.

Dr. Halfdan T. Mahler (Denmark), Director-General
20 Avenue Appia, 1211
Geneva 27, Switzerland

World Intellectual Property Organization (WIPO) promotes the protection of intellectual property (e.g., patents and copyrights). It encourages adherence to relevant treaties, provides legal and technical assistance to developing countries, encourages technology transfer, and administers the International Union for the Protection of Industrial Property and the International Union for the Protection of Literary and Artistic Works.

Dr. Arpad Bogsch (United States), Director-General
34 Chemin des Colombettes
CH-1211 Geneva 20, Switzerland

Universal Postal Union (UPU) sets international postal standards and provides technical assistance to developing countries.

Mohamed I. Sòbhi (Egypt), Director-General
Weltpoststrasse 4
Berne 1, Switzerland

The World Bank is actually three institutions: the International Bank for Reconstruction and Development (**IBRD**); the International Finance Corporation (**IFC**); and the International Development Association (**IDA**). IBRD lends funds to governments (or to private enterprises if the government guarantees repayment),

World Meteorological Organization (WMO) promotes the exchange and standardization of meteorological information through its World Weather Watch, and conducts research and training programs.

G.O.P. Obasi (Nigeria), Secretary-General
41 Avenue Giuseppe Motta
CH-1211 Geneva 20, Switzerland

OTHER AUTONOMOUS AFFILIATED ORGANIZATIONS

General Agreement on Tariffs and Trade (GATT) is a multilateral treaty establishing rules for international trade. As the postwar plans for an International Trade Organization never materialized, the GATT evolved into a forum for negotiations on international trade.

Arthur Dunkel (Switzerland), Director-General
Centre William Rappard
154 Rue de Lausanne
1211 Geneva 21, Switzerland

International Atomic Energy Agency (IAEA) was established under UN auspices but is autonomous and is not formally a specialized agency. It promotes the use of peaceful nuclear energy and provides safeguards on most of the world's peaceful nuclear materials to ensure that it is not diverted to military use.

Dr. Hans Blix (Sweden), Director-General
Vienna International Center
PO Box 100
A-1400 Vienna, Austria

THE 159 UN MEMBER STATES

Since the United Nations was founded in 1945, membership in the organization has more than tripled. There were 51 original member states; today, the membership numbers 159 countries. In the past decade, most new members have been ministates, which have joined as they have become independent—the end of the wave of decolonization that began after World War II. The vast majority of the world's nations are UN members. During the 39th General Assembly, Brunei became the newest member.

Afghanistan, Democratic Republic of
Albania, Socialist Republic of
Algeria, Democratic and Popular Republic of
Angola, People's Republic of
Antigua and Barbuda
Argentina, Republic of
Australia, Commonwealth of
Austria, Republic of
Bahamas, Commonwealth of The
Bahrain, State of
Bangladesh, People's Republic of
Barbados
Belgium, Kingdom of
Belize
Benin, The People's Republic of
Bhutan, Kingdom of
Bolivia, Republic of
Botswana, Republic of
Brazil, Federative Republic of
Brunei (Brunei Darussalam)
Bulgaria, People's Republic of
Burkina-Faso (formerly Upper Volta)
Burma, Socialist Republic of the Union of
Burundi, Republic of

Grenada
Guatemala, Republic of
Guinea, People's Revolutionary Republic of
Guinea-Bissau, Republic of
Guyana, Cooperative Republic of
Haiti, Republic of
Honduras, Republic of
Hungary (Hungarian People's Republic)
Iceland, Republic of
India, Republic of
Indonesia, Republic of
Iran, Islamic Republic of
Iraq, Republic of
Ireland
Israel, State of
Italy (Italian Republic)
Ivory Coast, Republic of
Jamaica
Japan
Jordan, Hashemite Kingdom of
Kampuchea, Democratic (formerly Cambodia)
Kenya, Republic of
Kuwait, State of
Laos (Lao People's Democratic Republic)

Romania, Socialist Republic of
Rwanda, Republic of
St. Christopher-Nevis
St. Lucia
St. Vincent and the Grenadines
Samoa, Independent State of Western
Sao Tome and Principe, Democratic Republic of
Saudi Arabia, Kingdom of
Senegal, Republic of
Seychelles, Republic of
Sierra Leone, Republic of
Singapore, Republic of
Solomon Islands
Somalia (Somali Democratic Republic)
South Africa, Republic of
Spain (Spanish State)
Sri Lanka, Democratic Socialist Republic of
Sudan, Democratic Republic of
Suriname, Republic of
Swaziland, Kingdom of
Sweden, Kingdom of
Syria (Syrian Arab Republic)
Tanzania, United Republic of
Thailand, Kingdom of

Byelorussia (Byelorussian Soviet
    Socialist Republic)
Cameroon, United Republic of
Canada
Cape Verde, Republic of
Central African Republic
Chad, Republic of
Chile, Republic of
China, People's Republic of
Colombia, Republic of
Comoros, Federal Islamic
    Republic of the
Congo, People's Republic of the
Costa Rica, Republic of
Cuba, Republic of
Cyprus, Republic of
Czechoslovakia (Czechoslovak
    Socialist Republic)
Denmark, Kingdom of
Djibouti, Republic of
Dominica, Commonwealth of
Dominican Republic
Ecuador, Republic of
Egypt, Arab Republic of
El Salvador, Republic of
Equatorial Guinea, Republic of
Ethiopia, Socialist
Fiji
Finland, Republic of
France (French Republic)
Gabon (Gabonese Republic)
Gambia, Republic of The
German Democratic Republic
    (East Germany)
Germany, Federal Republic of
    (West Germany)
Ghana, Republic of
Greece (Hellenic Republic)

Lebanon, Republic of
Lesotho, Kingdom of
Liberia, Republic of
Libya (Socialist People's Libyan
    Arab Jamahiriya)
Luxembourg, Grand Duchy of
Madagascar, Democratic
    Republic of
Malawi
Malaysia
Maldives, Republic of
Mali, Republic of
Malta
Mauritania, Islamic Republic of
Mauritius
Mexico (The United Mexican
    States)
Mongolia (Mongolian People's
    Republic)
Morocco, Kingdom of
Mozambique, People's Republic of
Nepal, Kingdom of
Netherlands, Kingdom of the
New Zealand
Nicaragua, Republic of
Niger, Republic of
Nigeria, Federal Republic of
Norway, Kingdom of
Oman, Sultanate of
Pakistan, Islamic Republic of
Panama, Republic of
Papua New Guinea
Paraguay, Republic of
Peru, Republic of
Philippines, Republic of the
Poland (Polish People's Republic)
Portugal, Republic of
Qatar, State of

Togo, Republic of
Trinidad and Tobago, Republic of
Tunisia, Republic of
Turkey, Republic of
Uganda, Republic of
Ukraine (Ukrainian Soviet
    Socialist Republic)
Union of Soviet Socialist
    Republics
United Arab Emirates
United Kingdom of Great Britain
    and Northern Ireland
United States of America
Uruguay
Vanuatu, Republic of
Venezuela, Republic of
Vietnam, Socialist Republic of
Yemen Arab Republic
    (North Yemen)
Yemen, People's Democratic
    Republic of (South Yemen)
Yugoslavia, Socialist Federal
    Republic of
Zaire, Republic of
Zambia, Republic of
Zimbabwe

The following countries maintain
    offices of permanent observers
    at the UN:
Korea, Democratic People's
    Republic of (North Korea)
Korea, Republic of (South Korea)
Monaco, Principality of
Switzerland
    (Swiss Confederation)
Vatican City, State of the

Index

Abbas, Abu, 10, 13, 14
Achille Lauro, 2, 10, 13–14, 146
Ad Hoc Committee on International
  Terrorism, 145
Ad Hoc Committee on the World
  Disarmament Conference, 61
Administration and budget, 151–158;
  budget and finance and, 151–154;
  personnel and administration and,
  154–158
Advisory Committee for the Coordination of Information Services
  (ACCIS), 83
Afghanistan, 2, 144, 157; human
  rights in, 115, 117, 118; Soviet intervention in, 36–39, 49, 58
Africa: boundary disputes in, 138;
  denuclearization of, 57; develop-
  ment of, 20–21, 22–26; food
  emergency in, 85, 86, 87, 89; food
  trade and, 88; per capita GDP of,
  67; population growth in, 94;
  refugees from, 21, 121–122, 123,
  124; southern, 21–22, 27–33, 115.
  See also South Africa
African National Congress (ANC), 27,
  29
African Priority Programme for Eco-
  nomic Recovery (APPER), 25,
  86–87
Agency for International Development
  (AID), 91
Agricultural products, trade in, 76
Agriculture, food policy and, 85–91
Ahmed, Rafeeuddin, 45
Ahtisaari, Martti, 2
Aid: to Afghanistan, 37; to Africa, 23,
  25–26; to Kampuchea, 40; to
  poorest countries, 72–73
Albania, 120
Algeria, 66
Angola, 2, 99; Cuban troops in, 30;
  food emergency in, 87; South
  African intervention in, 21, 23, 26,
  32, 115
Anguilla, 44
Antarctica, 102–103, 107–110

Antarctic Treaty, 102–103, 108–110
Antarctic Treaty Consultative Parties
  (ATCPs), 108
Anti-Ballistic Missile (ABM) Treaty,
  49, 50, 53
Apartheid, 26–30, 103, 108, 115,
  119; transnational corporations
  and, 81–82
Arab countries, 152
Arafat, Yasir, 8, 10, 18
Argentina, 35, 102; debt crisis and,
  70, 71, 72; Falklands/Malvinas
  conflict and, 44; nuclear weapons
  and, 55, 56, 57
Arms control and disarmament, 47–
  61; chemical, conventional and
  other weapons and, 58–60; com-
  prehensive disarmament and,
  60–61; nuclear weapons and super-
  powers and, 51–55; spread of
  nuclear weapons and, 55–58;
  weapons in outer space and, 49–51
Arusha Understanding, 106
ASAT systems, 49
Asia, 67, 77, 124
Assad, Hafez al-, 11, 12, 13
Association of South East Asian Nations (ASEAN), 39, 40
"Austral Plan," 70
Australia, 16, 58, 82, 102, 106, 141
Automated data processing, 143

Baker, James, 23, 64
Baker Plan, 68, 70, 71–72
Bank-Fund Interim Development Com-
  mittees, 72
Bar-Lev, Haim, 11
Bassas da India, 45
Belgium, 56, 102, 106, 139
Belize, 135
Berg, Elliot, 23
Berg Report, 23
Bermuda, 44
Berri, Nabih, 17
Biennialization, 100–101
Bill of International Human Rights, 112
Biological weapons, 58

Blix, Hans, 98
Body of Principles for the Protection
of All Persons under Any Form of
Detention or Imprisonment, 149
Boesak, Allan, 29
Bolivia, 69, 71
Botha, P.W., 28–29, 30, 32
Botswana, 21, 26, 27, 32
Brazil, 35, 55, 56, 57, 70, 71, 77,
102
Brunei, 39
Budget and finance, 151–154
Bulgaria, 60, 102, 144
Burkina Faso, 14, 22, 138
Burma, 157
Bush, George, 75
Byelorussia, 144

Cairo Programme for African Co-
operation, 101–102
Canada, 31, 74, 77, 82, 106, 138
Career development plan, 157
Cartagena Group, 70
Cash flow problems, 151–154
Cayman Islands, 44
Ceausescu, Nicolae, 132
Central America, 2, 33–36, 99, 124
Chad, 2, 21, 121
Chemical weapons, 2, 7, 58–59;
Geneva Protocol and, 2
Children: rights of, 114
Chile, 57, 71, 102, 105, 117, 118
China, 67, 72, 98, 102, 144; law
of the sea and, 108, 109; nuclear
weapons and, 55, 56, 58; popula-
tion program of, 91–93; Soviet in-
vasion of Afghanistan and, 36, 37;
Vietnamese invasion of Kampuchea
and, 39, 40
Chinh, Truang, 39
Cities, growth of, 95
Clausen, A.W., 90
Coalition Government of Democratic
Kampuchea (CGDK), 39–41
Cocaine, 135
Code of Offenses against the Peace
and Security of Mankind, 148
Collett, Alec, 157
Colombia, 33, 71, 135
Commercial arbitration, 143
Commission for Human Settlements,
136

Commission on Human Rights, 33,
35–36, 111, 114
Commission on Narcotic Drugs, 135,
136
Commission on the Status of Women
(CSW), 116, 126
Commission on Transnational
Corporations, 80, 81
Committee of 24, 44
Committee on Information, 130
Committee on Relations with the Host
Country, 144
Committee on Social and Cultural
Rights, 116
Committee on the Elimination of
Discrimination Against Women
(CEDAW), 125–126
Committee on the Elimination of
Racial Discrimination, 119
Committee on the Peaceful Uses
of Outer Space (COPOUS), 147
Commodity prices, 75
Common Fund for Commodities, 75–76
Communication(s), 128–131;
military, 49; satellites and, 147; on
science and technology, 83
Comorian Islands, 45
Comprehensive Nuclear Test Ban
(CTB), 53–54
Comprehensive Program of Dis-
armament, 61
Conable, Barber B., Jr., 71, 90
Conference (s): standard rules of
procedure for, 149
Conference on Disarmament, 50–51,
58, 59, 61
Conference on Population and Small
and Medium-Sized Cities, 95
Confidence-building measures
(CBMs), 55
Congress of South African Trade
Unions, 29
Consular missions, safety of, 146–147
Contadora Group, 33, 35
Convention against Torture, Other
Cruel, Inhuman or Degrading
Treatment or Punishment, 117
Convention on International Bills of
Exchange and International Pro-
missory Notes, 143
Convention on Psychotropic Sub-
stances, 136

Convention on the Conservation of Antarctic Marine Living Resources (CCAMLR), 102, 109
Convention on the Elimination of All Forms of Discrimination against Women, 116, 125
Convention on the Rights of the Child, 114
Cook Islands, 58
Cordovez, Diego, 36, 37, 38
Costa Rica, 33, 35
Cost-saving measures, 156
Covenant on Economic, Social and Cultural Rights, 116
Crime, 134
Crocker, Chester, 2
Cuba, 2, 14, 16, 30, 32, 57, 102, 144
Cyprus, 2, 4, 41–44
Czechoslovakia, 102, 125, 139, 144

Damascus Accord, 16, 17–18
de la Madrid Hurtado, Miguel, 70
Debt crisis, 23, 67–70, 68–70
Declaration of Basic Principles of Justice for Victims of Crime and Abuse of Power, 134
Declaration of the Indian Ocean as a Zone of Peace, 61
Declaration of Social and Legal Principles Relating to the Protection and Welfare of Children, 149
Declaration on the Human Rights of Individuals Who are not Nationals of the Country in which They Live, 115
Declaration on the Participation of Women in Promoting International Peace and Cooperation, 125
Decolonization, 44–46
Denktash, Rauf, 42, 43
Denmark, 16, 48, 60, 102, 125
Department of Technical Co-operation for Development (UN/DTCD), 99
Detainees, human rights of, 114
Development: African, 20–21, 22–26; military spending and, 61; refugees and, 88; women in, 87–88
Dhanapala, Jayantha, 69
Diplomatic bag, status of, 148
Diplomatic courier, status of, 148
Diplomatic missions, safety of, 146–147

Direct foreign investment (DFI), 79
Disabled persons, 133–134
Disarmament Week, 61
Discriminatory arrangements, 76
Dispute settlement and decolonization, 1–46, 140; in Afghanistan, 36–39; in Africa, 20–33; in Central America, 33–36; in Cyprus, 41–44; in Indochina, 39–41; in Middle East and Persian Gulf, 4–20; peacekeeping in, 1–4
Djibouti, 21, 121, 123
Dollar: depreciation of, 65; strength of, 74; value of, 100
Domestic violence, 127, 134
Draper, William H., III, 90–91
Drug abuse and trafficking, 135–136
Duan, Le, 39
Duarte, José Napoléon, 34
Dunkel, Arthur, 77

East Germany, 102, 106, 139, 144–145
East Timor, 2, 44, 45
Economic and Social Council (ECOSOC), 85, 96, 99, 133, 135, 154, 163–164; human rights and, 114, 119
Economic Commission for Africa, 86
Economic relations, 142–144
Economics and development, 63–84; money and finance and, 67–73; science and technology and, 82–83; technology transfer and, 83–84; trade and, 74–78; transnational corporations and, 79–82; world economy in 1986 and, 63–67
Ecuador, 105
Egypt, 13, 37
El Salvador, 33, 34–35, 117, 118
Elderly, 132–133
Electronic funds transfers, 143
Eminent Persons Group, 26
Energy, 98–100; financing development of, 100; renewable sources of, 99–100
Environment, 100–103
Equador, 71, 125
Eritrea, 21
Ermacora, Felix, 36
Espionage, in host country, 144–145
Esquivel, Manuel, 135

Ethiopia, 21, 87, 99, 120, 121
Europa, 45
Europe, 64, 78, 79, 105
European Economic Community (EEC), 76
Executions: summary or arbitrary, 116

Falklands/Malvinas, 2, 44, 60
Family planning, 91–93, 94–95, 96
February 11 Agreement, 8, 9, 11
Federated States of Micronesia, 45
Fiji, 58
Financial markets, 67
Finland, 102
First Committee, 47–48
Food Aid Convention, 85, 89
Food and Agriculture Organization of the United Nations (FAO), 85, 86, 87
Food Financing Facility, 89
Food policy, 85–91
Food trade, 88–89
Fornos, Werner, 95
France, 2–3, 16, 31, 48, 60, 61, 64, 65, 81, 105, 106, 141; Antarctic treaty and, 102, 103; disputes of, 45; law of the sea and, 105, 106; nuclear weapons and, 55, 57, 58

García, Alan, 34
Gaza Strip, 11, 157
Geagea, Samir, 17
Gemayel, Amin, 17
General Agreement on Tariffs and Trade (GATT), 64, 76, 77–78, 169
General Assembly, 160–162
Geneva Protocol, 2, 58
Geostationary orbit: regulation of, 148
Ghana, 16
Gibraltar, 45
Global Information and Early Warning System on Food and Agriculture, 85
Glorieuses, 45
Golan Heights, 3–4, 11
Good-neighborliness, 141
Gorbachev, Mikhail, 14, 51, 52, 53
Goulding, Marrack, 4

Great Britain. *See* United Kingdom
Greece, 43, 58
Greenpeace, 2–3, 58
Grenada, 50
Gross domestic product (GDP): in Africa, 22; of less developed countries, 66
Gross national product (GNP) growth: in industrial countries, 64
Group of High-Level Inter-Governmental Experts, 122, 152–153, 154
Group of 24, 72
Group of 77, 72
Guam, 44
Guatemala, 33, 35–36, 117–118, 157
Gulf Cooperation Council (GCC), 7, 8

Habib, Philip C., 35
Haiti, 120
Hartling, Poul, 91, 121
Helsinki Final Act, 55
Herndl, Kurt, 116, 117
Hijackings, 10, 12, 13–14, 146
Hobeika, Elie, 17
Hocké, Jean-Pierre, 91, 120–121, 123
Homeless, 136
Honduras, 33, 34, 35, 123
Hostage-taking, 2, 12, 146
Human rights, 111–120; in Central America, 35–36; country-specific issues in, 117–120; standard setting and, 113–117
Human Rights Commission, 112
Human Rights Committee, 115
Hungary, 102
Hussein, King, 8, 10, 11

Income, per capita, in Africa, 22
India, 4, 16, 48; Antarctic treaty and, 102, 108; debt crisis and, 72; law of the seas and, 105; nuclear weapons and, 55, 56, 58; population growth in, 94; trade and, 77
Indochina, 39–41
Indonesia, 39, 45, 66
"Industrial targeting," 78
Inflation, 67; in industrial countries, 64–65
Information, 128–131
Information networks: global, 83
Integrated Program for Commodities, 75

Inter-American Development Bank, 71
Interest rates, 67, 68
Intergovernmental Committee on Science and Technology, 82–83
Intermediate-range nuclear forces (INF), 53
International Atomic Energy Agency (IAEA), 52, 56, 98–99, 169
International Bank for Reconstruction and Development. *See* World Bank
International Civil Service Commission (ICSC), 155, 156
International Code of Conduct for Transnational Corporations, 80
International Code of Conduct on the Transfer of Technology, 84
International Commodity Agreements (ICAs), 75
International Conference for Assistance to Refugees in Africa (ICARA II), 88, 121–122
International Conference on Drug Abuse and Illicit Trafficking, 135
International Conference on Population and the Urban Future, 95
International Conference on the Relationship Between Disarmament and Development, 61, 103
International Convention on the Elimination of All Forms of Racial Discrimination, 119
International Convention on the Physical Protection of Nuclear Materials, 56
International Convention on the Protection of the Rights of All Migrant Workers and Their Families, 117
International Convention on the Suppression of the Crime of Apartheid, 119
International Court of Justice (ICJ), 30, 33, 34, 137–139, 165
International Development Association (IDA), 72, 85
International Development Strategy, 73
International Energy Agency (IEA), 98
International Finance Corporation (IFC), 100
International Fund for Agricultural Development (IFAD), 85, 88–89
International Law Commission (ILC), 142, 143, 148–149

International Monetary Fund (IMF), 20, 23, 24, 64, 69, 71, 72, 89
International Plan of Action on Aging, 133
International Planned Parenthood Federation (IPPF), 93
International Programme for the Development of Communication (IPDC), 130
International Research and Training Institute for the Advancement of Women (INSTRAW), 126–127
International Seabed Authority (ISA), 105
International Telecommunication Union, 148
International Union for the Conservation of Nature and Natural Resources (IUCN), 110
International Year of Peace, 115
International Year of Shelter for the Homeless (IYSH), 136
International Youth Year (IYY), 131–132
Iran, 7–8, 36, 37, 117, 118, 144
Iran-Iraq war, 1–2, 4–20, 59; in air, 7; armies in, 5; attacks on oil facilities and tankers in, 5–6
Iraq, 7–8, 59
Israel, 3–4, 37, 50, 103, 121, 145, 146; in Arab-Israeli conflict, 8–12; human rights and, 119–120; nuclear weapons and, 55, 56, 57–58; seizure of Libyan airplane by, 14, 145; withdrawal from Lebanon, 16–17, 18
Italy, 13–14, 64, 102, 106, 137, 139
Ivory Coast, 71

Japan, 102, 105, 106, 138, 139; economics and, 64, 65, 67, 68; trade and, 76, 77, 78
Jazairy, Idriss, 89
Jensen, D. Conell, 136
Jonathan, Leabua, 32
Jordan, 8, 10, 11
Juan de Nova, 45
Jumblatt, Walid, 17
Jurisdictional immunities, 148
Justice: administration of, 114
Juvenile delinquency, 134

Kampuchea (Cambodia), 2, 39–41, 58, 115
Karmal, Babrak, 36, 38
Kassebaum amendment, 152
Kenya, 94
Khmer People's National Liberation Front (KPNLF), 39–41
Khomeini, Ayatollah Ruhollah, 8
Kiribati, 58
Korea, 2
Kusumaatmadja, Mochtar, 40
Kyprianou, Spyros, 42, 43

Lagos Plan of Action, 25
Laos, 58
Latin America, 67, 68, 77, 129, 135
Law of the sea, 104–107
Law of the Sea Conference, 105–107
Law of the Sea Convention, 108
League of Nations, 30
Lebanon, 12, 15, 16–19, 146
Legal issues, 137–149; economic relations and, 142–144; effectiveness of United Nations and, 139–140; International Court of Justice and, 137–139; international law commission and, 148; international organizations and host country relations and, 144–145; outer space and, 147–148; peace and security and, 140–142; violence by individuals and groups and, 145–147
Lekhanya, Justin, 32
Lesotho, 21, 27, 32
Less developed countries (LDCs): development of energy resources of, 99; economic development in, 66–67; technology transfer and, 83–84
Li Luye, 92
Libya, 12–16, 60, 138, 139, 144, 146, 157
Limited Nuclear Test Ban Treaty, 49
Loans, 71–73; to Africa, 23, 29–30; to LDCs, 68–70
London Nuclear Suppliers' Group, 56–57
Long, Jay H., 113
Lopez-Rey, Manuel, 134
Luxembourg, 106

McCaffrey, Stephen, 148–149
Machel, Samora, 32

McPherson, M. Peter, 91–92
Madagascar, 45
"Magnet cities," 95
Malaysia, 39, 103, 108
Mali, 22, 138
Malta, 138
Mandela, Nelson, 28
Mandela, Winnie, 29
Manganese exploration, 105–107
Margan, Ivo, 158
"Market-opening, sector-specific" (MOSS) negotiations, 77
Marshall Islands, 45
Masri, Zafer al-, 11
Mauritania, 89
Mayotte, 45
M'Bow, Mahtar, 158
"Mega-cities," 95
Member states, 170–171
Mercenaries, 146
Mexico, 33, 48, 83; debt crisis and, 66, 68, 70, 71; oil prices and, 66, 74
Micronesia, 45–46
Middle East, 2, 57–58, 67
Milan Plan of Action, 134
Military spending, 51; in Africa, 24; food security and, 87; reduction of, 61
Mineral resources: of Antarctica, 109
Missiles: space-based, 49–50
Moi, Daniel T. Arap, 94
Mongolia, 125
Montserrat, 44
Morocco, 1, 22, 71
Morse, E. Bradford, 91
Most-favored-nation clauses, 143–144
Movement of Non-Aligned Countries, 119
Mozambique, 21, 23, 26, 32, 87
Mubarak, Hosni, 9
Multiyear restructuring agreements (MYRAs), 69
Mutual and Balanced Force Reductions (MBFR), 55

Najibullah, 36
Nakasone, Yasuhiro, 65
Nallet, Henri, 90
Namibia, 2, 121; South African intervention in, 21, 26, 30–32, 44, 81, 115

Nandan, Satya, 105
National Union for the Total Independence of Angola (UNITA), 31, 32
Naval disarmament, 60
Netherlands, 102, 106, 149
New International Economic Order (NIEO), 72–73, 142–143
Newly industrializing countries (NICs), 67; trade conflicts with, 78; trade restrictions and, 77
New World Information and Communication Order (NWICO), 128–131
New Zealand, 2–3, 58, 102, 139
News media: Western control of, 128–129
Nicaragua, 33–35, 69, 137, 138
Nigeria, 21, 66, 69, 71, 140
Niue, 58
No-first-use, 54
Non-use of force, 140–141
North Atlantic Treaty Organization (NATO), 14, 43, 54
North Korea, 56
Northern Marianas, 45
Norway, 3, 74, 98, 102
Nuclear and Space Arms Talks (NST), 51–52
Nuclear energy, 98–99; in outer space, 147
Nuclear weapons: spread of, 55–58; superpowers and, 51–55
Nuclear-weapons-free zones (NWFZs), 57–58
Nuclear winter hypothesis, 54–55
Nyerere, Julius, 25

Official development assistance (ODA), 73
Oil prices, 63–64, 66, 70, 74–75, 98
Oil reserves: in Antarctica, 102, 103
Oppenheimer, Tamar, 135
"Orderly marketing agreements" (OMAs), 76
Organization for Economic Cooperation and Development (OECD), 76, 88
Organization of African Unity (OAU), 1, 2, 119; development and, 20, 24–26, 86, 101

Organization of Petroleum Exporting Countries (OPEC), 63, 74–75, 88, 98
Outer space, 147–148
Outer Space Treaty, 49
Ozal, Turgut, 43

Pakistan, 4, 48, 120, 121; nuclear weapons and, 55, 56, 58; relations with Afghanistan, 36, 37, 38
Palau, 45–46
Palestine, 4
Palestine Liberation Organization (PLO), 8–11, 13, 14, 18, 146
Pan African Congress (PAC), 27
Panama, 33
Panel of Eminent Persons, 81
Papandreou, Andreas, 43, 58
Papua New Guinea, 102
Paraguay, 120
Partial Test Ban Treaty, 53
Peaceful Nuclear Explosions, 52
Peacekeeping, 139; financing of, 3; U.N. role in, 1–4
Pensions, 155
Peres, Shimon, 10
Pérez de Cuéllar, Javier, 1, 5, 7, 8, 13, 19, 38, 42, 43, 86, 92, 96, 133
Persian Gulf, 61
Persian Gulf war, 2
Personnel and administration, 154–158
Peru, 34, 35, 69, 71, 99, 102, 108
Philippines, 39, 71, 105, 140
Pioneer Investors, 105–107
Pisani, Edgard, 86
Poland, 69, 102, 129, 139, 144–145, 157
Pol Pot, 39
Population, 91–97; forecast for, 96–97; growth of, 22, 93–94; urban, 95; women and, 95–96
Population Council, 92–93
Population Institute, 92–93
Portugal, 45, 76, 103, 125
Proclamation of Teheran, 112
Programme of Action for African Economic Recovery and Development, 86
Prostitution, 127

Qaddafi, Muammar el-, 14, 15
Quotas, 77

Rainbow Warrior, 2–3
Reagan, Ronald, 2, 12, 13, 14, 15,
    33, 34, 40–41, 51, 52, 53, 76, 77,
    120, 146, 152
Refoulement, 124
Refugees, 120–124; Afghan, 121;
    African, 21, 121–122, 123, 124;
    armed attacks on, 124; Cambo-
    dian, 123; development and, 88;
    Ethiopian, 121, 123; Laotian, 123;
    legal protection of, 124; Namibian,
    121; Palestinian, 19–20, 121, 122;
    Salvadoran, 123; Ugandan, 123
Repatriation: forced, 124, voluntary,
    123
Republic of South Africa. See South
    Africa
Resource management, 85–110;
    Antarctica and, 107–110; energy
    and, 98–100; environment and,
    100–103; food and agriculture and,
    85–91; law of the sea and,
    104–107; population and, 91–97
Retirement benefits: amount available
    for, 155–156
Rhodesia. See Zimbabwe
Romania, 48, 102, 108, 140, 141
Roosevelt, Eleanor, 111, 112

Salaries, 154–155
SALT I, 52
SALT II, 52
Samoa: American, 44; Western, 58
Samrin, Heng, 39, 40, 41
Sarney, José, 70
Satellites, 147; military, 49
Saudi Arabia, 37, 63, 74
Savimbi, Jonas, 2
Schultz, George P., 92
Scientific Committee on Antarctic Re-
    search (SCAR), 110
Second Committee, 101
Secretariat, 166
Security Council, 1–2, 163
Self-determination: right to, 115
Services: trade in, 77–78
Shaaban, Sheikh, 19
Shevardnadze, E., 52
Sihanouk, Norodom, 39

Sihanoukist National Army (SNA), 39,
    40
Singapore, 39, 40, 158
Single Convention in Narcotic Drugs,
    136
Sixth Committee, 142, 145, 146,
    149
Skyjackings, 146
Snyder, Margaret, 127
Somalia, 21, 121
Somoza Debayle, Anastasio, 34
Son Sann, 39, 40
South Africa, 20–21, 59,
    121; Antarctic treaty and, 102,
    103; apartheid in, 26–30, 32–33;
    foreign investment in, 81; interven-
    tion in Namibia and Angola by,
    30–32, 115; law of the sea and,
    108–109; nuclear power and, 55,
    56, 57, 99; sanctions against, 81,
    108–109, 115, 119
South Atlantic war, 2, 44, 60
South West Africa People's Organiza-
    tion (SWAPO), 30, 31, 32
South West Africa. See Namibia
Soviet Union, 10, 43, 46, 48, 103,
    133, 138–139, 144, 147; Antarc-
    tica treaty and, 102; chemical
    weapons and, 58–59; International
    Court of Justice and, 137; interven-
    tion in Afghanistan by, 36–39, 49,
    58, 61, 118; law of the sea and,
    105; on non-use of force, 140–141;
    nuclear power and, 98; population
    of, 94; proposal for boundary of
    space, 147–148; relations with
    Iraq, 8; terrorism and, 14;
    weapons in space and, 49–55;
    withholding by, 3, 152
Space: weapons in, 49–51
Spain, 45, 76, 102, 139
Special Committee on Enhancing the
    Effectiveness of the Principle of
    Nonuse of Force in International
    Relations, 141
Special Committee on Peacekeeping
    Operations, 4
Special Committee on the Situation
    with Regard to the Implementation
    of the Declaration on the Granting
    of Independence to Colonial Coun-
    tries and Peoples, 44

Special Committee to Investigate
Israeli Practices Affecting the
Human Rights of the Population of
the Occupied Territories, 119–120
Special Facility for Sub-Saharan
Africa, 72
Special Programs of Emergency Relief
Assistance in Africa, 121
Special Session of the Critical Economic
Situation in Africa, 86
Special Sessions on Disarmament
(SSOD I and II), 61
Specialized agencies, 167–169
Spector, Arlen, 131
Speidel, Joseph, 93
Standard Minimum Rules for the Ad-
ministration of Juvenile Justice, 134
Standing Consultative Commission, 53
State responsibility, 149
Strategic Arms Reduction Talks, 51
Strategic Defense Initiative (SDI),
50, 52, 53
Structural Adjustment Facility, 72
Substantial New Programme of Action
for the 1980s for the Least
Developed Countries, 73
Sudan, 21, 69, 87, 121, 123
Sundquist, Don, 152
Supplier restraint: spread of nuclear
weapons and, 56–57
Swaziland, 27
Sweden, 48, 60, 102
Switzerland, 56, 81
Syria, 3–4, 14, 18, 157; assistance
in resolving hijacking, 12–13;
Damascus Accord and, 16, 17;
February 11 agreement and, 11

Taiwan, 55, 56
Tanzania, 106
Tariffs, 77
Technical Assistance and Cooperation
Fund, 98
Technology transfer, 83–84
Terrorism, 2, 10, 12–16, 145–146;
"state," 145
Thach, Nguyen Co, 40
Thailand, 39, 40, 123
Thiam, Doudou, 142
Third Committee, 131
Third Review Conference of the
Parties to the Treaty on the Non-

Proliferation of Nuclear Weapons,
55–56
Thomas, Jon R., 135
Threshold Test Ban Treaty, 52, 53
Tigrai, 21
Tin market, 75
Trade, 74–78; in food, 88–
89; in manufactures and services,
76–78; in oil commodities, and
agricultural products, 74–76
Transnational corporations (TNCs),
79–82; apartheid and, 81–82;
technology transfer and, 83–84
Trant, Gerald Ion, 90
Travel restrictions: in host country,
144–145
Treaty of Tlatelolco, 57
Treaty on the Non-Proliferation of
Nuclear Weapons (NPT), 55, 56,
57
Trust Territory of the Pacific Islands,
45–46
Trusteeship Council, 45, 46, 165
Turkey, 43, 58
Turks and Caicos Islands, 44
Tuvalu, 58

Ukraine, 144
United Kingdom, 10–11, 15, 16, 31,
50, 58–59, 65, 74, 81, 119, 138;
Antarctica treaty and, 102, 103;
economics and, 64, 66; in
Falklands/Malvinas conflict, 44;
Gibraltar and, 45; law of the sea
and, 104, 105, 106; nuclear
weapons and, 55; in UNESCO,
129, 158
United Nations: budget and finance
of, 151–154; Charter of, 111,
139–140, 141; effectiveness of,
139–140; personnel and administration of, 154–158; principal
organs of, 159–171
United Nations Association of the
United States of America (UNA–
USA), 153
United Nations Centre for Human
Settlements (HABITAT), 136
United Nations Centre for Science
and Technology for Development, 82
United Nations Centre on Transnational Corporations (CTC), 79

United Nations Commission on International Trade Law (UNCITRAL), 143
United Nations Conference for the Promotion of International Cooperation in the Peaceful Uses of Nuclear Energy, 57, 99
United Nations Conference on New and Renewable Sources of Energy, 99–100
United Nations Conference on Science and Technology for Development (UNCSTD), 80, 82–83
United Nations Conference on Trade and Development (UNCTAD), 73, 75, 80, 84
United Nations Congress on the Prevention of Crime and the Treatment of Offenders, 134
United Nations Convention on the Law of the Sea, 104–107
United Nations Convention on the Law of the Sea in the Southern Ocean, 108
United Nations Council for Namibia, 30
United Nations Decade of Disabled Persons, 133–134
United Nations Department of Disarmament Affairs, 48, 59
United Nations Department of Public Information (DPI), 131
United Nations Development Fund for Women (UNIFEM), 87–88, 126
United Nations Development Programme (UNDP), 122, 126; World Bank Energy Sector Assessment Programme of, 99
United Nations Disarmament Fellowships, 61
United Nations Disengagement Observer Force (UNDOF), 3–4
United Nations Economic Commission for Africa (ECA), 101
United Nations Educational, Scientific and Cultural Organization (UNESCO), 128–131, 157–158
United Nations Environment Programme (UNEP), 100–101
United Nations Food and Agricultural Organization, 23
United Nations Fund for Population Activities (UNFPA), 91–93, 95, 96

United Nations Group of Experts on the Reduction of Military Budgets, 61
United Nations Group of Governmental Experts on Nuclear-Weapons-Free Zones, 57
United Nations High Commissioner for Refugees (UNHCR), 88, 120–122
United Nations Industrial Development Organization (UNIDO), 82, 156
United Nations Institute for Training and Research, 142
United Nations Interim Force in Lebanon (UNIFIL), 3, 16, 18–19
United Nations Military Observer Group in India and Pakistan (UNMOGIP), 4
United Nations Office for Emergency Operations in Africa (OEOA), 89–90
United Nations Peacekeeping Force in Cyprus (UNFICYP), 4, 43
United Nations Pledging Conference for Development Activities, 133, 134
United Nations Regional Center for Peace and Disarmament in Africa, 61
United Nations Relief and Works Agency for Palestine Refugees in the Near East (UNRWA), 19–20, 122
United Nations Truce Supervision Organization in Palestine (UNTSO), 4
United Nations Trust Fund for Aging, 133
United Nations Voluntary Fund for Victims of Torture, 117
United Nations World Disarmament Campaign, 61
United States, 43, 48, 66, 68, 119, 133, 156, 157, 158; Antarctic treaty and, 102, 103; Arab–Israeli conflict and, 99–10; chemical weapons and, 58–59; economics and, 64, 65; foreign investments of, 81, 82; human rights and, 112, 125; law of the sea and, 104, 105, 106; Micronesia and, 45–46;

Nicaragua and, 33–34, 35, 138; nuclear weapons and, 141; relations with Iran and Iraq, 7–8; South Africa and, 30, 31, 81; Soviet invasion of Afghanistan and, 37, 38; terrorism and, 12–16, 145–147; trade and, 75, 76, 77–78, 79; travel restrictions imposed by, 144; in UNESCO, 129; Vietnamese invasion of Kampuchea and, 39, 41; weapons in space and, 49–55; withholdings by, 3, 91–93, 151, 152; World Bank contributions of, 72
Universal Declaration of Human Rights, 111–112
Urban Incentive Fund, 95
Urquhart, Brian, 4
Uruguay, 35, 71, 102, 109

Venezuela, 33, 66, 71, 125, 135
Vienna Convention on the Law of Treaties between States and International Organizations or between International Organizations, 144
Vienna Programme of Action, 82–83
Vietnam, 39–41, 58, 125, 144
Virgin Islands: British, 44; U.S., 44
Volcker, Paul, 65
"Voluntary export restraints" (VERs), 76
Voluntary Fund for the United Nations Decade for Women, 87
Voluntary Fund for the United Nations Decade of Disabled Persons, 134

Walters, Vernon, 13, 14
Walvis Bay and the offshore islands, 31–32
Warioba, Joseph S., 106
Warsaw Pact nations, 14, 48

Watercourses: non-navigational uses of, 148–149
West Bank, 11, 157
West Germany, 31, 50, 139; Antarctica treaty and, 102, 103; economics and, 64, 65, 68, 143; foreign investments of, 81; law of the sea and, 104, 105, 106; nuclear weapons and, 56; sanctions against South Africa, 81, 119
Western Sahara, 1, 2, 21, 22, 44
Wheat Trade Convention, 88
Whelan, Eugene, 90
Williams, Maurice J., 90
Women, 124–128; in Africa, 22; in development, 87–88; population issues and, 95–96; rural, 127; in U.N., 125–126, 156–157; as victims of crime, 134
World Bank, 64, 90, 95, 100; African development and, 20, 23, 24; debt crisis and, 68, 69, 71–72; food policy and, 87
World Conference on Sanctions against Racist South Africa, 119
World Court. *See* International Court of Justice
World Food Conference, 90
World Food Council, 90
World Food Security Compact, 87
World Programme of Action Concerning Disabled Persons, 133

Yakimetz, Vladimir V., 138
Yen, rise of, 65
Youth, 131–132
Yugoslavia, 71

Zaire, 21, 69, 120, 123
Zambia, 26, 29, 32
Zimbabwe, 21, 26, 31

A New Series from the Overseas Development Council

U.S.-THIRD WORLD POLICY PERSPECTIVES

Richard E. Feinberg & Valeriana Kallab, Series Editors

trade • investment • debt • aid • economic and social development • political and economic security • poverty alleviation • U.S. relations with Africa • Asia • Latin America

Now part of this series

U.S. FOREIGN POLICY and the THIRD WORLD: AGENDA 1985-86

Edited by John W. Sewell, Richard E. Feinberg and Valeriana Kallab

The Overseas Development Council's 1985-86 Agenda—the tenth of its well-known assessments of U.S. policies toward the developing countries of the Third World—analyzes recent U.S. policy performance and sets out policy options in the period ahead. Addresses itself to all who take an interest in U.S.-Third World relations and U.S. participation in international development. Extensive statistical annexes presenting the latest available data on U.S.-Third World economic transactions and indicators are again provided.

Titles in the *U.S.-Third World Policy Perspectives* series:

☐ **U.S. Foreign Policy and the Third World: Agenda 1985-86**
John W. Sewell, Richard E. Feinberg & Valeriana Kallab, editors
$12.95 (pbk.) ISBN: 0-87855-990-6　　　　　　　　March 1985 _____

☐ **Adjustment Crisis in the Third World**
Richard E. Feinberg & Valeriana Kallab, editors
$12.95 (pbk.) ISBN: 0-87855-988-4　　　　　　　　May 1984 _____

☐ **Uncertain Future: Commercial Banks and the Third World**
Richard E. Feinberg & Valeriana Kallab, editors
$12.95 (pbk.) ISBN: 0-87855-989-2　　　　　　September 1984 _____

☐ **Hard Bargaining Ahead: U.S. Trade Policy and Developing Countries**
Ernest H. Preeg, editor
$12.95 (pbk.) ISBN: 0-87855-987-6　　　　　　September 1985 _____

☐ **Development Strategies Reconsidered**
John P. Lewis, editor
$12.95 (pbk.) ISBN: 0-87855-991-4　　　　　　　　March 1986 _____

☐ **Investing in Development: New Roles for Private Capital?**
Theodore H. Moran, editor
$12.95 (pbk.) ISBN: 0-88738-644-X　　　　　　　　May 1986 _____

☐ **Between Two Worlds: The World Bank's Next Decade**
Richard E. Feinberg, editor
$12.95 (pbk.) ISBN: 0-88738-665-2　　　　　　　　July 1986 _____

☐ **The United States and Mexico: Face to Face with New Technology**
Cathryn L. Thorup, editor
$12.95 (pbk.) ISBN: 0-88738-663-6　　　　　　November 1986 _____

Payment Enclosed　　　　　　　　　　　　　　TOTAL $_____
Please make out check to **Overseas Development Council.**

Send prepaid orders to:　　　Name:_____
Overseas Development Council
1717 Massachusetts Ave., NW　Organization:_____
Washington, DC 20036
　　　　　　　　　　　　　　Street Address:_____

　　　　　　　　　　　　　　City:_____ State:_____ Zip:_____ Country:_____

Let UNA-USA put you in the corridors of power.

If you are among the 85% of Americans who say they want a stronger United Nations so it can do a better job solving the world's problems, then UNA-USA is for you! The United Nations Association of the USA is dedicated to making the U.N. work. In an increasingly dangerous and chaotic world, peace and prosperity cannot be secured without better international institutions and stronger U.S. leadership. UNA-USA is helping to achieve both through a unique blend of policy research, international dialogue, and public outreach.

UNA-USA is a national, nonpartisan, nonprofit "citizens' think tank." Through it, thousands of Americans

come together to weigh the choices facing U.S. foreign policy makers; and for more than twenty years, decision-makers at the highest levels of government have listened to them. Join us and you too can be heard.

UNA-USA has over 175 local chapters, each with a lively program of discussions, debates, speakers, and special events designed to inform and entertain you.

With your membership comes a subscription to *The Inter-Dependent*, UNA's

acclaimed bimonthly publication. Its timely investigative reporting takes you behind the headlines of today's news, and offers a range of views seldom found in the domestic press.

Also available, on request, are Fact Sheets, Reports, and Alerts derived from UNA's ongoing coverage of the United Nations, from its close contacts with business, labor, and government leaders, and from its high-level bilateral programs with the Soviet Union, Japan, and the People's Republic of China.

$35 ☐ Individual
$40 ☐ Family

$15 ☐ Retiree (if desired)
$10 ☐ Student

$100 ☐ Patron
$50 ☐ Sponsor

☐ Additional contribution for my local chapter: $_____

☐ Additional contribution for UNA's national programs: $_____

Dues and contributions are tax deductible. **Total enclosed $_____**

☐ My check is enclosed (Make check payable to UNA-USA) ☐ Please bill me

Name _____

Address _____

City _____ State _____ Zip _____

Return this form with your check to: **UNA-USA** 300 East 42nd Street New York, N.Y. 10017